Preface

This book is designed to teach beginners how to operate SPSS in either its PC+ or its Windows form. You have some data and some questions such as 'How do I get a frequency table, an average or a histogram?' The book gives you the answers, explaining the commands you need, and showing you the output the commands provide. It is not a text in statistical analysis; I have assumed that the person who comes to SPSS is likely to know, at least in general terms, what statistical analysis they want to do. What they do not know is how to get SPSS to do it for them!

The book is intended for the individual student or researcher who has access to a PC with SPSS/PC+ or SPSS for Windows installed; moving between the computer and the written explanation is the only way to develop skill at using the program. A set of hypothetical data is used in explaining how to obtain the results you want from SPSS. Do please carry out the various examples and exercises: it is only by having hands-on practice that you will develop an understanding of the way SPSS works, and become its master.

Finally, a word of hope: SPSS is very efficient, but it is complicated. Do not become discouraged if at first you find it confusing: we all do! Once you have mastered the general principles, you will soon find that it is comparatively straightforward to obtain the results you want. And remember that when you are able to drive SPSS, you have enormous power at your disposal.

Jeremy J Foster

Acknowledgements

Thanks are extended to SPSS UK Ltd for permission to use copies of *SPSS/PC+* and *SPSS for Windows* screens.

SPSS is a registered trademark and the other product names are trademarks of SPSS Inc.

Windows is a trademark of Microsoft Corporation

For information about SPSS, contact:

SPSS UK Ltd., SPSS House, 5 London Street, Chertsey, Surrey KT16 8AP.

Tel: 0932 566262; Fax: 0932 567020

STARTING SPSS/PC+
and
SPSS FOR WINDOWS

...ner's guide to data analysis

Jeremy J Foster

PRESS – Wilmslow, United Kingdom

First published in 1993 by

Sigma Press, 1 South Oak Lane, Wilmslow, Cheshire SK9 6AR, England.

British Library Cataloguing in Publication Data

A CIP catalogue record for this book is available from the British Library.

ISBN: 1-85058-509-1

Typesetting and design by: Sigma Press, Wilmslow

Printed by: Manchester Free Press

Distributed by: John Wiley & Sons Ltd., Baffins Lane, Chichester, West Sussex, England.

Acknowledgement of copyright names

CONTENTS

1

Aims of this book

1.1 Introduction

This book is intended to show you how to operate SPSS/PC+ and SPSS for Windows so that you can analyse data which you want analysed. The fact that you are reading it means that you are thinking of using SPSS/PC+ or SPSS for Windows, and are probably aware that SPSS is a set of programs that allows you rapidly to analyse huge amounts of data, and that it lets you carry out in a few moments statistical analysis that would be impractical without the aid of a computer.

This is not a book on statistics, because you are likely to know the analyses you want, if not how to obtain them. There is a brief account of the various statistical procedures, and you will find an explanation of the output that SPSS provides, as users do not always find the printed output completely clear. A summary of the basic principles of statistical analysis is given in Appendix B, and chapter 8 is intended to help you decide which analysis you require and which SPSS procedure will provide it for you.

You may have come across the SPSS manuals: those for SPSS/PC+ are particularly daunting! The ones for SPSS for Windows look much more appealing; the page size is smaller, the format and layout far clearer, the illustrations much more numerous and helpful. So one must commend SPSS for acknowledging the need for an easier style of manual, but there are still drawbacks. First, the order of topics reflects the order they are presented on the screen rather than any order of graded usefulness or difficulty. This means that essential, basic matters may not be dealt with until rather late. Second, lengthy and highly technical issues about statistical analyses precede the explanation of how to obtain any particular analysis. I have taken the view that the user is likely to know which analysis they require, and want to be informed how to achieve it.

This book covers most of the facilities offered by the Base modules of SPSS/PC+ and SPSS for Windows. I have structured the text by considering the questions that the user asks, moving from the simpler to the more complex procedures. (Manuals are often written the other way round; they explain the various commands one after the other, giving you the answer before you understand the question.)

Even the Base modules of SPSS offer you a very wide range of options when analysing your data. Saying that this book covers the facilities of the Base module, does not mean that I have attempted to describe every possible feature. There are thousands of different options which one can choose, and many of these can be explored at leisure once the basic mode of driving the package is understood. As in the first edition, I have tried to explain the structure of the system and describe very fully how beginners can obtain the analyses they are likely to require, so that they gain the fundamental skills from which they can explore further facilities for themselves.

I have tried to anticipate the problems that you are most likely to come across, and to explain how to deal with them. Some of the simpler problems that confuse beginners in SPSS/PC+ are listed in chapter 36, and others are described at appropriate points in the text. SPSS for Windows is less likely to lead users into a state of helplessness, since recovery from any situation is much easier. When Windows users have mastered chapters 17-20 they should be able to return themselves to a familiar location in the system wherever they are.

1.2 Versions of SPSS/PC+ and SPSS for Windows

The first edition of this book was written for SPSS/PC+ Version 3.1, which was superseded in 1990 by version 4.0. These two versions operated in a similar manner. There were some minor discrepancies between the printouts illustrated and what the user of version 4 would see on the screen, but these changes were comparatively trivial, and did not alter the way the package was used.

This edition has been up-dated so that it corresponds with version 4 of SPSS/PC+. If you have version 3, the ~ symbol in the on-screen menus is replaced by !, and some procedure commands will not have an = included when you select them from the menus. (The = does not have to be added, the procedures will run without it.) There are also some slight differences in the contents of some menus and the printouts of some commands. For example, in version 3 you ask for a chi-square test by using the sub-command /STATISTICS 1, which in version 4 is /STATISTICS CHISQ. The printout of the chi-square test in version 3 does include the phrase 'chi-square', but in version 4 it does not, confusing the user somewhat. These discrepancies are rather annoying for those writing a guidebook, but should not have too much impact on the beginning user.

The version 4.0 Base module included most of the procedures described in this book, but some had been made part of a separate Statistics option. These have now been returned to the Base module in version 5, SPSS for Windows.

The release in June 1992 of version 5, SPSS for Windows, has implemented a radical departure in the way that the user drives the system. For this edition, therefore, it has been necessary to add extensive sections for those whose first experience with SPSS is the Windows version. For those already familiar with SPSS/PC+, section 5.4 provides some information on upgrading to SPSS for Windows.

Whereas users of version 4 will soon learn how to use version 5, it looks unlikely that a user of version 5 will be able to use version 4 without extensive additional learning. It is rather like driving: someone who has learnt to drive a manual gear-change has little difficulty with an automatic, but drivers who have only ever used automatic transmission have a lot to learn if they want to use a manual one.

1.3 How to use this book

If you are unfamiliar with PCs, a simple description is given in chapter 2. This information may be helpful if you are uncertain about such things as the difference between a floppy disk and a hard disk, or what the less familiar keys on the keyboard do.

Users of SPSS/PC+ should remember that SPSS/PC+ operates from the DOS environment. If you are unfamiliar with DOS, with the difference between DOS and programs such as SPSS/PC+, do read chapter 3. I have found, when teaching SPSS/PC+, that many beginners get confused and try to run DOS commands from SPSS/PC+ or vice versa. So if you are unclear about the idea of directory structures, renaming and copying files or what a batch file is, take the time to go through chapter 3. Resist the temptation to get stuck straight into the chapter on Starting Out: you do need to understand the elementary features of DOS before you launch yourself into SPSS/PC+.

In order to make the book applicable to those facing both the new and the older versions of SPSS for the PC, chapters 5-8 cover topics relevant to all versions. SPSS/PC+ users should then follow chapters 9-16 to learn how to operate that version of the package, while Windows users should work through chapters 17-20.

In explaining how to use the package, I employ a set of hypothetical data, described in chapter 7. For users of SPSS/PC+, this set of data is referred to as exdat, and for SPSS for Windows users it is referred to as salesq. (The names are different, but the data is the same.)

Chapters 21-30 deal with various types of statistical analysis, and provide an explanation of how to obtain them using either version of the package. SPSS for Windows users will often need to refer to illustrations of printout originally generated with SPSS/PC+, and should remember that the explanations of the output refer to exdat, which they know as salesq.

The versions of SPSS have marked differences in their graphing facilities, and so there are separate chapters for each version on graphs (chapters 31 and 32). The reader will obviously use the chapter appropriate to whichever version of SPSS is being used.

The way you can obtain a neat printout of the results, merge sets of data and transfer files with other programs are covered in chapters 33 – 35. The final chapters are largely reference material, with subsections for the different versions.

SPSS/PC+ makes extensive use of the Function keys and of a complex menu system. A summary of what the Function keys do is provided in section 9.8, and a summary of the structure of the SPSS/PC+ and SPSS for Windows menu systems is provided in Appendix C.

1.4 Conventions used in the printing of this book

As you work through the exercises and examples, you have to key in material from the keyboard, and press specified keys to achieve particular results. When you have to type in words and numbers, they are printed like this:

`type 'a:exdat'`

This means that you should type in from the keyboard exactly what is shown in this format, including, in this example, the word type and the inverted commas, but no full-stop (period).

Pressing the Return key (also known as the Enter key) is shown as

↵.

If you are using SPSS/PC+, you will need to make regular use of the Function keys, marked F1 to F10 on your keyboard. These are named as F1, F2 etc.: remember this does not mean you press the letter F and then a number, but the appropriate Function key.

Your keyboard has a set of keys for controlling the movement of the cursor on the screen. They are labelled on the keyboard with arrows pointing up, down, left and right and are named in the text as up-arrow, down-arrow, left-arrow and right-arrow. The keys labelled PgUp, PgDn, Home, End, Ins are referred to by their names, as are the Esc (Escape), Alt and Ctrl keys.

Your keyboard contains two or three keys marked Del. The one needed most of the time is the –Del (backspace) key, which will be referred to as the Del key. When you need the Del key included in the number pad to the right of the keyboard, this will be referred to as the number/Del key.

There will be many occasions when you need to press two keys together, for example the Alt and E keys. To do this, you press down the Alt key and while it is depressed tap the E key, then release the Alt key. This is shown in the text as Alt+E, but remember it does not mean that you press the Alt key followed by the E key, and certainly does not mean that you press the + key: the Alt key must be held down when you press the E key.

2

Simple introduction to the PC

2.1 Hardware

You will be familiar with the basic physical components of the PC: a screen (VDU) and a keyboard which are attached to the unit housing the various electronic components that form the 'works' of the machine and which has a floppy disk drive incorporated in it. In addition there may be a mouse (essential for Windows), and to use SPSS you really need a printer.

'PC' is rather a simplification, since there are various kinds. There are, of course, many different makes of PC, but the name on the outside of the box is not particularly important: it is what is inside the box, the type of chip that forms the central processor, that distinguishes one kind from another. The original PCs, the PC XT, has an 8088 processor, whereas the more modern one, the PC AT has an 80286, 80386 or 80486 processor. At the time of writing (March 1993), machines with the 486 processor are rapidly becoming the norm.

Screens vary in terms of their physical size, and whether they are monochrome or colour. (Colour displays vary in terms of their sophistication, and you will come across terms such as EGA and VGA which describe different types, but you can happily remain ignorant of such matters.) The physical size of the screen is unimportant, as there will be 80 columns available in one line of characters whatever the physical dimensions of the screen. If you are using SPSS/PC+ with a colour display, you will find that the screen is divided into differently coloured sections; if yours is a monochrome display, the differences will be in whether the sections are light on dark or dark on light.

PCs vary in terms of the number and size of disk drives they have. The simpler machines have just one floppy disk drive (5.25" or 3.5"). The next grade up has two floppy drives, and the top category has one floppy drive and a hard disk incorporated inside the unit. You can only use SPSS on a PC that has a hard disk, which can store much more information than a floppy. Most 5.25" disks contain just over 360k, most 3.5" disks just over 720k; k here refers to thousands of bytes of information, so 360k means 360,000 bytes. High density disks, which require high density drives to use their full potential, contain 1.2 Mb and 1.44 Mb respectively. Mb denotes a megabyte, or million bytes of information, so 1.2 Mb is almost four times as much as 360k. You can use low density disks on a high density drive, but it is not possible to use high density disks on a low density drive. A hard disk will contain 40 or more Mb and is needed because SPSS itself takes up so much memory.

This book assumes you are sitting in front of a PC that has SPSS/PC+ or SPSS for Windows installed on it, which means it has a hard disk and at least one floppy disk drive. (Whether it uses 5.25 or 3.5 inch disks does not matter, so long as you have a disk of the correct size!)

2.2 The keyboard

There are different styles of keyboard, with the various sets of keys in different positions. Make sure you can identify the main letter and number keys which are in the traditional QWERTY layout, and the shift key which gives you upper case letters and the symbols written on the number keys above the numbers themselves. In addition to these, your keyboard will have a set of Function keys, labelled F1 to F10 or F12, and at least one set of keys on the right of the keyboard which control the movement of the cursor on the screen. They may have arrows and numbers on them. There is another key labelled NumLock. With NumLock on, these 'arrow keys' have the effect of entering numbers, but we shall be using the cursor movement facilities, so make sure the NumLock key is in the off position. (There will be an indicator light on the keyboard which is on when NumLock is on. Make sure it is off; if it is lit, press the NumLock key and it will go out.)

There are two or three Del (Delete) keys. One, the backspace key, is on the top right of the main section of the keyboard and may be marked –Del or have a left-pointing arrow. There is another in the number keypad on the right of the keyboard which can also function as a decimal point key. For most purposes use the backspace –Del key, which deletes the character to the left of the position where the cursor is placed. The number keypad Del, which will be referred to as number/Del, deletes the character at the point the cursor is placed when the key is pressed; characters to the right of the cursor position move left to fill the gap. If your keyboard has a grey key marked Delete it functions in the same way as the number/Del one.

The Alt and Ctrl keys are rather like shift keys in that they modify the meaning of pressing an ordinary key if that key is pressed while Alt or Ctrl is depressed. Esc (for Escape) is used to cancel certain operations. Ins (which stands for Insert) switches you from Insert mode to Overtype mode. When typing with Insert on, the material you key in is inserted in the file, and existing material moves right to make room for it. In Overtype mode, what you key in replaces any existing content.

The Return or Enter key has different effects, depending upon the task you are doing at the keyboard. When you are typing in, it causes the cursor to finish a line and move to the beginning of the next one. It is also used to instruct the computer to carry out the command and within SPSS/PC+ to select items from menus. In this book, pressing the Return key is shown by ↵.

2.3 Floppy disks

Once installed, the various programs that make up SPSS are stored on the hard disk in their own directory. It is perfectly feasible to store the data that you want analysed and the results of the analysis on the hard disk, but hard disks can 'crash' (i.e. fail) so whatever is stored on them is lost. Furthermore, if you store your files on the hard disk they are not portable. But when stored on a floppy, they can be taken to any PC that has SPSS/PC+ or SPSS for Windows installed on it, and used on that machine. So you are not tied to one PC, and can make copies of your data and command files so that you have a back up copy in case disaster strikes and your floppy gets damaged.

2.4 Formatting a floppy disk

When you buy a new disk, it cannot be used until it has been formatted, a process which divides into sections and creates a map telling the computer what is in the various sections. All this is electronic and invisible, of course. A disk needs to be formatted just once, so only if you have acquired a new disk do you need to do the following before using it. If the PC has one floppy disk drive, it is drive A. (On a PC with two drives, the upper or left one is drive A and the other is drive B. If you put the disk into drive B, then type B rather than A in the following instruction).

Do not put the disk into the drive

Make sure the machine is on and showing the DOS prompt:

`c:\>`

Put the disk into the drive and close the door. Type

`format a:` ↵

It is vital to have a space between t and a, but no space between a and :. If you type in the wrong instruction, the computer will probably come back to you telling you it could not read drive A and asking you 'Abort, Retry, Ignore?' If this happens, press A ↵ (for Abort); and when the prompt C:\> re-appears, try again after making sure the disk is in the correct drive and the door is closed.

The formatting process will take place (it takes a minute or so). When it is finished the screen will show how many bytes are available on the disk and ask if you want to 'Format another? (y/n)'. Type in n ↵ and the screen will return to the C:\> prompt.

2.5 Warning for beginners: switch on without a floppy disk

When switching the computer on, make sure the floppy disk is NOT in the disk drive. If you do switch on with a disk in the drive, the computer will try to read DOS programs from the disk, and unless it is a special type of disk it will not contain them; the computer will then tell you the drive contains the wrong type of disk (not a system disk). If this happens, take the disk out of the drive, switch the computer off, count to ten, and switch on again. When the prompt C:\> appears, put the disk into the drive.

Simple introduction to DOS

When the computer is turned on, it automatically loads a disk operating system, DOS, which is a set of programs that controls the way the computer operates. (Different PCs have different versions of DOS, but they are similar in the way the user interacts with them.)

It is important for those beginning SPSS, especially if they have SPSS/PC+, to appreciate the difference between DOS and the SPSS/PC+ programs, because one can do things in DOS that one cannot do in SPSS/PC+, and vice versa. There are different versions of DOS. The current one is version 6, but all versions will recognise the commands explained in this chapter.

You know that you are at the DOS level when you first switch the machine on, because the screen will display the prompt C:\>. (It is quite easy to alter this, so that the prompt contains some message. Your screen may show additional information such as the date.) This means the system is connected to drive C (the hard disk inside the computer box), and is ready to receive orders.

3.1 Typing in simple DOS commands

The most simple DOS commands are explained in the sections below. When you type in a DOS command, the case of the letters is unimportant, so DIR and dir have the same effect. But the spaces between components of the commands are crucial, as they distinguish one part of the command from another. So, for example, when using the rename command, the space between fn1 and fn2 in the command

```
rename a:fn1 fn2
```

is a necessity. If you typed in

```
rename a:fn1fn2
```

you would get a message indicating that DOS cannot understand the instruction, so do ensure you type in the commands with the spaces.

3.2 Seeing a list of the files on your disk: DIR

The various programs and files on the computer are stored on the hard disk, and the first thing one can do is see a list of the programs on the hard disk, by typing in

`dir ↵`

This tells DOS to put on the screen a list of the programs on the disk drive to which the system is connected. So when the machine has just been switched on, typing dir ↵ yields a list of the programs on the hard disk (drive C). The list may be longer than the number of lines on the screen, and it will scroll off the top. The machine will show the list one screenful at a time if one uses the command:

`dir/p ↵`

The listing of the files will pause when the screen is full; press any key to continue the listing. It is complete when the screen indicates the number of bytes available on the disk.

The list of programs is known as a directory list; think of it as a catalogue, showing the contents of a library of programs. Different kinds of items are listed, each with a name and many also have a suffix (known as a filename extension) listed in a second column on the screen. Examples of the extension are BAT, EXE, COM.

One program is shown as

`AUTOEXEC BAT`

The true name of this program is AUTOEXEC.BAT i.e. it is the name from the first column of the directory listing followed by a full stop and then the extension. The extension indicates what kind of program or file it is. For example, a file with the extension .BAT is a Batch File which contains a number of commands for the computer. Some kinds of file can be listed on the screen as recognisable words, but others (such as .EXE files) are written in a special code and any attempt to list them on the screen will give sets of meaningless symbols. Do not worry if this happens: it does no harm to the computer or the program file.

3.3 The directory structure

The directory shown after first switching on and then typing in dir ↵ is known as the root directory. Some of the entries in the list have the extension <DIR>, like this:

`SPSS <DIR>`

The <DIR> extension means that there is a subdirectory within the main directory. A subdirectory contains its own set of programs, and to see what they are it is necessary to move into that subdirectory.

There may be a large number of subdirectories, and a subdirectory can contain further subdirectories, so the structure resembles a tree with many branches and sub-branches as illustrated in Fig 3.1. To keep the filing system in reasonable order, programs or files associated with a particular application are usually stored in their own subdirectory. For example, all the files concerned with a word processor will be stored in one subdirectory, all the files concerned with SPSS in another, and so on.

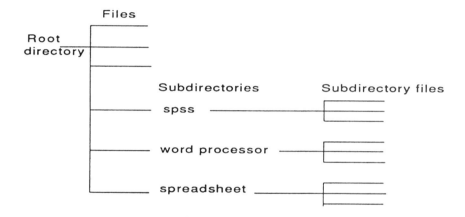

Fig 3.1 Diagram of the file structure of DOS

3.4 Changing directories

To change from the root directory to the subdirectory called SPSS, type

cd SPSS ↵

which means 'Change to the directory labelled SPSS'. The screen prompt will change to C:\SPSS>, indicating that the system is now in the subdirectory labelled SPSS. Note that the cd command does NOT tell the computer to run the programs contained in the subdirectory; it simply tells it to move to the subdirectory. To find out what is in that subdirectory, type in

dir ↵

and the contents of the subdirectory are shown on the screen.

To move back to the root directory, type in

cd\ ↵

The prompt will go back to C:\>. The back-slash character, \, indicates the system is in the root directory.

3.5 Creating a new subdirectory

To create a subdirectory called PROJECT on the hard disk, make sure you are in the root directory of the hard disk and type

md PROJECT ↵

A directory listing will then include PROJECT <DIR>, showing that there is now a subdirectory with that name.

3.6 Changing drives

When first switched on, the computer addresses the hard disk, drive C. The floppy disk drive is drive A (or A and B if there are two). To have the machine communicate automatically with the floppy disk drive, follow these steps:

Put a formatted disk into the drive. Type

A: ↵

The prompt will become A:\>. You can then obtain a directory listing of what is on the floppy disk by keying in

dir ↵

To return to communicating with the hard disk, type

c: ↵

and the prompt will become C:\>.

3.7 Telling the system where a file is

Most DOS instructions tell the computer to carry out some operation on a named file or program. For example, the command

type autoexec.bat ↵

instructs the system to list the file called autoexec.bat on the screen. When giving an instruction like this, you must remember which drive the system is addressing, and which drive contains the file or program it is to operate upon. The system will automatically look for a file or program in the drive and directory that it is currently connected to. For example, if the system is addressing drive C and is in the root directory (the prompt is C:\>), you can list a file that is in the root directory (such as autoexec.bat) by simply typing

type autoexec.bat ↵

When the file wanted is not in the current drive and directory, you must specify the drive and/or directory within the DOS instruction. If the system is addressing drive C and you want to list on the screen a file (suppose it is called ex.lis) that is on the floppy disk (drive A), you must tell DOS that the file wanted is on a different drive by preceding the name of the file with the drive name. So you would need to type in

`type a:ex.lis ⏎`

If the system is addressing drive A already, it shows the prompt A:\>. To list a file (ex.lis, for example) that is on the floppy disk (drive A), you do not have to specify the drive, and can just use the command

`type ex.lis ⏎`

Here is another example. In SPSS/PC+ the subdirectory SPSS on the hard disk contains a file called SPSS.LIS. How can you have it listed on the screen? The answer depends on where you are in the system. If you are connected to the C drive and are in the SPSS subdirectory, the screen prompt will be C:\SPSS>. You can then just type in

`type spss.lis ⏎`

If you are in the root directory of the hard disk, the prompt shows C:\> and you have to tell the computer that the file you want is in a subdirectory by preceding the filename with the subdirectory name like this:

`type \spss\spss.lis ⏎`

The \ characters are essential, as they tell DOS that in this line spss is the name of a subdirectory, and spss.lis is the name of a file.

If you are connected to drive A, and the screen prompt is A:\>, you have to indicate that the file you want is on a different drive and specify its directory by typing in

`type c:\spss\spss.lis ⏎`

If you asks the computer to apply a command to a file and receives the message 'File not found', this is often because the file is not in the drive or directory that the system is currently addressing. Another frequent error which produces the same message is to type in a filename that the system does not recognise, because the spelling is not exactly the same as the name under which the file is stored. If you receive the 'File not found' message, repeat the command, making sure that if necessary you specify the drive and/or directory of the file in the DOS instruction, and are using the correct filename.

3.8 Listing a file on the screen: TYPE

To list a file called fn on the screen use the DOS command

`type fn ⏎`

Use the name of the file which you want listed in place of fn. So to see the contents of the AUTOEXEC.BAT file, type in this line, including the word 'type':

`type AUTOEXEC.BAT ⏎`

Lengthy files will scroll off the screen. To pause the listing, use Ctrl+S. Use this combination again to restart the listing.

3.9 Printing a file from DOS

To print a file, make sure the printer is switched on, loaded with paper and is 'on line'. This means it has a channel of communication with the computer. There will be a button on your printer marked 'On Line', and an indicator light associated with it. This light must be on; if it is not, press the On Line button on the printer and check the indicator light is illuminated. Then use either the TYPE or PRINT commands, but type in the name of the file instead of filename:

`type filename >PRN ⏎`

or

`print filename ⏎`

If you use the PRINT command, DOS will put on the screen a message asked which printer should be used. In most instances you just press ⏎ in response to this message.

The main difference between TYPE and PRINT is that PRINT sends the file to a print queue, and rapidly allows you to carry out other tasks, whereas TYPE occupies the system until the command has been executed and the file has been printed.

3.10 Changing the name of a file

Changing the name of a file does just that: it simply alters the title, but does not alter the contents of the file.

From drive C, to change the name of a file which is stored on the floppy disk (drive A) from fn1 to fn2, type

`rename a:fn1 fn2 ⏎`

If the system is addressing drive A, so the prompt is A:\>, just type `rename fn1 fn2` ⏎

The space between fn1 and fn2 is crucial.

The file that was called fn1 will now be called fn2.

3.11 Copying a file

From the root directory of drive C, to copy a file called fn1, which is in subdirectory called subdir, to the floppy disk (drive A), type

`copy C:\subdir\fn1 A:`⏎

Remember to replace subdir with the name of the subdirectory in which the file is stored, and fn1 with the real name of the file to be copied. It is essential to include the space between the last character of the filename and the letter indicating the destination drive. As an example, the following command copies the file spss.lis from the subdirectory spss to the floppy disk:

`copy \spss\spss.lis a:` ⏎

If one were in the spss subdirectory on drive C, the copy could be achieved with this instruction:

`copy spss.lis a:` ⏎

To copy a file named fn from the floppy disk into the subdirectory called subdir on the hard disk, get into the root directory of drive C and type

`copy a:fn c:\subdir` ⏎

Put the name of the subdirectory into which the file is to be copied in place of the word 'subdir' in this instruction. For example, to copy a file called mydat from the floppy disk (drive A) into a directory on the hard disk called PROJECT, type

`copy A:mydat C:\PROJECT` ⏎

The directory called PROJECT must exist on the hard disk before this command is used. Section 3.5 explains how to create a subdirectory.

3.12 Deleting a file from the floppy disk

To remove a file from the floppy, ensure that DOS is showing the C:> prompt and type, using the full name of the file in place of fn,

`del a:fn` ⏎

Simple introduction to Windows

The user of SPSS for Windows will almost certainly know how to use the Windows interface. This chapter is merely intended to remind you of some of the techniques.

Operating the mouse involves four different techniques: pointing, clicking the mouse button, double-clicking (click twice in rapid succession), click/drag, which means you press the mouse button and while it is depressed move the mouse.

Windows is usually started by typing in win ↵ at the DOS prompt. Initially it presents the Program Manager, and applications are run by double clicking on their icon. Applications (such as SPSS for Windows) run in their own applications window.

When using Windows, one has to interact with windows and dialogue boxes. The components of these are described in the following sections.

4.1 The components of a window

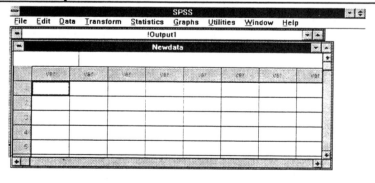

Fig 4.1 The screen when SPSS for Windows is started

The *title bar* is at the top and includes the title of the window. At the left edge there is a control-menu box, and clicking on this will open the control menu which can also be opened using Alt followed by Spacebar on the keyboard. The control-menu entries allow you to restore a window to its previous size, move it via the keyboard, alter its size, reduce it to an icon, enlarge it to its maximum size or close the application.

At the right edge of the title bar there are the minimise and maximise buttons which allow you to reduce the window to an icon or enlarge it to its largest possible size. You can alter the size of a window more precisely by placing the mouse pointer in the bottom right corner and use the click/drag technique to reduce or increase the size of the window. The position of a window on the screen can be altered by click/dragging the title bar.

The menu bar is the bar below the title bar. It includes a number of menu headings (such as File, Edit*)*. Each menu can be opened by moving the mouse cursor over it and clicking the left mouse button, or by using the keyboard: press and release the Alt key and then press the letter key corresponding to the underlined letter in the menu's title. To select one of the entries in the selected menu, put the mouse cursor over it and click the mouse, or type in the underlined letter of the entry name which is underlined (you do not press Alt for submenu entries). A menu is closed by moving the pointer so it is outside it and clicking.

Some windows in SPSS for Windows have an *icon bar*. This contains some command buttons and/or icon buttons (command buttons with an icon rather than a verbal label to indicate their function).

The *scroll bars* are used to reveal information that is outside the limits of the window. You can scroll the information by clicking on the scroll arrows at the end of the scroll bar, click on the space between the scroll box (which shows which part of the file is being shown in the window) and the arrows, point at the scroll arrow and hold the mouse button down, or by click/dragging the scroll box to position the window where you want it to be in the file.

4.2 The components of a Dialogue Box

Dialogue boxes are presented when you have to enter information about the task to be performed. A dialogue box is illustrated in Fig 4.2. It has a number of components.

Scroll bars are provided down the side and (when needed) along the bottom when a window or a drop-down list box cannot show all the information available.

Text boxes are areas where you type in text from the keyboard. Move the pointer into the text box, and an insertion point (flashing vertical bar) appears. Anchor the insertion point by clicking the mouse, and then type in material.

List boxes display a list of options; if there are more options than can be shown, the box has scroll bars which you use to scroll the list. To select one of the options, click on it: it will be highlighted. To select a number of adjacent items, use the click/drag technique to highlight the set of options you want. To select a number of non-adjacent items, hold down Ctrl while you click on each one you wish to select.

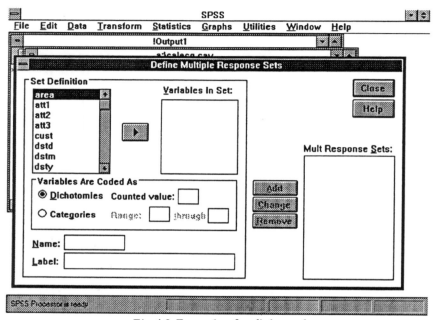

Fig 4.2 Example of a dialogue box

Drop-down list boxes show a selected option, but if you click on the down-pointing arrow at the top right of the box, a list of alternatives will be revealed. You can select one of these by clicking on it. You may need to click in the text box at the top of the list to insert the highlighted item into it. In some cases a double click on the entry in the text box invokes the entry in the text box.

Check boxes are small squares adjacent to a label indicating their function. By clicking on them, you either delete or insert an X into the box. If there is an X, the option is in force, and if the box has no X it is not.

Command buttons are shaded rectangular areas which you click on to initiate an action or to reveal another dialogue box. Those buttons not available at the present time are dimmed.

Most dialogue boxes in SPSS for Windows contain a Help button; clicking on this will open a window showing information about the topic with which the dialogue box is concerned. Further information about the Help facility is given in chapter 20.

Option buttons (sometimes known as radio buttons, these are circular: see Fig 4.1) are organised in sets. The members of a set are exclusive: if you click on one of them, any other previously selected one will be deselected, since only one of the set can be operative at any one time.

4.3 Using the keyboard if there is no mouse

In the windows:

❏ To move to the menu bar, press Alt or the F10 key

❏ To move along the menu bar, use the left or right arrow keys

❏ To move down a menu, use the down arrow key

❏ To select an item in the menu, have the cursor over it and press ↵

❏ To cancel a selection, press Esc

❏ To open Help, press F1

In the Dialogue Boxes

❏ Move between items with Tab (to move forward) or Shift+Tab (to move backward)

❏ To move up or down a list, use the down arrow and up arrow keys

❏ To move up or down a list of radio buttons or check boxes, use the down arrow and up arrow keys

❏ To select an item, use the underlined letter in the item name

❏ To select a highlighted item, press ↵

❏ To activate the OK or Continue buttons, use the Tab keys to have them highlighted and press ↵

❏ To cancel and close the dialogue box, press Esc

❏ To open Help, press F1

What is SPSS?

SPSS is a suite of computer programs, which has been developed over many years. The original SPSS and SPSSx were only available on main-frame computers. The PC version is now one of the most widely-used programs of its type in the world. The main development over the main-frame versions was SPSS/PC+ V2.0, which incorporated a menu-driven front end. Further modifications are appearing regularly, with version 5 being the current one: the general structure of the program is likely to remain stable, but the interface between the package and the user is dramatically altered between SPSS/PC+ and SPSS for Windows. (A Macintosh SPSS/PC+ is available, using the familiar Mac front end, which is similar to the Windows interface.)

All users will have the Base system of whichever version of SPSS they have available. In addition, one can purchase extra modules such as Data Entry and the Tables module. These are not considered in this book, which relies mainly on the Base system. Even this consists of a large set of programs.

As a beginner, you do not need to know much about the actual SPSS programs; the important thing is learning to drive rather than learning how the car works! But SPSS is rather complicated, and it is important to understand the general characteristics of the structure of the program and the files that are used and created by the program.

If you are learning SPSS/PC+, read section 5.1 and then 5.3-5.6. If you are upgrading or learning SPSS for Windows read sections 5.2-5.6.

5.1 Overview of the structure of SPSS/PC+

Fig 5.1 indicates the way in which the files are organised. (In this book it is assumed the data and command files are stored on a floppy disk, and that one of the output files, the .LIS file is also sent to the floppy disk.) Essentially, SPSS/PC+ sits on the hard disc, usually in a directory called SPSS. In order to use SPSS/PC+ you must provide it with data to be analysed, and this is stored in a data file. When you want the data to be analysed, you have to tell SPSS/PC+ how the data in the data file is organised and what analysis you want done on it. This set of data descriptions and instructions is included in a command file. The user has to create the data and command files.

When SPSS/PC+ runs, it reads the commands from the command file and makes a copy of the data from the data file in another file known as the Active File. It then follows the commands from the command file, using the copy of the data in the *Active File*. The Active File is lost when you leave SPSS/PC+.

When it is running, SPSS/PC+ creates two output files. One is the file that holds the results of the analysis it has performed; unless you tell it otherwise, this results file is called SPSS.LIS. The other output file is named SPSS.LOG, and records a list of the commands which SPSS/PC+ is carrying out.

There is one important fact to understand about the .LIS and .LOG files. When you first enter SPSS/PC+, the SPSS.LIS and SPSS.LOG files in the subdirectory SPSS on drive C are wiped clean, ready for the results of a new run of the program. So you need to make sure you have saved the results of any previous run of the program in a file that will not be wiped. How this is done is explained as you work through this book.

Remember that SPSS/PC+ is distinct from DOS. The various DOS commands that were described in chapter 3 cannot be entered directly from SPSS/PC+. So you cannot be in SPSS/PC, type in a DOS command such as type a:ex1.lis>prn ↵ and expect it to work: it won't! There are ways of entering DOS commands into a set of SPSS/PC+ commands, but they do require a special form. For the moment, try to remember that DOS and SPSS/PC+ are different!

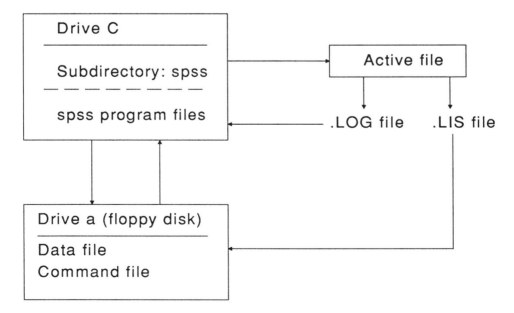

Fig 5.1 Diagram of the structure of SPSS/PC+ files

5.2 Overview of the structure of SPSS for Windows

If you are learning SPSS for the first time with the Windows version, you have an easier task than those who have to learn SPSS/PC+. The Windows interface means that you can operate the package with little awareness of how it is structured and functions. But this can be dangerous: you do need to appreciate how the package uses and creates various components, so that you can understand the explanation of its facilities: a driver, however ignorant of the principles of the car's transmission system, does need to know what a clutch pedal is and does!

Like earlier versions, SPSS for Windows consists of a number of components. First, there are the programs making up the package itself; these read the data, carry out the analysis, produce a file of the results. The normal user needs to know little about these programs, just as a driver needs to know little about the structure of the internal combustion engine or the physical characteristics of a differential. Second, there are the numbers that the user wants analysed, and these have to be entered into a data file. Third, there are the commands which tell the package which analyses the user wants performed on the data. Fourth, there are the results of the analysis.

With the Windows version, entering the data, providing the instructions on which analyses to perform, and examining the output can all be carried out on screen with the data, commands and results being available in separate windows at the same time.

Fig 5.2 indicates the way in which the files are organised. (In this book it is assumed the data and command files are stored on a floppy disk, and that one of the output files, the .LST file is also sent to the floppy disk.) Essentially, SPSS itself sits on the hard disc. In order to use it you must provide it with data to be analysed, which is entered into a spreadsheet presented on the screen and is then stored in a data file which has the filename extension .SAV. When you want the data to be analysed, you have to tell SPSS which analysis you want done by issuing commands. The commands can be entered by selecting from the Window menus, and they can be stored in a syntax file. The user must create the data file by entering data into a spreadsheet and may create a syntax file. It is not essential to save one's commands, but I strongly urge you to do so, as you then have a record of the instructions which were used to generate the output you obtain.

When SPSS for Windows runs, it either reacts to the commands selected from the menus directly and applies them to the data in the spreadsheet or it reads the commands from the syntax file and responds to them by applying them to the data. The spreadsheet of data is lost when you leave SPSS unless you save it (as you always will) in a data file.

When it is running, SPSS for Windows creates two output files. One holds the results of the analysis it has performed and is put into a window on the screen entitled !Output1, !Output2 etc. You will almost always want to save this file, and it will be saved with the filename extension .LST.

The other output file is named SPSS.JNL, and records a list of the commands which SPSS carries out. Every time you use SPSS for Windows, the record of the commands you use is added to the end of the .JNL file so over a series of sessions it can become very lengthy. You can turn off the process of recording the journal file, or you can ask the system to record only the .JNL file for the current session, overwriting any previous version. You can also have the .JNL file stored on the floppy disk rather than the hard disk. To do any of these, you use Edit /Preferences: the way to achieve these alterations to the way the .JNL file is saved will be clear once you have experience at using SPSS for Windows.

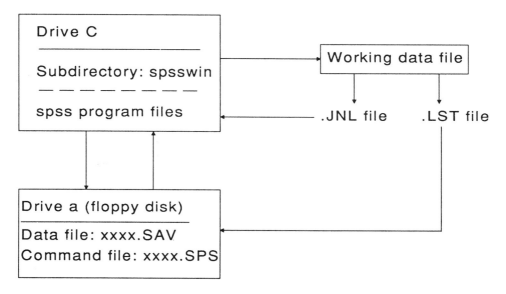

Fig 5.2 Diagram of the structure of SPSS for Windows files

5.3 Essential terminology for all SPSS users

The previous sections of this chapter have indicated the distinction between data, commands, output and the SPSS or SPSS/PC+ programs. You also need to appreciate some of the terminology that is used when explaining how the package operates.

The case

When you approach SPSS, you have some data to be analysed, and this is in the form of responses or scores from a number of different respondents. Each respondent is known as a *case*, and the results from one case (respondent) form one line in the data file. In SPSS/PC+ the data for a single case can be spread over more than one line on the screen, but functionally it is a single line of numbers. In SPSS for Windows, the data from one case forms one row in a spreadsheet.

Variables and levels

You will have a number of responses from each case, such as the respondent's age, sex, income, score on an intelligence test, number of heart attacks etc. Each of these is a score on a *variable* (age, sex, income etc). Each variable has to have a name, which cannot be more than 8 characters long and must not contain a space. (So you could name a variable intell, but not intelligence since the full word has more than 8 letters. And you cannot call a variable score 1, as that contains a space; you would have to use score1 as the name.) In SPSS/PC+ you have to specify the name of each variable, but in the Windows version they are automatically named var0001, var0002 etc until you rename them (which you should always do).

When you tell SPSS to analyse the data from the data file, you have to tell it which variables to analyse by indicating their names. So if you have a variable which indicates the respondent's gender, you might name this variable sex. Then when you want to analyse the responses on this variable (for example, to find out how many respondents were male and how many female), you have to tell SPSS to analyse the variable sex ie you must use the name that has been given to that variable. Users of Windows and experienced users of SPSS/PC+ will think this so obvious that it is hardly worth mentioning, but there are many beginner users of SPSS who do not appreciate the need for this consistency: having once given a variable a particular name, that same name must be used when referring to that variable later on.

It is important to be clear about the difference between *variables* and *levels* of a variable. The variable is whatever aspect of the respondent you have measured: age, sex, number of times admitted to hospital, intention to vote for a particular party etc. Each variable has a number of levels. There are two levels of sex, male and female. Age can have many levels; if you record the age in years, it can vary from 0 to about 105, so there would be 106 levels. Usually, age is put into categories such as 0-20, 21-40, 41-60, over 60 and in this particular case this gives 4 levels of the age variable. (It is quite simple to enter the actual ages into SPSS and then have the program code the values into a smaller number of categories, using the RECODE procedure.)

System missing and user-defined missing values

You need to appreciate the concept of the system-missing value, and how it differs from a user-defined missing value. If you enter data into the SPSS/PC+ data file and leave out the score on a variable because the respondent failed to provide a response, when SPSS analyses the data, it will record this respondent as having the 'system missing' value on the variable. In the SPSS for Windows Data Editor spreadsheet, if you leave empty one of the cells in a column or a row that contains data, the empty cell will be filled with a full-stop (period). This cell will be detected as containing no data, and SPSS for Windows will give it the 'system missing' value. So the system-missing value is automatically inserted by SPSS/PC+ or SPSS for Windows, when a number is expected but none is provided by the data.

But when some respondents have not answered all the questions asked, or have failed to provide a measure on one of the variables, it is sensible (for reasons that will become clear later) to record a no-response by entering a particular number. So one might record male as 1, female as 2 and then use 3 to indicate that the person failed to indicate their sex. The value of 3 on the variable sex would then be a user-defined 'missing value'. Of course one has to tell SPSS that this value does represent 'no response': how to do this is explained in the chapters on the data file.

When choosing a number to represent 'data missing', it is essential to use a number that cannot be a genuine value for that variable. If one wanted to define a missing value for age, for example, one would use a number that could not possibly be genuine, such as -1.00 or 150.

Case number

When entering data from a set of respondents, it is nearly always worth inserting a variable that represents the identification number of the respondent. You can then readily find the data for any respondent you need, and check the entries against the original record of the responses. This identification number has to be entered as a 'score' on a variable, just like any other.

But SPSS also assigns its own identification number to each case, numbering each case sequentially as it reads the data file. This is the *$casenum* variable, which you may see listed when you ask for information about the variables in the data file. The first case in the data file, which may have any user-defined identification number you wish, will have the *$casenum* of 1, the next one will have *$casenum* 2 and so on.

Procedures

When SPSS analyses data, it applies a *procedure*: for example, that part of SPSS which calculates a correlation coefficient is one procedure, the part which reports the average score on a variable is another. Most of this book is concerned with explaining how you decide which procedure you want in order to achieve a particular type of analysis, and how you run that procedure on your data.

5.4 Upgrading to SPSS for Windows from SPSS/PC+

Users familiar with SPSS/PC+ will probably find that after an initial feeling of confusion, the Windows version is easy to use, and that the transfer up from earlier versions is comparatively painless. The way that SPSS operates does not appear to have altered very much, there are some additional facilities, and the main contrast is the interface to the user. After a little practice, one appreciates how much easier it is than the previous interface, even though one is presented with so many choices that at first one feels overloaded with options.

There are a few points worth bearing in mind when making the transition to SPSS for Windows, particularly regarding the files. Fig 5.2 demonstrates that the file structure for SPSS for Windows is similar to that for SPSS/PC+, but that the filename extensions are different: .LIS has been replaced by .LST, and .JNL (for Journal) replaces .LOG. Command files, now known as syntax files, automatically have the extension .SPS. Perhaps the most notable feature is that in SPSS for Windows, data files created by saving the spreadsheet in which data has been entered are system files; these used to have the extension .SYS, but now it is .SAV.

Some of the names given to procedures in the menus have been changed. For example, the EXAMINE procedure of SPSS/PC+ is now the EXPLORE procedure of SPSS for Windows. (In fact this difference is only in the menu entries: when EXPLORE is invoked, the SPSS processor is actually running EXAMINE, as is shown in the status bar at the bottom of the applications window.)

Upgraders should note that some of the facilities available are not accessible from the SPSS for Windows menus, but have to be written into syntax files. So if you are looking for a particular subcommand and cannot find it, it is probably accessible but only indirectly. Paste the commands into a syntax file, as described in section 19.7, and then edit them (see section 19.11). Help on the structure of syntax file commands is available from the Syntax button of the Syntax window.

The output generated by some procedures is not identical with that obtained from those same procedures in SPSS/PC+. In most cases the differences are unimportant or self-explanatory. Where there are notable differences for the procedures explained in this book, the SPSS for Windows output is illustrated.

Finally, SPSS for Windows has much more sophisticated facilities for dealing with some kinds of material – graphs are the obvious example, and date/time data is another. Explanations of these are provided at appropriate points in this book.

5.5 Seeing what your SPSS contains

The particular version of SPSS installed on your system may have optional modules in addition to the Base system. You can find out which parts of the package are on your computer by following these steps. You are advised to do this only when you have had some experience with the package.

SPSS/PC+ users

Select session control and info *from the main menu, go right and select* SPSS MANAGER, *go right and select* STATUS . *Press* ↵ *and the whole command* SPSS MANAGER STATUS *will be pasted into the scratchpad. Running this command will provide a list of the SPSS/PC+ procedures installed.*

SPSS for Windows users

Access the SPSS for Windows Setup procedure from the File Manager of Windows by double-clicking on the Setup icon or by selecting Run from the program manager File menu and typing into the Run text window `c:\spsswin\setup`. (If neither of these methods work, you will need to seek local advice. Since procedures can be added or deleted from Setup, if you are using a network, it may have been disabled to prevent computer vandals disrupting the package.) The Setup window displays the procedures installed in SPSS for Windows.

Obtaining the data

SPSS makes it possible to analyse large sets of data in very brief time, once the data file has been created. Any type of research that generates quantitative data can be analysed by SPSS, as it allows you to count and tabulate the responses, calculate averages and variances, apply a very wide range of tests of statistical significance, use multiple regression, and (with the optional modules) perform factor analysis, time series analyses etc. It is especially useful for analysing the results of surveys, where each of a large number of respondents may yield a large amount of data. Since many users are concerned with questionnaires, this chapter provides guidelines on how they should be constructed and the responses coded for SPSS analysis.

6.1 Designing a survey response form

It is sensible to consider, when designing a survey response form, the person who is going to have to type the responses into a data file. This job of keying the data into a data file can be a large task in its own right, and the researcher can produce some gains by designing the response forms from the outset so that keying the data is made as easy as possible. This involves two aspects of form design: first, asking questions in such a way that the respondent gives clear and unambiguous responses; second, laying the form out so that the keyboard operator has as straightforward a task as possible.

Designing questionnaires that are effective is not a simple job, and the first attempt is almost never the optimal solution. Questionnaires should always be piloted, given to a small sample of people of the same type that are to be given the final version, so that any ambiguities or mistakes can be identified and corrected before the form is given to the final users. There are a number of simple rules that the questionnaire designer should follow, although experience suggests that even those who know what the rules are find it very difficult to implement them (which is why a pilot study is always necessary!).

Questions should be unambiguous, and ambiguity is not always apparent to the person who devises the questions For example, 'are you aged over 65?' may seem clear, but people who are 65 may be unsure how to respond. Does the question mean 'have you had your 65th birthday?' or does it mean 'are you aged 66 or more?'

Ambiguity is more likely if the question-setter makes the mistake of combining clauses. For example, one should not use questions like this: 'Are you a fluent speaker of English and Spanish?' It is better to use separate questions, each with a yes/no possibility.

People find it more difficult to interpret negatives and passive sentences than positives and active ones. It is wise to avoid such questions as 'Do not fill in this form if you are aged under 16'; it is preferable to use the positive equivalent: 'Fill in this form if you are aged 16 or over'.

Imprecise terms such as 'often' and 'frequently' are inherently ambiguous. A question such as 'do you often have sleepless nights?' is unlikely to produce clear answers, since the respondents concept of 'often' may not correspond with the questioner's- does it mean once a week, once a month, once a year? The term 'sleepless night' is also unclear – does it mean literally having no sleep at all, or being awake for 2 or more hours after trying to go to sleep?

The kind of response required also influences the way people answer questions. One should avoid having respondents 'delete whichever does not apply'; instead, have them tick or underline or circle the alternative that does apply. This is another aspect of avoiding negatives, and is particularly important if there is any risk of presenting the respondent with a double negative as here: 'Delete whichever does not apply .... I am over 16 / I am not over 16'.

When offering alternative answers, one must be sure that all possible answers are offered, even if this means allowing the respondent to write in a response not catered for. If asking about people's marital status, one must allow for the separated, the divorced, the widowed, and (depending on the purpose of the research) for those living together on a long-term basis who are not legally married. It should be clear what is to be done about coding the response if the respondent ticks two or more of the alternatives.

The completed forms are going to be transformed into a data file, so it is important to arrange the design so that the keyboard operator has a clear task. Most, if not all responses will be transformed into numbers, so the numbers corresponding to each question and each response to each question must be known in advance, and it can be helpful to have them indicated on the form or to provide a template which can be used when the keying is being done. It is important to ensure that the responses to any question are placed in the appropriate columns of the SPSS data file, that a failure to respond is indicated by a number, that allowance has been made for multiple answers and free responses. Answers should be clearly located next to the questions, and questions clearly differentiated from the adjacent ones. Although having alternative responses arranged in columns does save paper, a set of similar rows is likely to cause keyboard operators to lose their place, with the danger that the responses to one question may be keyed in as the responses to a different question.

6.2 Numeric and string (alphanumeric) variables

SPSS does accept alphanumeric (known as string) data, in which the data is coded in the data file not as a number but as a series of letters (or letters and numbers). If the data contains any letters, it is a string variable. SPSS divides string variables into two types: short ones, which have 8 characters or less, and long ones.

There are some drawbacks to using alphanumeric variables. First, typing in strings takes longer than typing in numbers. Second, there are limitations on what SPSS can do with string variables: one cannot use them in most statistical procedures. Consequently, it is usually more convenient to use numerical coding of all variables. For example, when recording a respondent's sex you might code male as 1 and female as 2. (It is simple to obtain in the printout a verbal label corresponding to any numerical score so the printout shows that a score of 1 on sex means male and a score of 2 means female.)

There is an important point to bear in mind when using numbers instead of a string label, such as coding male as 1 rather than 'm' and female as 2 rather then 'f'. When numbers are used like this, the magnitude of the numbers has no correspondence with the magnitude of the feature they represent: the numbers are merely acting as labels or names. This is known technically as a nominal scale.

The danger is that one may forget that in a nominal scale the size of the numbers has no meaning. Once you have numbers, you can apply arithmetic and statistical operations to them even if they are not appropriate. For example, if you have coded sex of respondents as 1 for male and 2 for female, you can calculate the mean 'score' on the sex factor. If you have an equal number of men and women the mean 'score' will be 1.5. But this is nonsense: 1.5 does not mean anything at all. A mistake like this occurs when the researcher forgets that the numbers for this variable are only a nominal scale, and wrongly applies procedures that are only relevant to more sophisticated types of scale in which the magnitude of the numbers does reflect the size of the variable. (These are known as interval scales and ratio scales.)

You can refer back to the information given here once you are familiar with using SPSS. If you are using a string variable in your data file, you have to tell SPSS that the variable is a string variable. In SPSS/PC+, you do this in the DATA LIST line by adding (A) after the variable name:

```
DATA LIST FILE = 'a:smoke.dat'/id 1-3 brand 5-15(A) age 17-20.
```

Here id and age are numeric, but brand is a string variable.

It is possible to transform string variables into numeric ones by a slightly indirect method. Suppose, for example, that one has a data file in which sex has been coded as 'M', 'F' or 'U' (for 'unknown'). One can create a new numeric variable, gender, which codes sex as a number by using the IF procedure:

```
IF (sex = 'M') gender = 1.
IF (sex = 'F') gender = 2.
IF (sex = 'U') gender = 3.
```

Gender is a numeric variable and can be used in FREQUENCIES, DESCRIPTIVES and the other procedures which require numeric variables.

In SPSS for Windows you use the Define Variable dialogue box, as described in section 18.5, to tell the package that you are using a string variable. You can convert a string variable into a numeric one using the Automatic Recode procedure described in section 28.4 or using Compute If: the idea of this is explained above, and the procedure covered in section 29.4.

6.3 Know what you want to find out

SPSS provides the opportunity to carry out a wide range of statistical procedures very rapidly and with little effort. The danger is that because it offers such power, the researcher is tempted to comb the data: "Let's do a factor analysis / multiple regression / 100 t-tests... and see what happens."

It must be emphasised that there are real dangers in this approach. First, there is the statistical problem of interpreting significance levels when one has done a series of significance tests after the data has been given a preliminary examination. Practically, there is a risk that one obtains masses of analyses which overwhelm one's ability to interpret and understand them: faced with a 4-inch pile of listing paper, many researchers, after the first flush of enthusiasm, have regretted their unrestrained proliferation of analyses!

Decide before you get to the computer what you want to find out, what statistical analyses you wish to apply. The power of the program is not a substitute for clear thinking. Without a definite idea of what you are looking for and how to find it you are likely to generate confusion rather than understanding. Chapter 8 is intended to help you decide which analyses you need, and therefore which SPSS procedures you require, in order to obtain the results you want from your data.

The data used in this book

The data file is simply the stored record of the numbers (data) which are to be analysed. The way you create a file of your data is quite different depending on whether you are using SPSS/PC+ or SPSS for Windows, so detailed explanations are given in the appropriate chapters (chapter 10 and chapter 18). In explaining how to create, store and use a file of data, it is helpful to have an example to refer to, and I shall be using the data described here.

Imagine that we have carried out a piece of research in which we gave a questionnaire to each of a group of 22 salespeople. They were employed by three different employers, and the respondents were asked their sex, the name of their employer, the area of the country they work in (either North or South), and then three questions intended to reveal their attitude towards their job. Each of these questions (numbers 5-7 in Fig 7.1) invited a response on a scale from 1 to 5. The questionnaire also asked the number of customers each salesperson had visited during the previous month, the total sales for the previous month and the date the respondents started working for their company. Fig 7.1 shows an example of a completed questionnaire from one respondent, and in all there are 22 questionnaires like this.

When encoding these responses for SPSS, all the responses were encoded as numbers. Although the respondents indicated whether they are male or female, the answers were expressed as a number, with 1 representing male and 2 representing female. Similarly, each employer was given a number and the respondent's employer was recorded as 1, 2 or 3; the value 1 was used to represent Jones and Sons etc. The area of work was also coded numerically with 1 for North and 2 for South. (The package can deal with responses that are coded as letters or words, see section 6.2, but there are drawbacks so whenever possible just use numbers. It is straightforward to have the verbal meanings of the numbers displayed in the printout, using the VALUE LABELS command.)

Although this type of investigation may not be of any interest to you, the kind of responses obtained are similar to those yielded by many kinds of research. Essentially, we have series of numbers. Here they are used to represent sex, employer, area of country, attitude expressed on each of three questions, two performance measures (customers visited and sales), and the date when the person started with the company. We could have data on socio-economic status, number of children, or a thousand other things which can be represented as numbers.

The responses shown in Fig 7.1 can be represented numerically as:

`01 2 1 1 4 5 1 043 03450.60 010688`

(The spaces are put in to make it easier to check the figures, and are highly recommended!) The 01 at the beginning of the line is the respondent number, the 2 indicates that the sex is female, and so on. Imagine we have 22 lines of data like this, corresponding to the responses of our 22 salespeople. The amount of data is small, but once you have learned to use SPSS on a small set, there should be no problems with a much larger set, since the principles are the same.

```
Where there are alternative answers, please underline the one
relevant to you. For the other questions, please fill in your
answer.

                                     Respondent number:   01

1  What is your name?              K Smith

2  Are you male or female?         (1) M      (2) F

3  What is the name of your employer?
   (1) Jones and Sons     (2) Smith and Company     (3) Tomkins

4  In which area of the country do you work?   (1) North  (2) South


Please indicate your reponse to the following three questions by
underlining one of the numbers, using the following scale:
     1 means that you strongly agree with the statement;
     2 that you agree with it;
     3 that you are uncertain;
     4 that you disagree;
     5 that you strongly disagree with the statement.


5 In general I enjoy my job              1    2    3    4    5

6 In my company, hard work gets rewards  1    2    3    4    5

7 I often wish I was doing a different job 1   2    3    4    5


8 How many customers did you visit last month?    43

9 What was your total sales value last month?    3450.60

10 Enter the date you started working for your present employer:
                              01 day 06 month 88 yr
```

Fig 7.1 Completed Sales Personnel Questionnaire

Which analysis do you need, and how do you obtain it?

Faced with a package such as SPSS, beginners are likely to be over-awed by the power at their disposal. If they have only had experience of simple computer statistical packages, or even had to calculate statistics by hand (which nowadays means by calculator!), it is rather exciting to realise you can, with a few key presses, obtain statistics such as multiple regression or analysis of variance, procedures which would previously have taken hours of error-prone activity. But, as I mention elsewhere, this means that the user must understand the statistical analyses they are asking for. One can readily obtain nonsensical figures, such as the mean of nominal variables, and can be thoroughly confused by the power of the package.

Appendix B provides a short refresher in the principles of statistical analysis, but it is worth summarising here the major types of statistical question, and the way one answers them using SPSS.

This is not a complete list of all that SPSS can do, by any means; but it should help you identify the procedure you want in order to answer the question you have. You can then turn to the appropriate point later in this book to find out just how any procedure is applied.

How Many Respondents Gave That Response?

In many types of investigation, the investigator wants to know *how many* respondents gave a particular answer or response. For example, how many cases in the data file were female, how many were female and under 40 years of age? Answers to this kind of question are provided if you use the FREQUENCIES procedure (chapter 22).

You may want to obtain a table showing the number of cases that had certain scores on one variable subdivided according to their scores on another variable. For example, suppose you want a table showing the number of males and females coming from the North and the South. This type of table is provided by CROSSTABS (chapter 22).

Having produced a table showing the number of people of each sex coming from each part of the country, you might ask whether there is a significant relationship between these two factors: do proportionally more men than women come from the North? To see whether this type of relationship exists with frequency data, you need the chi-square test, which can be obtained within the CROSSTABS procedure.

How Are The Scores Distributed? What Are The Percentile Scores?

If you want to see how the scores are distributed (do they form a normal distribution?) or discover the percentile scores, then in SPSS/PC+ you use EXAMINE (chapter 21), and in SPSS for Windows you use EXPLORE (chapter 21).

Averages: What Are The Means And Medians?

You may want to know what was the average score on a certain variable: what, for example, was the average age of all the cases in the data file? This data can be found using DESCRIPTIVES (chapter 23). Note carefully that if you want the means of subgroups of respondents, such as the average age of males and then of females you need the MEANS procedure (see next paragraph).

Averages: What Are The Means For Subgroups Of Respondents?

If you want the average score of subgroups of respondents, such as the average age of men and of women, or the average income of people below 40 and the average income of people over 40, then you need the MEANS procedure (chapter 23).

Is There A Significant Difference Between Scores?

A large part of statistical analysis is involved with evaluating the differences between sets of scores, and determining whether they are statistically significant. (The concept of statistical significance is summarised in Appendix B.) For example, is the average score on one test of performance significantly different from the average score on another test of performance?

There are many different tests that are used to answer this question, and which one you use depends on a number of factors: is the data amenable to parametric analysis? are you comparing two sets of scores or more than two sets? are the sets of scores from different respondents or from the same respondents? Depending on the answer to these questions, you decide whether you need a paired (within-subjects) t-test, an independent-groups (between-subjects) t-test, an analysis of variance, or one of the various non-parametric tests.

Chapter 24 covers the t-test, analysis of variance for comparing three or more sets of scores of different respondents on one variable (the ONE-WAY procedure), and ANOVA which is needed if you have a two-factor study, and so have four or more means to compare with different respondents in each of the subgroups.

Many studies have 'repeated measures'. Imagine you have measured the performance of males and females on test1 and test2: the sex factor is between-subjects, but as the same people did both test1 and test2, type of test is a within-subjects or repeated measures variable. To compare the means of the four groups in a study like this, you need the MANOVA procedure- which is NOT included in the Base module of SPSS.

Is There A Significant Difference Between Nonparametric Scores?

If you need to use nonparametric analysis, the NPAR TESTS procedure (chapter 26) offers a number of tests including the Kruskal-Wallis, Mann-Whitney and others.

Are Two Sets Of Scores Correlated?

As scores on one variable increase, do scores on another variable increase or decrease? This type of question is asking whether there is a correlation between the scores on the two variables, and is answered by using the CORRELATIONS procedure (chapter 25). Rank correlations are also obtained from CORRELATIONS. If you have to rank the data, you use RANK (chapter 27).

How Well Can I Predict One Score From Respondents' Other Scores?

If you want to see whether scores on one variable predict scores on another, this also involves studying correlations. You may want to investigate whether responses on test1 and scores on test2 predict scores on test3, and this is a problem in multiple regression, which is dealt with using the REGRESSION procedure (chapter 25).

How Do I Analyse Subgroups Of Respondents Separately?

You will frequently want to analyse the data for just some of the respondents: perhaps compare the scores on test1 and test2 only for people over 40, for example. To do this, you have to tell SPSS which subgroups you want to select, and then which analysis you wish to be carried out. In SPSS/PC+, this is achieved by using the PROCESS IF or SELECT IF commands (chapter 30) to select the subgroups, and then specifying the particular analysis (such as FREQUENCIES, T-TEST) you want. In SPSS for Windows, you can use SELECT IF or SPLIT FILE (chapter 30).

How Can I Use The Data To Calculate 'new' Scores, Such As Each Respondent's Average On A Number Of Variables?

You will often find that you want to obtain a 'new' score from the data provided by your respondents. Suppose, for example, that you have scores on test1 and test2; you might want to find the average score of these two scores for each respondent. To do this, use the COMPUTE procedure (chapter 29).

How Do I Put The Scores Into A Particular Order?

This is achieved using the SORT procedure (chapter 27).

Can I Change The Way Scores Are Coded?

Suppose you have asked your respondents to indicate their age in years, and you find that their ages vary from 16 to 85. To make the data more manageable, you might decide that you would like the respondents grouped into categories of 16-35 years, 36-55 years, 56 and above: you want to put the respondents into just three different age groups. This can readily be achieved using the RECODE procedure (chapter 28).

If you want the scores transformed into ranks, use RANK (chapter 27).

How Do I Obtain Graphs?

In SPSS/PC+, the EXAMINE, FREQUENCIES and PLOT procedures provide boxplots, simple barcharts and scattergrams which will display the distribution of scores, the number of people obtaining particular scores or the relationship between two sets of scores (chapter 31).

The graphing facilities for SPSS for Windows are considerably more sophisticated than for previous versions, and allow you to create barcharts, histograms, box plots, line graphs, area charts and pie charts, using the GRAPHS procedure (chapter 32).

How Do I Get A Neat Table Of The Results?

SPSS has a procedure called REPORT which allows you to generate clean displays of tables and output (chapter 33). Alternatively, you can transfer your output file to a word-processor and edit it there (chapter 35).

I Have Data In Different Files- How Do I Merge Them Into One?

This is performed using JOIN MATCH or JOIN ADD in SPSS/PC+. With Windows, it is rather easier to use these procedures, which are covered in chapter 34.

Even the Base module of SPSS provides you with enormous power to modify, tabulate and analyse your data. If you have any of the optional, additional modules on your system, then further facilities will be available, such as factor analysis, discriminant analysis, log-linear analysis, reliability analysis, repeated-measures analysis of variance, time-series analysis. This book only covers what is included in the Base modules: note that some of the facilities in the Base module of SPSS/PC+ are not in the SPSS for Windows' Base module and vice versa. So your particular version may not allow you to use all the analyses described, but most of them will be available to you.

SPSS/PC+: Starting out

9.1 What you need to run SPSS/PC+

Assuming SPSS/PC+ is installed on your hard disk, there are six things you need in order to use it:

1. To know how to get to the SPSS/PC+ programs

2. A file of data to be analysed, which you will write

3. A set of commands telling SPSS/PC+ how the data is laid out and precisely what analysis you want it to do. These are included in the Command File, which you write

4. To know how to get SPSS/PC+ to apply the command file to the data file; in other words, how to run SPSS/PC+

5. To know how to examine the contents of the output (.LIS) file;

6. To know how to get the .LIS file stored on the floppy disk, and in such a way that it will not be overwritten the next time SPSS/PC+ runs.

These requirements are covered in the following chapters. To begin, how do you get into SPSS/PC+ (and how do you get out of it)?

9.2 Getting to SPSS/PC+

If SPSS/PC+ has been installed on your PC in the usual way, it will be stored on your hard disc in a directory entitled SPSS. To get into the program:

Switch on

At the C:\> prompt, type

cd SPSS ↵

The screen prompt will become C:\SPSS>

Type SPSSPC ↵

The program will then load; you will first of all see the title screen, and after a few moments the main entry screen, shown in Fig 9.1 will appear. Before you do anything else it is worth taking a few moments just to look at the screen, as it has a number of components.

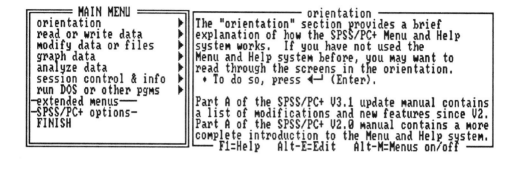

```
╔═══════ MAIN MENU ═══════╗ ┌──────────── orientation ────────────
║ orientation           ▶ ║ │The "orientation" section provides a brief
║ read or write data    ▶ ║ │explanation of how the SPSS/PC+ Menu and Help
║ modify data or files  ▶ ║ │system works. If you have not used the
║ graph data            ▶ ║ │Menu and Help system before, you may want to
║ analyze data          ▶ ║ │read through the screens in the orientation.
║ session control & info ▶║ │ • To do so, press ◄┘ (Enter).
║ run DOS or other pgms ▶ ║ │
║─extended menus────      ║ │Part A of the SPSS/PC+ V3.1 update manual contains
║─SPSS/PC+ options─       ║ │a list of modifications and new features since V2.
║ FINISH                  ║ │Part A of the SPSS/PC+ V2.0 manual contains a more
╚═════════════════════════╝ │complete introduction to the Menu and Help system.
                            └─── F1=Help   Alt-E=Edit   Alt-M=Menus on/off ───
```

```
═══════════════════════════════════════════════════Ins════════════Std Menus= 01
                                        ...        scratch.pad
```

Fig 9.1 The initial SPSS/PC+ screen

9.3 The entry screen

The screen is divided into four sections. In the upper left there is a section headed MAIN MENU, with one entry (orientation) highlighted in light on dark; other entries are dark on light. When SPSS/PC+ starts, it automatically goes into menu mode, and you can move this highlighting cursor up and down the menu using the arrow keys on the keyboard.(If your version of the program has been modified so that the screen you are now looking at does not contain the Main menu, press Alt+M. The screen will then look like Fig 9.1)

In the upper right part of the screen there is a window that shows information about whatever is highlighted in the menu. As the cursor in the menu is moved using the arrow keys, the information in the information window changes. As you use SPSS/PC+, do keep referring to the information window: it is helpful!

The lower half of the screen is the Scratchpad, which is where you write in data or commands when you are creating files. When you first enter SPSS/PC+, the scratchpad is empty.

The last section of the screen is the bottom two lines. As you use the system, various messages and minimenus will appear on the bottom line. At present it simply reads `scratch.pad` the name of the file in the lower part of the screen.

The line above the bottom line contains information. There is a small window which says `Ins`; this means you are in Insert mode. If you press the Ins key on your keyboard, this message will disappear (you will be in Overtype mode). Get back to Insert mode by pressing the Ins key again. There is also a counter on the far right which tells you the column in which the cursor in the scratchpad is placed; at the moment it says 01 because the cursor is in column 1, the top left of the lower half of the screen.

9.4 Menu mode and edit mode

SPSS/PC+ can be run in different modes. In menu mode, when you move the cursor with the up-arrow and down-arrow keys (or the mouse), the cursor in the menu moves up and down, and you can select items from the menu and paste them into the scratchpad. (When you are familiar with using the package you may find the menu system is rather laborious and it easier to do without it. But for beginners it is very helpful and we shall be using it throughout this book.) In menu mode you can NOT type from the keyboard directly into the scratchpad. If you want to do that, you must be in edit mode. Similarly, when you are in edit mode you can type directly into the scratchpad, but cannot select items from the menu in the upper left quadrant.

In edit mode, you can type from the keyboard directly into the scratchpad. There is a range of editing facilities available that allow you to correct or alter the text or data you type in. You move the typing cursor around in the scratchpad by using the arrow keys, and type in new material which will be inserted at the point where the cursor was placed. The fact that you are in Insert mode is shown by `Ins` being displayed at the bottom of the screen. To switch to Overtype mode, where what you type will overwrite the existing characters, press the Ins key on the keyboard; the `Ins` message on the screen will disappear.

9.5 Switching between menu and edit modes

At various times you are likely to try actions when you are in the wrong mode. If you try to select a menu item when you are in edit mode, the cursor will not move around the menu as you expect; pressing the arrow keys will move the scratchpad cursor, not the menu cursor. On the other hand, if you try to type in when you are in menu mode, you will get a warning beep and the message `Not found,` followed by a window showing the characters you typed will appear on the bottom line. Remove this window by pressing the Escape key. On other occasions you will try to do something but the system will tell you that it is not possible to do it when you are in menu mode. (This occurs with some of the Function keys, which are explained a little later on).

Whenever you are in the 'wrong' mode, you need to switch to the other mode, using Alt+E, before trying the instruction again. When switching from menu mode to edit mode, the message Edit mode- press Esc to resume menu mode will appear on the left of the bottom line of the screen, and the cursor in the scratchpad will become a flashing underline character. When switching from edit to menu mode, the message Loading menu will appear briefly at the bottom left of the screen, and the cursor will become a flashing square.

9.6 Using the menus

In menu mode, move up and down the menu using the arrow keys on the keyboard. Words in CAPITALS in the menu are SPSS/PC+ commands. You select these commands and add them to the file being built up in the scratchpad by moving the cursor until the command is highlighted and then pressing ↵.

If a menu entry has an arrowhead to its right, there is a subsidiary menu; to reach it, put the menu cursor over that item and press the right-arrow key on the keyboard. The subsidiary menu will then appear in the menu quadrant, and relevant information will appear in the information window. For example, the starting position is shown in Fig 9.1. If you move the cursor down to the entry read or write data and then press the right arrow key you will find the screen changes. The menu now has a different title (read or write data, in this example) and a fresh set of entries: DE, GET etc.

The menu system goes to six levels, and it is easy to get lost! To get back up a level in the menus, press the left-arrow key on the keyboard. To jump straight back to the top level Main Menu press Alt+Esc.

Although the menu system is intended to be helpful (and is, once you become familiar with it!), the titles of the menus are not always self-explanatory; commands can be difficult to find. Chapter 38 provides a summary of the menu structure, showing where the main commands are.

The menu system which operates when you first enter SPSS/PC+ is known as the standard menus. You can ask for an even larger menu system by pressing Alt+X, which invokes the Extended Menus. A window in the bottom right of the screen will indicate if you are using extended menus. In this book, we shall use the Standard Menus, but you can explore the Extended menus at any time by pressing Alt+X.

9.7 Removing and restoring the menus

To remove the menu, press Alt+M. The menu and information windows will disappear, you will be put into edit mode, and the top half of the screen will show the output .LIS file. (If you remove the menus before you have run an SPSS/PC+ application, the top half of the screen will be blank.)

To restore the Menus, press Alt+M again. You will automatically be put into menu mode.

9.8 What the Function keys do

Various facilities are available if you press the Function keys (F1 – F10), each of which produces a minimenu along the bottom line of the screen. When you press F9, for example, this minimenu appears:

```
file:     write Whole file     Delete
```

To select any of the options available, move the cursor along the line with the arrow keys, and when the cursor is over the desired choice press ↵. Alternatively, each option has one capital letter in its title, and you can select that entry by typing the capital letter.

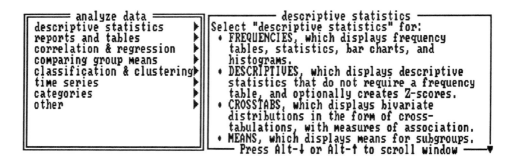

Fig 9.2 The screen when F9 has been pressed

NOTE: The analyze data entry from the main menu has been selected and the right arrow key pressed to reveal the submenu shown in the menu section of the screen.

The uses of the Function keys are shown in Fig 9.3 (by key) and Fig 9.4 (by function). A screen display showing the uses of the Function keys is obtained by pressing F1 and selecting Review help. To remove the display, press Esc.

Note that all the F keys are available in edit mode, but when you are in menu mode you only have F1, F2, F7, F9 and F10 available. Pressing the other Function keys while in menu mode, will produce the message Not available in menu mode at the bottom of the screen. To remove this message, press the Del key. (Pressing Esc does not work here). Then switch modes (Alt+E) and press the F key you want again.

If you press the wrong Function key and have not pressed ↵, cancel the operation and remove the minimenu by pressing Esc on the keyboard. If you press ↵ and select the wrong item, the action to take to cancel the operation is sometimes shown on the screen; Esc will often retrieve the situation.

9.9 The Help system

To obtain some on-screen help to using the system, press F1 and select the first entry: Review help by pressing ↵. You will be shown a reminder of what the function keys do, and a guide to menu commands. If F1 is pressed again, a screen is displayed showing how to move the cursor around the file being edited. The bottom line of the screen says:

Enter command or press F1 for more help or Escape to continue.

If you enter a command, it does NOT provide help information on that command, but invokes it. You are most likely to want Esc to return to where you were when you pressed F1.

9.10 The Glossary

SPSS/PC+ contains a glossary explaining the meaning of technical terms you may come across. These terms are concerned both with the operation of SPSS/PC+ itself, and with statistical analysis. To see a definition of a term such as 'mode', press F1 and select Glossary from the minimenu. A window will appear on the screen. Type in the item you want, and an explanation will be shown. To move up and down the glossary, use Ctrl+PgUp or Ctrl+PgDn. To remove the glossary display, press Esc.

9.11 Working from the system prompt

There is another mode for using SPSS/PC+ in addition to the menu and edit modes, which build up a series of commands into a command file. If you select the option Exit to prompt from the minimenu obtained by pressing F10, the screen goes blank except that on the bottom line you will see:

SPSS/PC:

This is known as the system prompt, and shows you are in direct mode. In direct mode, you type in commands directly, one at a time, and press ↵. SPSS/PC+ will carry out the command and then come back with the prompt, waiting for the next command. When you are experienced at using SPSS/PC+ you may find that using this direct mode of interacting with the program is easier than using menus or using the scratchpad in Review (SPSS/PC+'s editor), but beginners are advised to avoid it.

If you find yourself faced with the system prompt, get back into Review by typing

`review.` ⏎

Do not forget the full stop! You will then get back into Review, and be faced with a screen like Fig 9.1 except that the scratchpad may contain entries.

9.12 Leaving SPSS/PC+

There are two major methods for leaving SPSS/PC+. If you are in menu mode, start at step 1 in the list below; if you are in edit mode start at step 4.

1. In menu mode, move the cursor to the `FINISH` command at the bottom of the menu

2. Press ⏎ to select that command. It will be pasted into the scratchpad (the bottom half of the screen).

3. Go to step 6

4. In edit mode, type the word `finish.` into the scratchpad. Make sure you put a full stop after the word. (All SPSS/PC+ commands must end in a full stop.)

5. Go to step 6

6. Ensure the cursor is on the line containing the word `finish`, and press F10. A mini-menu will appear on the bottom line of the screen, with two entries:

`run from Cursor     Exit to prompt`

(If you do not have this minimenu on the bottom line, because you pressed some key other than F10, press the Esc key and then press F10.) The `run from Cursor` entry will be highlighted (dark on light). This is the option required.

7. Press ⏎

SPSS/PC+ will obey the command `finish.`, and the system will return to DOS.

The sequence F10 followed by ⏎ is always used to run the instructions shown in the scratchpad.

You have now run your first SPSS/PC+ command! But to do anything worthwhile you must start by creating a data file, covered in chapter 10.

F1 for obtaining Help information, a list of files on your floppy disk, using the Glossary.
Submenu:
info: Review help   Var list   File list   Glossary   menu Hlp off

F2 for switching between windows and changing window size.
Submenu:
windows: Switch   Change size   Zoom

F3 for retrieving files to edit from your floppy disk.
Submenu:
files: Edit different file   Insert file

F4 for inserting blank lines or deleting lines in a file.
Submenu:
lines: Insert after   Insert Before   Delete   Undelete

F5 for finding or changing strings of characters in a file.
Submenu:
look:Forward find   Backward find   fOrward change   bAckward change

F6 for moving to a particular place in a file.
Submenu:
goto: after executed Line   Output pg

F7 to mark a block of lines in a file.
Submenu:
mark/unmark area of: Lines   Rectangle   Command

F8 to operate upon a marked block in a file.
Submenu:
area: Copy   Move   Delete   Round

F9 to save a file or to delete a file from disk.
Submenu:
file: write Whole file   Delete

F10 to run a command file or to exit to system prompt.
Submenu:
run: run from Cursor   Exit to prompt

Fig 9.3 Main uses of the Function keys by key (the way these facilities work is described as you work through this book.).

Change size of window	F2
Change strings in a file	F5
Delete a block of lines	F8
Delete a file from disk	F9
Delete a single line from a file	F4
Find strings in a file	F5
Glossary	F1
Go to particular page in a file	F6
Insert a single line in a file	F4
List of files	F1
List of variables in the Active File	F1
Mark columns of figures in a file	F7
Mark a block of lines in a file	F7
Move a block of lines in a file	F8
Move a single line in a file	F4
On-screen help	F1
Retrieve a file from floppy disk	F3
Round numbers off	F8
Run SPSS/PC+	F10
Save a file	F9
Switch windows	F2
System prompt	F10

Fig 9.4 Main uses of the Function keys by function

10

SPSS/PC+: The data file

The data which is used as an example throughout this book is described in chapter 7.

10.1 General features of a data file

The first thing to do in preparing the data for SPSS/PC+ is to lay out the data for each respondent in a consistent order, in a line like this:

```
01 2 1 1 4 5 1 043 03450.60 010688
```

The first numbers (01) are the respondent identification number; it is useful to give every respondent a unique identifying number and start the line of data with it. This helps later if you need to check the data (and you almost certainly will!) The third number (2) represents the respondent's sex, with 1 meaning male and 2 meaning female. The next 1 is the code number of the employer, and the following 1 shows the respondent was working in the North. The numbers 4 5 1 are the responses to the three attitude questions (questions 5, 6 and 7), while 043 is the number of customers visited. 03450.60 is the sales, and the last set of numbers is the date of starting at the company expressed as day, month and year (so 010688 represents the first of June, 1988).

Table 10.1 shows the complete set of data for the 22 respondents in our survey. Each line of the file is a case (usually each line is the data from one subject), and it is essential that the data for each respondent, known as a *case*, is laid out in the same sequence. (In Table 10.1, the data for the respondent is in the same order as they appear on the data sheet; this is not necessary, but is usually the most convenient way of arranging things.)

The second point to note is that it is essential that if an item of data occupies two columns for one respondent it must occupy two columns for every respondent. For example, you cannot indicate the first day of the month as a 1 for some people and the tenth day as 10 for other people; you must always use two columns to indicate day of month. This is why the leading zeros are included in the dates, and 1st June 1988 is written as 010688. (You can omit the leading zeros and have a blank column instead, but this confuses the appearance of the data and makes it easier to make mistakes, so insert the leading zeros!)

Table 10.1 The data used in this book laid out in SPSS/PC+ style

```
01 2 1 1 4 5 1 043 03450.60 010688
02 1 2 2 4 4 3 046 04984.42 080690
03 1 1 2 2 3 5 048 10432.82 090690
04 1 3 1 2 3 4 083 08235.21 010690
05 3 2 2 2 2 4 071 06441.38 080690
06 2 3 2 3 3 3 072 06497.05 090690
07 2 1 2 3 2 5 042 03835.26 010690
08 1 2 2 4 5 3 028 03819.00 080690
09 1 1 1 2 3 4 041 05723.52 090690
10 1 3 2 1 2 5 076 07937.45 080690
11 2 2 1 2 3 3 039 04582.44 090690
12 1 1 1 2 3 4 030 02005.30 010690
13 1 3 2 2 2 4 068 08914.50 030691
14 2 2 2 1 2 4 033 03124.20 050691
15 2 2 2 5 4 1 036 04222.45 030691
16 2 3 1 2 2 4 079 08881.28 310591
17 1 1 2 3 4 3 038 03449.35 050691
18 2 1 1 2 3 4 048 07882.60 310591
19 2 3 1 4 3 1 058 08779.00 030691
20 2 2 2 1 3 4 060 05822.68 310591
21 1 2 2 3 4 3 039 04004.80 030691
22 2 1 1 2 3 3 040 05886.40 050690
```

The data must be in the same columns for all cases (respondents). If column 4 contains the sex of respondent 1, the same column must contain that data for all the other respondents. (This is not strictly necessary, but I strongly recommend you use this consistent spacing style because it does make it much easier to check your data file if you ever need to do so... as you probably will!)

In Table 10.1 the numbers are laid out in series separated by blanks; this is not necessary, and the data for respondent 1 could be written as:

`0121145104303450.60010688`

This is definitely not recommended: you may need to check your data later, and it is much easier to do so if the figures are divided into short sequences rather than being one uninterrupted line.

Where there is a lengthy set of data for each respondent, it will be too long to fit onto one line. This is not a problem, the data can just continue on the next line. The data shown in Table 10.1 could have been laid out like this:

```
01 2 1 1 4 5 1 043
   03450.60 010688
02 1 2 2 4 4 3 046
   04984.42 080690
```

and so on.

The indentation of the second line for each case is not necessary, but I recommend that you do indent because it does make it much easier to check your data file should you ever need to do so. Remember to be consistent for every case (respondent). If the data extends over two lines, the command file must indicate that this is so, as explained in section 13.5.

10.2 Writing the data file

To write the data as a file that can be analysed later, proceed as follows:

❑ Get into SPSS/PC+ and put your floppy disc into the drive

❑ Get into Edit mode by pressing Alt+E

❑ Type in the lines of data as shown in Table 10.1, pressing ↵ at the end of each line EXCEPT THE LAST ONE. Start each line in column 1, and use the spacing shown in Table 10.1, with one blank column between items of data.

❑ When the last line is typed in, do not press ↵, but save the file, as described in chapter 11. Call the file `exdat`.

If you type ↵ at the end of the line and the cursor does not move down to the next one, you have almost certainly inadvertently switched off the Ins (Insert) mode: press the Ins key on the keyboard, check that the message `Ins` appears on the bottom line of the screen, and now press ↵.

If you make a mistake, refer to chapter 12 for an explanation of how to correct errors when typing in and how to edit a file that has been saved.

You have now written a data file and saved it on the floppy disk. The next task is to write the command file which informs SPSS/PC+ of the structure of the data file and instructs it which analyses to perform on the data. How to create the command file is described in chapter 13.

11

SPSS/PC+: Saving and retrieving files from the floppy disk

11.1 Saving a file

To save a file, proceed as follows:

❑ Press F9 and a minimenu will appear on the bottom line of the screen. The option
write Whole file will be highlighted

❑ To select this option press ↵ and a box will appear at the bottom of the screen,
inviting you to type in a name for the file.

❑ Type in, but using the filename you want instead of fn, a:fn ↵

The a: writes the file to the floppy disk. Use whatever name you want the file to be
called in place of fn, for example: a:exdat. It is sensible to give a data file a
name ending in 'dat' so you know whenever you see a list of files that this is a data
file. When the file has been saved, the message done (including nn lines
from memory) appears at the bottom left of the screen.

When saving a revised version of an existing file which has been retrieved from disk,
it is not necessary to type in the file name, as it will be offered in the window at the
bottom of the screen when F9 ↵ has been keyed in. So you can just press ↵. The
revised version will then replace the previous version on the floppy disk. To keep
both the old version and the revised version, type in a new filename when saving the
revised version.

The file is now stored on the floppy disk (drive A). One annoying feature is that
although the file has been saved as exdat, you are still actually editing scratchpad, and
that is the name of the current file that is shown in the bottom right of the screen.
You can check that the file has indeed been stored on the floppy by using the
procedure for viewing the list of files on the floppy described in section 11.4.

11.2 Filenames

A filename cannot be longer than eight characters+full stop+three letters for the filename extension. So `exerc.dat` is acceptable, and so is `exercdat`. But `exercise1dat` will be shortened to the first eight characters and will be `exercise`.

11.3 Retrieving a file from disk

To retrieve a file that has been stored on the floppy disk, follow these steps:

❑ Ensure you are in edit mode

❑ Press F3, and a minimenu will appear on the bottom line of the screen. The first entry, `Edit different file` is highlighted.

❑ To select this entry press ↵. A box will appear at the bottom of the screen, inviting you to type in the name of the File to edit.

❑ Type in, but replacing fn with the name of the file you want, `a:fn` ↵

If the filename has an extension (e.g. `spss.lis`), the complete name, including the extension, must be typed in.

The file will be retrieved and appear in the scratchpad, with the filename given on the bottom right of the screen.

11.4 Finding out what is on the floppy disk

When you have forgotten the name of the file you want to retrieve from the floppy disk, SPSS/PC+ will display a list of all the files on the floppy if you proceed as follows:

❑ Ensure you are in edit mode, and press F1

❑ Move the cursor along the mini-menu at the bottom of the screen until it is over `File list` *and press* ↵*. A typing window will appear on the bottom line of the screen, asking for a File specification*

❑ To indicate that the files on the floppy disk (drive A) should be listed, type `a:` ↵

A list of the files on the floppy is shown in the top half of the screen. The first file in the list is highlighted, and details of its size and creation date are shown in a window just above the centre of the screen. When the cursor is moved over the list of filenames using the cursor-movement keys, details of the file highlighted are shown in the window. To remove the list press Esc. (Note that you cannot retrieve a file and put it into the scratchpad by selecting it from this list and pressing ↵. To retrieve one of the files, use the F3 key as described in the previous section.)

11.5 Deleting a file from the floppy disk

To delete a file, follow these instructions:

❑ Press F9 and a minimenu will appear on the bottom line of the screen

❑ Move the cursor so it is over the entry Delete.

❑ To select this option press ↵. A box will appear at the bottom of the screen, inviting you to type in the name of the file to be deleted from the floppy disk.

❑ Type in, replacing fn with the name of the file you wish to delete, a:fn ↵

The file named will be deleted from the floppy disk.

An alternative procedure is to leave SPSS/PC+, and delete the file from DOS, as explained in section 3.12.

12

SPSS/PC+: Editing and correcting errors in a file

12.1 Correcting errors when typing in

To correct errors, put the cursor over the character or space after the error and press the –Del (backspace) key, or put the cursor over the error and press the number/Del key: the wrong character will then be removed and the correct figure can be typed in.

At the bottom of the screen, toward the right hand edge, there is a window with the letters Ins, indicating Insert mode. When a new number or letter is typed in, it will be inserted at the cursor position and the rest of the line will shift right to make room for it.

Switch between Insert and Overtype modes by pressing the Ins key on the keyboard. When in Overtype mode, the Ins on the bottom line of the screen disappears. Now if the cursor is positioned in the centre of a line and a new character keyed in, it will replace the one that was there before, rather than making extra room for the new one.

Moving the cursor in the file is speeded up by using Ctrl+left-arrow and Ctrl+right-arrow, which take the cursor to the start and end of the line. Home moves it to the top of the window, Ctrl+Home to the first line of the file.

12.2 Editing a file stored on the floppy disk

To alter (edit) a file stored on the floppy disk, follow these steps:

❑ If necessary, retrieve the file from the disk as described in section 11.3

❑ Make the changes required

❑ Save the file as explained in section 11.1.

When a file has been edited, the revised version can be saved under the original name or under a different name. If it is saved with the original name, the revised version will overwrite the original. If a new name is used, the old version and the new version will both be kept.

12.3 Inserting blank lines in a file

To insert a blank line in a file:

❏ Move the cursor to the line above or below the point where the blank line is to be inserted

❏ Press F4 and a menu appears at the bottom of the screen

❏ Move the cursor so it is over Insert after or insert Before, whichever is appropriate

❏ Press ↵. A blank line will appear above or below the line at which the cursor was positioned when F4 was pressed.

12.4 Removing lines from a file

To remove a single whole line from the file:

❏ Move the cursor so it is on the line to be deleted

❏ Press F4 and a menu appears at the bottom of the screen

❏ Move the menu cursor until it is over Delete

❏ Press ↵ and the line will be removed.

To remove a set of successive lines (known as a block):

❏ Mark the block, as explained in section 12.5

❏ Press F8 and a menu appears at the bottom of the screen

❏ Move the menu cursor until it is over Delete

❏ Press ↵ and the marked block will be deleted.

12.5 Marking a block of lines

❏ Put the cursor on the first line of the block to be marked

❏ Press F7 and a minimenu appears along the bottom of the screen. The first entry is Lines

❏ To select this press ↵. The line in the file will flash

❏ Move the cursor to the last line of the block to be marked

❏ Press F7 and the block of lines will be highlighted.

If you make a mistake marking a block, cancel the marking by pressing F7 again.

12.6 Joining lines

If you have the cursor in the middle of a line and press ⏎, the part after the cursor will become a new line. Frequently this is not what was intended! To join the line back to its root, put the cursor at the end of the upper line and press the number/Del key on the keypad (not the Del (backspace) key on the main part of the keyboard).

12.7 Moving lines

To move one line in a file:

❑ Go through the procedure for deleting the line described in 12.4

❑ Move the cursor to the line below the position where you want the line to be inserted

❑ Press F4

❑ Select the entry `Undelete` from the minimenu on the bottom line of the screen

❑ Press ⏎ and the line will be inserted above the line on which the cursor rested when ⏎ was pressed.

To move a block of lines:

❑ Mark the block as described in section 12.5

❑ Move the cursor so it is at the position where the marked block is to appear

❑ Press F8

❑ Select the minimenu entry `Move`

❑ Press ⏎ and the marked block will be moved to the new location.

12.8 Saving some lines as a separate file

When a block of lines has been marked, as described in section 12.5, it can be saved as a separate file:

❑ Mark the block of lines

❑ Press F9. The minimenu contains a new option: `write Marked area`

❑ Move the cursor so it is over this entry

❑ To select it, press ⏎ and a window appears asking for the filename to be used when the block is saved

❑ Type in the filename, preceding it with `a:` to have the file stored on the floppy disk.

❑ Press ⏎.

12.9 Removing or moving columns

When editing a file of data containing columns of figures, you can remove or move some columns of numbers. In practice, this is very rarely necessary, but can be done using the Rectangle function from the F7 key:

❑ Position the cursor over the top left corner of the block to be marked

❑ Press F7

❑ Position the cursor over Rectangle in the minimenu on the bottom line of the screen

❑ Move the cursor to the bottom right corner of the rectangular block

❑ Press F7. The area marked will be highlighted

❑ If the rectangle is being moved, put the cursor at the new location for the block

❑ Press F8 and a minimenu appears on the bottom of the screen

❑ Move the cursor so it is over Move or Delete, whichever is appropriate

❑ Press ⏎.

12.10 Saving some columns of data as a separate file

To create a data file containing just some of the columns of data from the original file:

❑ Mark a rectangular block as described in section 12.9 above

❑ Press F9

❑ Select the option write Marked area from the minimenu by putting the cursor over it

❑ Press ⏎ and a typing window appears at the bottom of the screen

❑ Type in the name for the new file

❑ Press ⏎.

12.11 Obtaining a clean, empty file to write to

To get a clean, new file (eg to write your first Command File), proceed as follows:

❑ Ensure you are in edit mode (If you are in Menu mode, use Alt+E)

❑ Press F3. At the bottom of the screen the cursor will be over a minimenu entry Edit different file

❑ To select this entry press ⏎. A typing window titled File to edit appears at the bottom of the screen

❑ Type in the name of the new file, remembering to use the name you want in place of fn, a : fn ↵.

The scratchpad will be cleared and you have a new file to write to. The file is called whatever you used instead of fn, and the name is shown at the bottom right of the screen.

13

SPSS/PC+: The Command File

13.1 What the command file is

The file exdat holds the data to be analysed. You now have to write the command file. This contains the instructions which tell SPSS/PC+ about the data in the data file (data definition commands), where the output from the analysis is to go (operation commands), and which analysis SPSS/PC+ is to perform (procedure commands).

These instructions have to be entered into the command file in a particular form and a proper order. The order is as you would expect. For example, you must explain which data file to use before you order the program to analyse the figures. Similarly, it is no good telling the program to compare the scores of males and females if you have not already told it that the data for sex is in column 4 of the data file.

The data definition section of the Command File tells SPSS/PC+

❏ Where the data file is

❏ The way the data is laid out in the data file (e.g. that the data in column 4 indicates the respondent's sex)

❏ The names of the variables included in the data file (e.g. that the data in column 4 is to be referred to as sex, gender or whatever name you want to give it).

In exdat we have data on the following variables: id number, sex, employer, area, attitude questions 1, 2 and 3, customers visited, sales, date started job. But these names cannot be used, because within SPSS/PC+ a variable name cannot contain a blank space (so id number is not acceptable), and must be no more than 8 characters long. So names that fit these rules must be used.

It is sensible to use names that are informative. Names like var1, var2 etc can be confusing later, so use names that are recognisably related to the 'real-life' names of the variables. For exdat, these might be: id, sex, employer, area, att1, att2, att3, cust, sales, datest (for date started job). There is a special command (YRMODA, covered in section 29.8) for dealing with dates which needs the year, month and day of a date to be listed separately, so we shall divide the date of starting the job into three components: dstd, dstm and dsty for day, month and year.

13.2 Command file example 1 (excom1)

You are going to create the very simple Command File, shown in Fig 13.1, that will enable you to analyse the data stored in exdat.

Note that all command lines must end in a full-stop. In Fig 13.1, the line beginning DATA LIST FILE occupies three lines of screen and paper, but is one SPSS/PC+ command line which ends with 'dsty 33-34'.

```
DATA LIST FILE 'a:exdat' FIXED /id 1-2 sex 4 employer 6 area 8
att1 10 att2 12 att3 14 cust 16-18 sales 20-27 (2) dstd 29-30
dstm 31-32 dsty 33-34.
SET / LISTING 'a:ex1.lis'.
LIST.
```

Fig 13.1 The command file excom1

The DATA LIST FILE line is essential. The first part DATA LIST FILE 'a:exdat' tells the program to get the data for analysis from the file exdat which is in drive A (the floppy disk). The second part of this line, FIXED /id 1-2 sex 4 etc tells the program how the data in each row of the data file is laid out: id is in columns 1-2, sex in column 4, employer in column 6 etc. Sales are in columns 20 to 27; the (2) indicates that there are two decimal places in these figures. The Manual states that it is not necessary to specify that numbers are decimals if the decimal point is keyed in, but problems can occur if this specification is omitted.

The SET / LISTING 'a:ex1.lis'. line tells the program to send the output to a file called ex1.lis on drive A (the floppy disk). If this instruction is not included, the output will go to a file called SPSS.LIS on drive C.

The last line, LIST. is an example of a PROCEDURES command. These instruct SPSS/PC+ to carry out some analysis on the data. Much of the rest of this book will be concerned with explaining what the various procedures do. LIST tells SPSS/PC+ to list the data. It is useful when first creating a new command file because it lets you check that the program is reading the data file correctly, and has understood your commands about the way the data is laid out.

So this is a (very simple) complete Command File. The question is, how do you create it? There are two different ways. One way is to be in the edit mode and type all the lines into the scratchpad. The other way is to use the menu system.

13.3 Creating the command file excom1 with the menu system

To write the Command File, start with a 'clean', new file; it is like starting on a fresh sheet of paper. Do NOT simply add the Command File lines to the Data File; it will not work! To get a clean, new file to write your Command File, follow the instructions given in section 12.11, using as the name of the new Command File: a:excom1. The a: tells SPSS/PC+ to store the file on the floppy disk (drive A); the name of the file is excom1.

The scratchpad will be cleared, providing a new file to write to. The name of the new file, excom1, will be shown on the bottom line of the screen.

To create the command file lines, get into menu mode, put the cursor over the appropriate line in the menu and press ↵. The menu entry is then pasted into the scratchpad. At certain points, information has to be typed in from the keyboard.

To get the first line of the Command File, proceed as follows:

❑ Make sure you are in menu mode and that the first-level main menu (headed MAIN MENU) is in the top left of the screen

❑ Move the cursor down so it is over the entry read or write data

❑ Press right-arrow to enter the submenu

❑ Move cursor to DATA LIST entry

❑ Press ↵ to paste DATA LIST into scratchpad. The submenu of DATA LIST will automatically be shown in the screen's menu area

❑ Move cursor to FILE"

❑ Press ↵ to paste FILE" into scratchpad. A window appears in the centre of the screen

❑ Type in the filename a:exdat ↵. Remember to include the a: since this tells the program the file is on the floppy, and do not put a full-stop at the end as this is already included by the system

❑ Move the cursor in the menu so it is over FIXED

❑ Press ↵ to paste FIXED into scratchpad. The cursor will move to numeric variables in a submenu

❑ Press Alt+T to enter type-in mode;

❑ Read the next paragraph and then type in the details on the layout of the data:

```
id 1-2 sex 4 employer 6 area 8 att1 10 att2 12 att3 14 cust 16-18 sales
20-27 (2) dstd 29-30 dstm 31-32 dsty 33-34
```

You will have to press ↵ before the input gets to the right edge of the window, as you cannot type in a line longer than the window's length. When you press ↵, the material you have typed in is pasted into the scratchpad. Press Alt+T again to bring the typing window back, and key in the rest of the line. When you reach the end of the line (dsty 33-34), do not put a full-stop; just press ↵.

All this takes much longer to describe than to do, once you know what you are supposed to be doing! If you find you have pressed the wrong key at any stage, refer to 13.4 below.

You should have in the scratchpad a line which is the same as the first line in Fig 13.1. If you are having problems, see section 13.4.

To write the SET /LISTING line, first check that you are still in menu mode, with the cursor in the scratchpad immediately before the full stop at the end of the DATA LIST FILE line you have just written. If the cursor is not located there, go into edit mode (Alt+E), and use the arrow keys to position the scratchpad cursor at the end of the DATA LIST FILE line. Get back into menu mode (Alt+E again), and follow these steps:

❑ Press Ctrl+Escape, to move to the first level of main menu

❑ Move the cursor down until it is over the entry `session control & info`

❑ Press the right arrow key. The cursor will be over the entry `SET` in the submenu

❑ Press the right arrow key again, to reveal a submenu

❑ Bring the cursor down until it is over `output` and press the right arrow key. You will see yet another submenu, and the eighth entry down the list is `/LISTING`

❑ Move the cursor down until it is over `/LISTING` and press the right arrow key. This will reveal another submenu, and the cursor will be over `' '`

❑ Press ⏎. `SET /LISTING ' '.` is added to the scratchpad file, and a typing window appears in the centre of the screen

❑ Type in (without a final full stop) `a:ex1.lis` and press ⏎.

The scratchpad line will now be `SET /LISTING 'a:ex1.lis'`.

NOTE: Every time this command file is run, the output will be sent to ex1.lis. If it is run twice, without leaving SPSS/PC+, the second set of outputs will be added on to the end of ex1.lis. But if you leave SPSS/PC+ and then start it again from the DOS level by using `SPSSPC` ⏎, on the next run a new version of ex1.lis will be created. This will OVERWRITE the first- you will have lost the results of your first analysis.

To overcome this, there are two alternatives. One method is to alter the output filename in the SET /LISTING line every time you enter SPSS/PC+, before you run a command file. When creating a second command file the output file can be changed to ex2.lis, so that running that command file does not overwrite ex1.lis. The second method for ensuring ex1.lis is preserved is to change its name after leaving SPSS/PC+, using the DOS rename command, as explained in section 3.10.

The last line, LIST. is obtained as follows:

❑ Press Ctrl+Escape to go back to the first level main menu

❏ Move the cursor so it is over `analyze data`

❏ Press the right arrow key to reveal a submenu

❏ Move the cursor down so it is over `reports and tables`

❏ Press the right arrow key again. You will now see another submenu, and the first entry, which has the cursor over it, is `LIST`.

❏ Press ↵ to paste `LIST .` into the scratchpad

Assuming the command file is as shown in Fig 13.1, save it as described in section 11.1, i.e. press F9 ↵ and ↵ again. The file is now saved on the floppy as excom1.

Both the data file, exdat, and the command file, excom1, are now stored on the floppy disk. The next task is to tell SPSS/PC+ to run the command file. How to do this is described in chapter 14.

13.4 If you run into problems

There is a danger that the complexity of this task will overwhelm you; for the beginner, creating the lines of the command file seems a very complicated and laborious business. But do persevere: after a little practice you will find it is much easier than it looks now.

Remember to look at the Help window in the upper right of the screen; it offers you useful information about the commands that are highlighted in the menu and sometimes provides examples of what command lines should look like.

If you find that you are not where you want to be in the menu system, you can always move up a level by pressing the left arrow key, or can jump to the top level menu by pressing Ctrl+Esc.

If you make an error when typing into the typing window, you can edit it using the usual procedure of moving the cursor within the window, deleting characters, inserting characters in the middle of a line and so on. To remove the typing window and not have its contents pasted into the scratchpad, press the Esc key; get the window back with Alt+T.

As you try to create the command lines, you may obtain some lines that you know are wrong. Do not worry, they can easily be removed later using the technique described in section 12.4 of putting the cursor on the faulty line, pressing F4 and selecting the `Delete` option.

If all else fails, you can get into edit mode (Alt+E) and type in the command lines from the keyboard. But you can make more mistakes this way; you may make a lot of mistakes with the menu system, but it does not let you make some real howlers!

Be careful when you are typing in information in menu mode: you do NOT need to type full-stops at the ends of lines when using the menu system, as they are generated automatically. Look at the screen to see if you have inadvertently obtained two full-stops at the end of a line. If so, you can edit the file to remove one of them, by getting into edit mode, moving the cursor so it is over the second full stop and pressing the –Del key.

If you end up in real chaos and want to start again, the easiest thing to do is go through the procedure of obtaining a new file to write to (section 12.11). So long as you have not saved your chaotic attempt at creating the command file, you can as before call the new file a:excom1. When you press F3 and select Edit different file from the minimenu, the program will tell you (on the bottom line of the screen) that there are unsaved changes in the file you are writing, and ask if it is alright to exit. To abandon your error-filled attempt, press y (for yes) and ↵. The system will then give you another clean file called a:excom1, and you can have another try.

If you have saved an error-filled version of excom1 and want to delete it before beginning again, follow the procedure described in section 11.5.

13.5 If the data occupies more than one line in the data file

The example data used in this book occupies one line per case (respondent). Real data may be longer and occupy two or more lines of the data file. In such a case, it is necessary to tell SPSS/PC+ to read data from the second line for each case, by separating the two lines with / in the DATA LIST FILE line. For example, suppose each case in exdat had been written as follows, with two lines per respondent, the first line ending with the data on att3:

```
01 2 1 1 4 5 1
   043 03450.60 010688
02 1 2 2 4 4 3
   046 04984.42 080690
.........
```

The second line starts with the data on customers visited (cust). The DATA LIST line in the command file would have to be written like this:

```
DATA LIST FILE 'a:exdat' FIXED /id 1-2 sex 4 employer 6 area 8
att1 10 att2 12 att3 14 /cust 2-4 sales 6-13 (2) dstd 15-16 dstm 17-18
dsty 19-20.
```

The / in the list of variables, after the description of att3, tells SPSS/PC+ to go to the next line to read the next variable (cust). Note that the numbers following the name of each variable indicate which columns in the line of the data file contain the relevant scores. So when the second line of data for each respondent is being defined, the numbers must specify the columns used in that second line.

13.6 Data and command files combined

The command file and data files are kept separate in this book, because it easier to explain the way SPSS/PC+ operates if you think of them as separate. But they can be amalgamated, as shown in Fig 13.2. Note that the order of the various parts is vital.

Do NOT copy this File – it is only an example!!!

```
TITLE 'Example data+command files'.
DATA LIST FIXED /id 1-2 sex 4 age 6-7.
VALUE LABELS sex 1 'male' 2 'female'.
MISSING VALUE sex(3).
SET /LISTING 'a:\myd.lis'.
BEGIN DATA.
01 1 20
02 1 15
........
19 3 19
END DATA.
FREQUENCIES /VARIABLES sex.
FINISH.
```

Fig 13.2 Example (NOT to be copied) of a data file and command file amalgamated.

13.7 Running a DOS command from SPSS/PC+

DOS commands can be run without leaving SPSS/PC+. To insert a DOS command (such as del a:ex.lis, which deletes the ex.lis file from the floppy disk) into a command file, follow this procedure:

❑ Select run DOS or other pgms from the main menu

❑ Press the right-arrow key to move to the submenu

❑ To paste DOS into the scratchpad, ensure the cursor is over it and press ↵. A typing window appears

❑ Type in the DOS command and press ↵.

When the command file is run, it will execute this single DOS instruction and then continue with the other SPSS/PC+ commands.

14

SPSS/PC+: Running the analysis

14.1 How to invoke SPSS/PC+

The floppy disk now contains both the data file (exdat) and the command file. The next step is to tell SPSS/PC+ to apply the commands in the command file to the data. There are two ways of doing this.

Method 1

1a Make sure the floppy containing the data and command files is in the disk drive

1b If the command file is in the scratchpad go to step 1g

1c Ensure you are in menu mode

1d Press F3

1e To select `Edit diff file`, press ↵

1f To bring excom1 into the scratchpad, type `a:excom1` ↵

1g Press Ctrl+HOME to position the cursor on the first line of the file

1h Press F10 and a minimenu appears on the bottom line of the screen. There are two options, and the first one, `run from Cursor`, is highlighted

1i To invoke this command, press ↵

Method 2

2a Make sure the floppy containing the data and command files is in the disk drive

2b Ensure the scratchpad is empty. If it is not, delete the lines using the procedure described in section 12.4

2c Ensure you are in edit mode

2d Type, with the full stop, `INCLUDE 'a:excom1'.`

2e Leave the cursor on this line or move the cursor so it is on this line. Press F10 and a minimenu appears on the bottom line of the screen. There are two options, and the first one, `run from Cursor`, is highlighted

2f Press ↵

With either technique, SPSS/PC+ will try to follow the commands in the command file. The screen shows what is happening: the system lists the commands as it comes to them and writes the results of the commands on the screen. At various times it will stop, and the word MORE will appear in the top right of the screen. Press any key on the keyboard and the program will go on to the next stage.

If all is well, the program will follow the commands, and show the table illustrated in Fig 14.1 on the screen. When a key is pressed at the last MORE sign, it will return to the original entry screen.

If all is not well, the program will stop trying to run the command file; a message indicating the problem will be shown and the entry screen will re-appear. (If Method 1 of invoking the run was used, the scratchpad will be empty. If Method 2 was used, the scratchpad will contain the INCLUDE `a:excom1'`. command.) Do not worry: this is a very common event! See section 14.3 if the run has failed.

When the analysis is complete, the floppy will contain the output file, ex1.lis. If you have followed the instructions given here, you are still in SPSS/PC+ and faced with the entry screen. There are easy ways of looking at the output file without leaving SPSS/PC+ (see chapter 15), but for the moment return to DOS following the procedure described in section 9.12, and examine the output file from there.

14.2 Examining the output of excom1

From the DOS level, inspect the contents of the output file ex1.lis by typing (not forgetting the word type)

`type a:ex1.lis` ↵

The file ex1.lis will be presented on the screen. It scrolls up, and to make it pause press Ctrl+S; restart the scrolling by pressing Ctrl+S again.

To obtain a printed copy of ex1.lis, type:

`print a:ex1.lis` ↵
or
`type a:ex1.lis>prn` ↵

If the run of excom1 was successful, the output file looks like Fig 14.1. The commands that were carried out are listed, as are the results of the commands. In this simple first example SPSS/PC+ carried out the LIST procedure which gives a listing of the data in a table that shows the variable names at the head of the columns.

You have now succeeded in 'driving' SPSS/PC+: you have written and saved a data file, written and saved a command file, had the program apply the commands to the data and create an output .LIS file. Of course it may seem rather a lot of effort to obtain such a small outcome, but once you understand the basic principles of driving

SPSS/PC+ they apply to much larger sets of data and it is comparatively simple to obtain more complex forms of output.

As mentioned earlier, the LIST procedure is a helpful check that you have written the data and command files correctly. Do look carefully at the output and confirm that the system is reading the correct figures for the variables you have put into the data file.

```
LIST.
The raw data or transformation pass is proceeding
      22 cases are written to the uncompressed active file.
----------------------------------------------------------------
Page    2                          SPSS/PC+                 4/30/91

ID SEX EMPLOYER AREA ATT1 ATT2 ATT3 CUST      SALES DSTD DSTM DSTY

   1   2        1    1    4    5    1   43   3450.60    1    6   88
   2   1        2    2    4    4    3   46   4984.42    8    6   90
   3   1        1    2    2    3    5   48  10432.82    9    6   90
   4   1        3    1    2    3    4   83   8235.21    1    6   90
   5   3        2    2    2    2    4   71   6441.38    8    6   90
   6   2        3    2    3    3    3   72   6497.05    9    6   90
   7   2        1    2    3    2    5   42   3835.26    1    6   90
   8   1        2    2    4    5    3   28   3819.00    8    6   90
   9   1        1    1    2    3    4   41   5723.52    9    6   90
  10   1        3    2    1    2    5   76   7937.45    8    6   90
  11   2        2    1    2    3    3   39   4582.44    9    6   90
  12   1        1    1    2    3    4   30   2005.30    1    6   90
  13   1        3    2    2    2    4   68   8914.50    3    6   91
  14   2        2    2    1    2    4   33   3124.20    5    6   91
  15   2        2    2    5    4    1   36   4222.45    3    6   91
  16   2        3    1    2    2    4   79   8881.28   31    5   91
  17   1        1    2    3    4    3   38   3449.35    5    6   91
  18   2        1    1    2    3    4   48   7882.60   31    5   91
  19   2        3    1    4    3    1   58   8779.00    3    6   91
  20   2        2    2    1    3    4   60   5822.68   31    5   91
  21   1        2    2    3    4    3   39   4004.80    3    6   91

----------------------------------------------------------------
Page    3                          SPSS/PC+                 4/30/91

ID SEX EMPLOYER AREA ATT1 ATT2 ATT3 CUST      SALES DSTD DSTM DSTY

  22   2        1    1    2    3    3   40   5886.40    5    6   90


Number of cases read =    22    Number of cases listed =    22
----------------------------------------------------------------
Page    4                          SPSS/PC+                 4/30/91

This procedure was completed at   9:52:15
----------------------------------------------------------------
Page    5                          SPSS/PC+                 4/30/91

FINISH.

End of Include file.
```

Fig 14.1 The output (ex1.lis) from running excom1

Check that the table indicates there were 22 cases. You may find that your ex1.lis output indicates that there were 23 (or even more) cases in the data file rather than 22. This is because you may have pressed ↵ at the end of line 22, so that when the data file was saved the cursor was on line 23. (Sometimes this empty line seems to be added unpredictably.) Although line 23 has nothing on it, it is accepted by SPSS/PC as a case, but one with no data.

You will have to edit the data file, exdat, and remove this line.

Recall the data file for editing, as explained in section 11.3 and chapter 12. When a file is recalled, the end of the file is shown on the screen, with the cursor on the last line. If the cursor is on an empty line, remove it using F4 as described in section 12.4. Note that simply moving the cursor up to the last line of data and saving the file does NOT remove the empty line at the end! The cursor should now be on the last line (22) of the data file. If it is not, and you are still on an empty line, repeat this method for removing lines until the cursor is on the last line of figures in the data file.

Save the data file in its revised form (F9 and ↵), and then run excom1 again, using one of the methods described in 14.1.

Although this is a simple beginning, it demonstrates the way the menu system works, and how to use it. We now want to create a slightly longer command file, which will include additional information about the data file and will carry out a useful statistical analysis. This next stage is covered in 14.4.

14.3 When the run fails

If the analysis has failed, the output file will indicate why and where. A problem is usually due to an error in the command file. The error message gives you a clue as to what the problem might be. For example, you may have made a mistake by naming a variable in the DATA LIST line and then using a different (perhaps misspelt) name in a PROCEDURE command later on. You will then have to get back into SPSS/PC+, correct the command file and run SPSS/PC+ again.

To edit excom1, see chapter 12. Editing is most easily done from the edit mode rather than the menu mode. When any corrections to excom1 have been made, make sure it is saved (F9, ™, ™), and run it by moving the cursor to the top line, pressing F10 and ™.

Sometimes there is an error in the data file. This can be harder to spot, because the program will tell you that it could not run a command but it is not always clear that the error is in the data rather than the command file. The commonest mistake in the data file is to have typed in the letter o rather than the number 0. If there is a letter in the data file when there should have been a digit, the program will tell you Invalid digit read with F Format. Check your data. This could perhaps have been phrased in a more helpful way, since it is an invalid letter rather than an invalid digit that has caused the problem! If there is an error in the data file, you need to retrieve and edit it as described in chapter 12.

14.4 Command File example 2 (excom2)

The Command File for the second analysis of exdat is shown in Fig 14.2.

```
DATA LIST FILE 'a:exdat' FIXED /id 1-2 sex 4 employer 6 area 8
att1 10 att2 12 att3 14 cust 16-18 sales 20-27 (2)
dstd 29-30 dstm 31-32 dsty 33-34.
SET /LISTING 'a:ex2.lis'.
TITLE 'SPSS Exercise 2'.
VARIABLE LABELS cust 'Customer visits' dsty 'Year started'.
VALUE LABELS sex 1 'male' 2 'female' /area 1 'North' 2 'South'.
MISSING VALUE sex(3).
FREQUENCIES /VARIABLES sex area.
```

Fig 14.2 The second Command File (excom2)

The DATA LIST FILE line is identical to the one in excom1. When a series of analyses are run on one set of data, keep the same DATA LIST line since the same data file is used every time.

SET /LISTING is the same as in excom1, except that it specifies a new output file: ex2.lis. This ensures that the file of results of the earlier analysis (ex1.lis, the output of excom1) will not be lost when excom2 is run, and reminds you that the output of excom2 is ex2.lis.

The TITLE line means the title 'SPSS/PC Exercise 2' is printed at the top of each page of printout.

VARIABLE LABELS tells the program the labels to use when printing out the results. Although the data in columns 16-18 is called cust, when it is printed it will have the written label 'Customer visits'. Similarly, dsty will be labelled 'Year started'.

VALUE LABELS has the effect of including in the printout a verbal description of the value of a variable. Remember the difference between variables and values. In exdat, sex is one of the variables, and in column 4 of exdat all the numbers are 1, 2 or 3. These numbers are the values of the sex variable, with 1 representing male, 2 denoting female, and 3 meaning we do not know the sex of that respondent. The line shown here instructs the program to give the label 'male' to the value 1 of the sex variable, and the label 'female' to the value 2 when it presents the results. Similarly, area has been coded as 1 or 2, with 1 meaning North and 2 meaning South. The second part of this line, following the / will give the appropriate labels to these values on the variable area.

MISSING VALUE is nearly always needed. Often some respondents have not answered all the questions asked, or have failed to provide a measure on one of the variables. It is sensible (for reasons that will become clear later) to record a no-response as a particular number. When choosing a number to represent 'data missing', use a number that cannot be a genuine number for that variable. For the sex variable in exdat, 1 represents male and 2 female, so 3 can be used to indicate no response. This MISSING VALUE line tells SPSS/PC+ that a score of 3 on sex means 'sex unknown'. If one wanted to define a missing value for sales, one would use a number that could not be genuine, such as –1.00.

FREQUENCIES invokes the FREQUENCIES procedure. This particular instruction tells SPSS/PC+ to 'produce frequency tables for the value of the variables sex and area'. What this actually does will be clear when this command file has been run.

14.5 Creating the second command file (excom2)

The simple method of writing excom2 is to edit excom1. Enter SPSS/PC+ and retrieve excom1 from the floppy as described in section 11.3. It will be listed in the scratchpad. The DATA LIST FILE line can be left as it is.

To change the name of the output file from ex1.lis to ex2.lis, switch to edit mode and move the cursor so it is over the full stop in ex1.lis. Press the –Del (backspace) key so that ex1.lis is changed to ex.lis, with the cursor over the x, and type in the number 2.

To remove the LIST line:

❑ Check you are in edit mode

❑ Move the cursor so it is on the LIST line

❑ Press F4 and a minimenu appears along the bottom of the screen

❑ Move the cursor so it is over Delete

❑ Press ↵

You now have to add the extra lines shown in Fig 14.2.

To create the TITLE line of excom2:

❑ In edit mode, move the cursor to the end of the SET /LISTING line

❑ Enter menu mode

❑ Move to the top level Main Menu (Ctrl+Esc)

❑ Move the menu cursor so it is over session control & info in the main menu

❑ Press the right-arrow key to reveal the submenu

❑ Move the cursor down until it is over titles and comments and go right again

❑ Move the cursor down so it is over TITLE"

❑ Go right, and the cursor will be over ' ' in the submenu entitled TITLE

❑ Press ↵. TITLE" will be pasted into the file and a typing window will open in the centre of the screen.

❑ Type in the title you want, with no inverted commas, apostrophes or full stop (period)

❑ Press ⏎. The title will be inserted between the inverted commas in the `TITLE` line.

To create the VARIABLE LABELS line: *Ctrl*

❑ Move back to the main menu by pressing Alt+Esc

❑ Put the cursor over `read or write data` press the right arrow key

❑ Move the cursor down until it is over `labels and formatting`

❑ Press the right arrow key to reveal the next submenu.

❑ The cursor should be over `VARIABLE LABELS`.

❑ Press ⏎ to paste `VARIABLE LABELS` into the scratchpad

❑ Press Alt+T, which causes a typing window to appear in the centre of the screen

❑ Type in `cust 'Customer visits' dsty 'Year started'`

❑ Press ⏎

The VARIABLE LABELS line should now be as shown in Fig 14.2. Press left arrow to return to the menu entitled `labels and formatting`.

To obtain the VALUE LABELS line:

❑ Check you are in the menu `labels and formatting`

❑ Move the cursor down so it is over `VALUE LABELS`

❑ Press the right arrow key

❑ Move the cursor down so it is over `~VARIABLES`

❑ Press ⏎. `VALUE LABELS`. will be pasted into the scratchpad

❑ Use Alt+T to obtain a typing window;

❑ Type in: `sex 1 'male' 2 'female' / area 1 'North' 2 'South'`

❑ Press ⏎

The scratchpad should now contain the line shown in Fig 14.2.

To create the MISSING VALUE line:

❑ Press left arrow key to return to the `labels and formatting` submenu

❑ Move the cursor down so it is over `MISSING VALUE`

❏ Press right arrow key

❏ Ensure cursor is over ~variable(s);

❏ Press ↵ to paste MISSING VALUE into the scratchpad

❏ Press Alt+T to obtain a typing window

❏ Type in sex(3)

❏ Press ↵

To create the FREQUENCIES line:

❏ Make sure the cursor is over or past the full stop at the end of the MISSING VALUE line

❏ In menu mode, press Alt+Esc to get to the first level of main menu

❏ Move the cursor down so it is over analyze data

❏ Press right arrow key to reveal the submenu

❏ Ensure the cursor is over descriptive statistics

❏ Press right arrow key. Another submenu is revealed, with the cursor over FREQUENCIES

❏ Press right arrow key. There is another submenu and a useful help screen

❏ Move cursor down so it is over ~/VARIABLES

❏ Press ↵ to paste FREQUENCIES /VARIABLES into the scratchpad;

❏ Press Alt+T to obtain a typing window

❏ Type in, without a full-stop, sex area

❏ Press ↵

The command file in the scratchpad should now be the same as Fig 14.2. Even if it is not, save it (F9 and ↵) as excom2. If you need to make any changes, get into edit mode (Alt+E), make the alterations and save the file again.

14.6 Running excom2

Run the command file excom2 by moving the cursor to the top line (Ctrl+Home while in edit mode), then pressing F10 and ↵.

Watch the screen as the program runs, and try to follow what is happening. When MORE appears in the top right of the screen, press any key to continue the program run.

14.7 The output of excom2

If the run of excom2 has failed, you will be given some indication of what was wrong. You can then correct the command file, using the editing procedures described in chapter 12, and run it again.

The main outcome of this run is two tables, which are reproduced in Fig 14.3. The first table shows the number of cases having each value of the sex variable. The first column shows the value labels, the second the values for the variable. The third column (Frequency) shows the number of cases having that value for the variable. The data file included 10 males, 11 females and 1 *'missing values'*, the case where sex was coded as 3 because this individual had not responded to the question asking whether the respondent was male or female. Observe that the table shows that a value of 1 means male, 2 means female: this is the result of the VALUE LABELS command.

The Percent column shows the frequencies expressed as percentages of the total number of cases (22 in this instance).

The next column is headed Valid Percent. The data file has one case where the data is missing, the sex score of 3 having been given identified as a MISSING VALUE score. So there are fewer valid cases of data on this variable than there are cases in the data file. SPSS/PC+ sees that there are 21, not 22 sets of data for the sex variable, and puts the percentage out of 21 (the number of valid cases) in this Valid Percent column.

```
SEX

                                          Valid     Cum
    Value Label    Value  Frequency  Percent Percent  Percent

male                 1         10      45.5    47.6    47.6
female               2         11      50.0    52.4   100.0
                     3          1       4.5  MISSING
                            -------  ------- -------
               TOTAL          22     100.0   100.0

Valid Cases     21      Missing Cases      1
------------------------------------------------------------------


AREA

                                          Valid     Cum
    Value Label    Value  Frequency  Percent Percent  Percent

North                1          9      40.9    40.9    40.9
South                2         13      59.1    59.1   100.0
                            -------  ------- -------
               TOTAL          22     100.0   100.0

Valid Cases     22      Missing Cases      0
------------------------------------------------------------------
```

Fig 14.3 The output tables from excom2 command FREQUENCIES

The final column shows the valid percentages expressed in cumulative form.

Below the table there is a statement of the number of valid cases and the number of missing cases.

The second table shows the number of cases for each area, with 9 from the North and 13 from the South. The VALUE LABELS command in excom2 ensures the table shows that 1 means North and 2 means South.

You should now be faced with the initial entry screen, and are probably wishing you could see the output file on your screen.

Chapter 15 explains how to examine the output (.LIS) file and how to edit it.

Exercise 14.1

Imagine you have carried out a survey of alcohol intake among young people, and have data on 1000 respondents. For each person, you have a four-digit identification number, their age (in whole years), their sex (1 is male and 2 is female), and a measure of their weekly alcohol intake where 1 means none, 2 mean low, 3 means medium and 4 means high level of consumption. For all variables except id, −1 means the data is missing (missing values). The results of the survey have been stored in a file called alcdat on the floppy disk. The data for one respondent looks like this:

`0629 17 2 2`

Write a command file which would produce a table showing the number of respondents with each level of intake.

The answer is given in Appendix A.

14.8 Using Alt+V to select variables

When using the menu system to create the command file, the information window frequently suggests using Alt+V to produce a screen listing of the variable names that can be used to save typing them in. This will only work if the system has created an Active File i.e. you must have run SPSS/PC+ in the current session. If you are editing a command file after having run SPSS/PC+, Alt+V will operate correctly. But if you have not run the program, Alt+V will produce an error message: `No variables-execute a DATA LIST or TRANSLATE command`. In this case, press Esc and then use Alt+T to open a typing window and key in the variable names.

The list of variables shown when Alt+V is pressed includes some in addition to those defined in the DATA LIST line. These additional variables are automatically created by the program. The one you may need is *$casenum*, which is the system's number for the case or set of data, described in section 5.3. When the data file is read, the cases are allocated a *$casenum* with 1 being given to the first case read, 2 to the second and so on. For exdat, *$casenum* is the same as the id of each respondent, but this would not be true if the id numbers had not been in sequential order in the original data file.

14.9 Adding comments in the command file

If you are creating a complex command file, it can be very helpful to include lines which explain what the various comands do. This is done by beginning the line with * which has the effect of making SPSS/PC+ skip that line and go on to the next one.

14.10 Running parts of the command file

As mentioned earlier, when SPSS/PC+ runs a command file for the first time, it creates a copy of the data file, the active file, and uses that in the analyses. If you then edit the command file, perhaps adding some extra procedure lines, you do not need to run the complete file: the commands which tell the package where to obtain the data (DATA LIST FILE) and which provide details on the labels, missing values etc have already been run and their effect is still in operation because the active file is still in memory. So you can place the cursor on the first of the extra lines you have added, press F10 and ↵ to run from cursor, and the program will carry out just the additional commands. This is much quicker than putting the cursor on the top line of the command file and running the whole set of commands again, because when that happens a complete new active file has to be created.

You can also run part of the command file by marking it as a block (see section 12.5), and then pressing F10 and selecting run marked Area from the minimenu.

But remember that the first time you run a command file you must put the cursor on the first line and run from there, in order to create the active file.

If you try to run a procedure command other than the DATA FILE LIST before the active file has been created, you will receive an error message:

```
ERROR 34, Text: xxxx.

This command is not permitted until a file is defined via DATA LIST,
IMPORT, GET, JOIN or TRANSLATE.

This command not executed.
```

The program will be showing MORE in the top right of the screen, so press keys until you are returned to the usual SPSS/PC+ screen. Retrieve the command file, move the cursor to the first line of the file (Ctrl+Home in edit mode), and try F10 again.

🗍🗍

SPSS/PC+: The output

15.1 Examining the output (.LIS file) on screen

When SPSS/PC+ runs it creates two output files, the .LOG file and the .LIS file. The .LIS file contains the results of the analysis, and is the one of most interest. Excom2 saves the .LIS file, ex2.lis, on the floppy disk.

As it runs, SPSS/PC+ shows on the screen the commands it is executing, and the results of the command. (It is possible to suppress the screen output, but I always like to see what is going on!). When the run has finished, or is stopped because of an error in the commands, SPSS/PC+ returns to the Review mode, and the initial entry screen. You will have noticed that at the end of the run the .LIS file appears briefly in the top half of the screen but is then hidden by the menus.

To remove the menus and reveal the .LIS file, press Alt+M. (To get the menus back, press Alt+M again.) The end of the .LIS file is revealed in the top half of the screen. This is probably not informative, and does not show the part of the output you are interested in. To move around in the .LIS file it is necessary to move the cursor so that it is in the top half of the screen, not in the scratchpad in the bottom of the screen.

15.2 Switching the cursor between the top and bottom of the screen

To move the cursor into the top of the screen, proceed as follows:

❏ Press F2. The minimenu shown along the bottom of the screen has:

```
Switch       Change size      Zoom
```

(Note that Zoom may not be available, as earlier versions did not contain it.)

❏ With the `Switch` option highlighted, press ↵ and the cursor will move to the bottom line of the top half of the screen.

(The same effect can be obtained without pressing F2 if you use Alt+S.)

It is helpful to have the .LIS file fill the screen, rather than just forming the top half:

❑ Press F2

❑ Select Zoom from the minimenu or select Change size

❑ Press ⏎. If Zoom was selected, the upper window will fill the screen. If Change size was selected, type in the number of lines the upper window is to occupy and press ⏎.

To return to the normal setting, where the scratchpad is in the lower half of the screen, press Esc. Then press F2 and select Switch from the minimenu (or just press Alt+S) to move the cursor back into the scratchpad.

15.3 Moving around in the screen .LIS file

The up and down arrow keys or the PageUp and PageDown keys move the cursor up or down in the file, which scrolls in the window. Ctrl+left-arrow and Ctrl+right-arrow move the cursor to the start and end of a line. Home moves it to the top of the window, Ctrl+Home to the top of the file.

.LIS files can be lengthy, but are divided into pages. To jump to a particular page:

❑ Press F6, which reveals a window at the bottom of the screen displaying go to: Output pg

❑ Press ⏎

❑ Type in the number of the page to jump to

❑ Press ⏎ and the page requested will be shown.

15.4 Printing the output (.LIS) file

The .LIS file can be printed as SPSS/PC+ runs the command file, but is undesirable, for three reasons. First, it makes the whole process of running SPSS/PC+ very slow, as it keeps having to wait for the printer to catch up. Second, in its raw state the .LIS file contains a lot of material such as page headings that are not really wanted, so it is very extravagant on paper. Third, there are many occasions when the program fails because of some mistake in the command file, and it is wasteful to have a record of all these mistakes!

The easiest method of obtaining a printed copy of the .LIS file is to leave SPSS/PC+ and return to DOS. You can then use one of the usual commands, replacing fn with the name of the file to be printed:

```
print a:fn.lis ⏎
```

or

```
type a:fn.lis>prn ⏎
```

15.5 Editing the .LIS file

The original .LIS file contains a lot of unnecessary material such as page headings, messages about the time the task was completed etc. If you intend to use the .LIS output from SPSS/PC+ in reports it is necessary to edit the .LIS file to get a 'clean' version. (There are other ways of obtaining output in a form suitable for including in reports, considered in chapter 33).

The simple way of obtaining a 'clean' .LIS file is to word process it. Run your word processor in the usual way, and call up the .LIS file for editing. You can then remove unwanted sections, apply all the word processing facilities such as **bold**, *italic*, margination etc, and print it out in the form you want. The word processing technique is probably the most convenient method for editing the .LIS file, especially as you are likely to be familiar with the conventions of your own word processor.

It is also possible to edit the .LIS file within SPSS/PC+. As explained above (15.2), you can position the cursor in the top half of the screen where the .LIS file is shown, and use the zoom or change size facility to have this window fill the whole screen. Editing is done using the function keys. For example, deleting single lines or blocks of lines is accomplished using the F4 or F7 and F8 keys, as described in chapter 12.

Other editing functions can be used: F5 accesses a Search and Replace facility so you can change any string of characters into a different one. This is achieved by pressing F5 and then selecting fOrward change or bAckward change from the minimenu. So it is possible to edit the .LIS file within SPSS/PC+, and save the edited file using the F9 Write whole file route in the usual way. (Note that if you have zoomed the .LIS file so it fills the whole screen, you will need to 'unzoom' it by pressing Esc before F9 operates and allows you to save the file.) When you press F9 ↵, take the opportunity to type in a new name (such as a:clean2.LIS) for the file being saved, so there is no danger of losing it when SPSS/PC+ runs again. The edited file (clean2.lis) can then be printed when you have returned to DOS.

The illustrations of SPSS/PC+ output (.LIS) files in this book have all been edited, using either the editing procedures within SPSS/PC+ or a word processor, to remove page headings and irrelevant items of information that are automatically included in the output. This is why the illustrations do not match exactly the full .LIS files produced by running the command files.

15.6 The .LOG file

The .LOG file created when SPSS/PC+ runs is stored on the hard disk (drive C), and is a list of the commands that SPSS/PC+ has carried out during the session. It can be inspected from DOS in the usual way if you are in the SPSS directory of drive C by typing

type SPSS.LOG ↵

From the root directory of drive C, type

```
type \SPSS\SPSS.LOG ⏎
```

The .LOG file from running excom2 is illustrated in Fig 15.1. It shows which page of the .LIS file contains the results of each command. It can be copied to the floppy disk, or printed out.

```
[Next command's output on page 1
DATA LIST FILE 'a:exdat' FIXED / id 1-2 sex 4 employer 6 area 8 att1 10
att2 12
att3 14 cust 16-18 sales 20-27 (2) dstd 29-30 dstm 31-32 dsty 33-34 .
SET /LISTING 'a:ex2.lis'.
TITLE 'SPSS Exercise 2'.
VARIABLE LABELS cust 'customers visited' dsty 'year started job'.
VALUE LABELS sex 1 'male' 2 'female' /area 1 'North' 2 'South'.
MISSING VALUE sex(3).
FREQUENCIES /VARIABLES sex area.
[Next command's output on page 5
FINISH.
```

Fig 15.1 The .LOG file produced when excom2 is run

16

SPSS/PC+: The .SYS file

16.1 Uses and benefits of a .SYS file

Using the technique described so far, every time SPSS/PC+ is invoked it has to go through the procedure of reading the data file, interpreting the layout of the data, obeying the instructions on missing values, variable labels etc before it gets to the stage of doing the analysis. With large data files these preliminaries take some time, and it is frustrating to have to wait while the program deals with them before it gets round to doing one simple task that you forgot to ask for the last time. The way to abbreviate this is by creating a .SYS file.

A .SYS file is a special version of the data file, which incorporates the data description elements of the command file including VARIABLE NAMES and VALUE LABELS and the effects of some other commands such as RECODE which are explained later. When you have created a .SYS file, you can tell SPSS/PC+ to read the .SYS file and apply procedures to it, as though it were the original data file. But .SYS files are processed much faster than normal data files.

There is a second benefit from using .SYS files. If you have two sets of data and want to join them together into one set, you have to use .SYS files to do it.

16.2 Creating a .SYS file

Find SAVE *by selecting* read or write data *from the main menu and moving right. Move cursor to* SAVE *in the submenu and press the right arrow key; the next submenu contains* /OUTFILE".

To create a .SYS file, you write a command file that includes the data specifications (FILE LIST, VALUE LABELS, etc), and then add the line:

SAVE /OUTFILE 'A:fn.sys'.

using the actual filename you want instead of fn in this line.

The complete command file to create a .SYS file of the data in exdat is:

```
DATA LIST FILE 'a:exdat' FIXED / id 1-2 sex 4 employer 6 area 8 att1 10
att2 12 att3 14 cust 16-18 sales 20-27 (2) dstd 29-30 dstm 31-32 dsty
33-34.
TITLE 'SPSS Exercise 2'.
VARIABLE LABELS cust 'Customer visits' dsty 'Year started'.
VALUE LABELS sex 1 'male' 2 'female' /area 1 'North' 2 'South'.
MISSING VALUE sex(3).
SAVE /OUTFILE 'a:ex1.sys'.
```

When this command file is run, the .SYS file ex1.sys will be written on the floppy disk.

Exercise 16.1

Write the command file shown above to create a .SYS file of the exdat file. All except the last line are included in the command file excom2. Retrieve it and delete the SET /LISTING and FREQUENCIES lines. (In edit mode, put the cursor on the line to be deleted, press the F4 key and select `Delete` from the minimenu.) With the cursor on the MISSING VALUE line, move it to the end of that line by pressing Ctrl+right arrow. Return to menu mode, use Alt+Esc to get to the main menu, and add the `SAVE /OUTFILE 'a:ex1.sys'` line. Save the file as syscom on the floppy disk, and run it. The file ex1.sys will be stored on the floppy.

16.3 Using the .SYS file

Find GET /FILE" by selecting `read or write data` from main menu and pressing the right-arrow key. Move the cursor to GET in the submenu and press the right-arrow key. The submenu contains FILE".

Once the data has been stored in the form of a .SYS file, writing the command file for subsequent data analysis becomes much simpler. The .SYS file is retrieved with the GET command:

```
GET /FILE 'a:fn.sys'.
```

and procedures can then follow this line.

To use ex1.sys, you need these commands in your command file:

```
GET /FILE 'A:ex1.SYS'.
SET /LISTING 'a:sysout.lis'.
...Procedure lines....
```

(Remember that SET /LISTING is under `session control & info` in the main menu.)

16.4 Modifying the .SYS file

There is one major drawback to .SYS files: they cannot be edited. They are stored in a particular format that can only be read by SPSS/PC+, and they cannot be brought into the scratchpad or listed on the screen. At first, this inability to edit a .SYS file may seem a major problem. If the data has a mistake in it, how can it be corrected? In fact, this is no problem at all. Remember the .SYS file was created by having the command file syscom (Exercise 16.1) read the original data file and then create the .SYS file with the SAVE /OUTFILE command. If one needs to change the data, go back to the original data file (exdat) and edit that. Then retrieve the command file syscom, and run it again. It will save an outfile ex1.sys just as before, but this ex1.sys will be a version of the corrected data file.

Now that you are aware of .SYS files, you will probably use them almost all the time. (The remainder of this book uses ex1.sys rather than the original exdat file.) They are considerably more convenient than using the original data file, but of course the data and data definition commands must be correct before the .SYS file is created.

16.5 Viewing the contents of a .SYS file

To find SYSFILE INFO from the Main menu, select session control & info and go right.

As it is not possible to list .SYS files directly on the screen, it is easy to forget what each one contains. The technique for obtaining a summary of the contents of a .SYS file is to use the SYSFILE INFO ' ' command. Paste it into the scratchpad, and type into the typing window the name of the .sys file. When the command is run, using the usual F10 key, details of the file will be shown, including a list of the variables and the variable labels.

17

SPSS for Windows: Starting out

17.1 What you need to run SPSS for Windows

Assuming SPSS for Windows is installed on your hard disk, there are six things you need to know in order to use it:

1. How to get to the SPSS programs;

2. How to create and save a file of data to be analysed;

3. How to obtain the commands (procedures) you want to apply;

4. How to get SPSS to apply the commands to the data file;

5. How to save the contents of the output (.LST) file on the floppy disk;

6. How to save the commands in a syntax file.

These requirements are covered in the following chapters. To begin, how do you get into SPSS for Windows (and how do you get out of it)?

17.2 Getting to SPSS for Windows

The first task is to run Windows, which usually means that when your system is running and you are faced with the DOS prompt you type in win and press ↵. You will then see the Windows logo while the windows programs are initialised, and then the Program Manager screen. This may contain a group icon labelled SPSSv5. Open the group by double-clicking on it; the group will contain a number of icons, including SPSSv5, Sample Data and Sample Chart. (Sample Data and Sample Chart are used in the manual for SPSS for Windows to explain how the package operates.) To start the package, double click on the SPSS/PCv5 icon. (As it is possible to rename groups and move applications from one group to another, the arrangement on your system may not be the same as the original one. You will need to ask locally if you have problems initiating SPSS for Windows.)

17.3 The SPSS for Windows screen

When SPSS for Windows first starts, it presents the screen shown in Fig 4.1 (chapter 4), which has three major components: the Application window, the Output window and the Data Editor window, titled **Newdata**. These are seen as lying one on top of the other, the Application window being the rear one that fills the screen, and the other two lying on top of it.

The Application window

The top line contains the usual Windows control box in the top left, the title bar showing that it is SPSS you are using, and the two boxes in the top right corner for minimising or maximising the size of the window. The second line is the Menu bar, and lists a number of Menu headings from **File** to **Help**. The **File** menu is used for retrieving and saving files, and therefore controls the way the package interacts with the hardware. The **Window** menu is used to alter the way that the items on the screen are organised and displayed, and the Menus between these two, **Edit** to **Utilities** are used to have the package perform operations on the data. The **Help** menu provides access to information which can assist you use SPSS for Windows; further information on Help is given in chapter 20.

As is generally true in Windows, the contents of the menu are revealed by moving the mouse pointer to the menu heading and clicking; items in the drop-down menu which is then revealed are selected by clicking on them. (If you select a drop-down menu and it is not the one you want, just click outside it and it will be folded up.)

Each menu heading in the menu bar has an underlined letter in its title; this indicates that one can reveal the drop-down menu by holding down the Alt key on the keyboard and while it is depressed tapping the underlined letter. So to have the **Help** drop-down menu revealed, hold down Alt and tap the H key on the keyboard.

The items in the drop-down menu also have an underlined letter which can be used to select that entry *without* using the Alt key.

The bottom line of the Application window, the status bar, presents messages indicating what the package is doing. When first started, it reads *SPSS Processor is ready*.

The Output window

The second window shown in Fig 4.1 is entitled !Output1. The results of the analyses are put into this window, and the contents can be examined, edited, and the file then saved. When the package is started up, the window contains the first line of the output file, giving the date and stating that the file comes from SPSS 5. The output window has a number of items in its menu bar (**Pause**, **Scroll** etc); their function is described in section 19.2.

At start up, the output window is behind the Data Editor. To make it active and bring it to the front, move the mouse pointer on to the title bar (!Output) or the scroll bar down the side, and click. When the Data Editor needs to be made active, clicking in its title bar or in its scroll bars will bring it to the front.

The Output window has scroll bars down the right side and along the bottom, so one can move the contents of the file within the window to reveal parts of it not otherwise visible.

The Data Editor window

The window at the front of the screen in Fig 4.1 is the one where you insert the data to be analysed. Initially it is titled Newdata, and contains no figures, but it can be seen to be a spreadsheet, with columns headed var and rows labelled 1,2 etc. (If you have not come across spreadsheets, read section 17.6 below.) Like the Output window, it has scroll bars down the right side and along the bottom, so one can move the contents of the file within the window to reveal parts of it not otherwise visible.

Active and designated windows

When using SPSS for Windows, you can have a number of output windows and a number of syntax windows on the screen simultaneously. (No syntax window is shown when the package first begins, but they are used for recording the commands you use in analysing the data: see sections 19.6 and 19.7).

For the moment, assume you have two output windows visible. One of these is the one that will receive the results of the analysis you are performing, and this is known as the designated window. It is identified by having a ! before its verbal title, so the title reads !Output1.

The active window is the one that is currently selected: it is the 'front' one, with the darkened (blue) title bar. You can make any window currently on the screen the active window by clicking in it: it will then come to the 'front'. You might have a data window as the active window, but a different one, such as an !Output1 window, as the designated one, the one that will receive the results of the analysis you are currently performing.

17.4 Rearranging the screen windows

When you first start SPSS for Windows, the windows are arranged to overlap, like a stack of cards. The 'front' window is for data input, and is entitled Newdata; behind that is the output window, !Output1, and the largest window, at the 'back' of the stack is the Application window, titled SPSS. This stacked arrangement is known as cascading. If the screen becomes cluttered, and you cannot see the window you want, you can have the cascade re-arranged by clicking on the Window menu heading in the menu bar of the Application window, and selecting the Cascade option.

You may want the windows arranged side-by-side. This is known as the tile arrangement, and can be selected from the Window menu of the Application window. When the windows are tiled, they are narrower than usual. You can scroll the contents of the window with the scroll bars along the bottom and down the right-hand side. If you want one of the windows to fill the screen, click on the small square button with an upward pointing arrow in the top right of the window (the maximise button). This will mean the other windows will be covered up, but they can be revealed by clicking on the double-headed arrow button in the menu bar or by using the Window /Cascade or Window /Tile commands from the menu bar.

17.5 Leaving SPSS for Windows

To leave the package, you can either double click on the control box at the left edge of the application window title bar, or select File /Close from the application window menu. In either case you will be asked whether you wish to save the files that are at present in use: the data file, output file, and syntax and chart files if they are present.

17.6 Basic principles of a spreadsheet

SPSS for Windows' Data Editor resembles a spreadsheet. Spreadsheets were one of the facilities that convinced people that computers had the potential to make a real benefit to business and commerce. Over the last 10 years they have become increasingly sophisticated, and modern spreadsheet programs such as Borland's Quattro or Microsoft's Excel provide a huge range of facilities for dealing with tables of numbers. But despite this, the essential principles of a spreadsheet are fairly simple.

A spreadsheet can be thought of as a table, made up of columns and rows, where the columns are labelled with a letter or name, and the rows by number. So if the first column is column A, and the first row is number 1, the top left of the table is cell A1, the one to its right is B1, the one below that is B2 and so on. You can put numbers or words (labels) into a cell by moving the cursor so it is over the cell you want and then typing in the numbers from the keyboard. When you move the cursor (cell indicator) to another cell by pressing one of the arrow keys on the keyboard, the number you typed in appears in the cell you just left, and you can type in the numbers for the cell now highlighted. So entering series of numbers is quite simple.

The major feature of a conventional spreadsheet is that you can tell the program to manipulate the entries in the table by specifying the cells to use and not their contents. Suppose we had entered the numbers 6, 7, 8 and 9 into cells A1, A2, A3 and A4 of the sheet. We could obtain the total of these numbers by moving the cursor to cell A5 and typing as its contents the formula +A1+A2+A3+A4; when we press Enter, the result of this calculation (30) will appear in the cell. Note that we are not asking for the total of 6, 7, 8 and 9 but for the total of whatever values are in cells A1, A2, A3 and A4. It just happens that those cells contain 6, 7, 8 and 9. If we go back to cell A1 and type in 16, the total shown in cell A5 will become 40 (=16+7+8+9), the total of the numbers which are now in cells A1, A2, A3 and A4 . It is this ability to deal with the contents of cells by referring to the 'name' of the cell rather than its particular contents at any one time that gives spreadsheets their power. A conventional spreadsheet will allow you to use particular expressions, known as functions, to obtain particular answers. For example, the total of the values in cells A1, A2, A3 and A4 might be obtained by typing into cell A5 the function @SUM(A1..A4).

The spreadsheet in SPSS is more limited than a standard spreadsheet, as the cells can only contain values, not formulae or functions. To obtain totals, means etc, one has to use the SPSS commands, and these are not entered into the data spreadsheet itself.

18

SPSS for Windows: The data file

In SPSS for Windows, data is entered into the spreadsheet which is automatically presented in the Data Editor (Newdata) window. When putting data into the Data Editor, each row of the sheet should contain the results from one respondent; SPSS refers to each line as a case.

Each column contains the results on one variable; for example the second column, var00002, might contain the data indicating the respondent's sex. The cell entries are values, usually numbers. (If you wish to use letters, refer to section 6.2.)

18.1 Creating the data file

To enter data:

Ensure the Data Editor window is active; if necessary, click on its title bar

Check that the top left cell is highlighted. If it is not, press the Ctrl+Home key combination to move the cell selector to this cell

Type in the first set of numbers for the first case of your data set: I advise you to have an identification number as the first 'score' for each respondent.

Press the ↵ key or the down or right arrow keys on the keyboard.

If you press the right arrow key, the cell selector moves to the next cell on the right of the one you have just been addressing. It is usually more convenient to enter the data for each respondent rather than each variable, so pressing the right arrow key is normally the easiest procedure. If you press Enter or down arrow, the cell selector will move down to the cell below the one you have just been addressing.

The first cell will now contain the figures you typed in, and the column will now be headed var00001. You then type in the figures for the second cell, press the arrow key and so on until all the figures have been entered in to appropriate row and column positions. Each time you put a number into a column for the first time, the column will be given a label: column 2 is labelled var00002, column 3 is var00003 and so on.

Exercise 18.1: Entering a set of data into the Data Editor

The data I shall use to explain how SPSS for Windows operates has been described in chapter 7, and in covering SPSS for Windows this set of data will be referred to as salesq (for Sales Questionnaire). (Remember that for those using SPSS/PC+, the file of data is called exdat, and so the illustrations of the printouts may use that name instead of salesq.) The table of data is shown in Table 18.1, and your first task is to enter it into the Data Editor. Put the first number (1, the id for the first respondent) into the top left cell of the spreadsheet, the number 2 (representing the sex of respondent number 1) into the top cell of the second column. Then continue entering numbers until all the data has been put into the sheet. The complete number for sales (3450.60 for the first case) goes into one cell in column 9 of the sheet The three sets of numbers representing the date started go into separate columns, so you will have 12 columns of numbers altogether. (SPSS for Windows has special ways of dealing with dates, but these require you to be familiar with some aspects of the program we have not yet covered. Section 29.9 gives a more detailed explanation.)

Table 18.1 Data from the sales questionnaire study.

				response to			customer		date started		
id	sex	empl oyer	area	q5	q6	q7	visits	sales	(day, month, year)		
id	sex	empl	area	att1	att2	att3	cust	sales	dstd	dstm	dsty
1	2	1	1	4	5	1	43	3450.60	01	06	88
2	1	2	2	4	4	3	46	4984.42	08	06	90
3	1	1	2	2	3	5	48	10432.82	09	06	90
4	1	3	1	2	3	4	83	8235.21	01	06	90
5	3	2	2	2	2	4	71	6441.38	08	06	90
6	2	3	2	3	3	3	72	6497.05	09	06	90
7	2	1	2	3	2	5	42	3835.26	01	06	90
8	1	2	2	4	5	3	28	3819.00	08	06	90
9	1	1	1	2	3	4	41	5723.52	09	06	90
10	1	3	2	1	2	5	76	7937.45	08	06	90
11	2	2	1	2	3	3	39	4582.44	09	06	90
12	1	1	1	2	3	4	30	2005.30	01	06	90
13	1	3	2	2	2	4	68	8914.50	03	06	91
14	2	2	2	1	2	4	33	3124.20	05	06	91
15	2	2	2	5	4	1	36	4222.45	03	06	91
16	2	3	1	2	2	4	79	8881.28	31	05	91
17	1	1	2	3	4	3	38	3449.35	05	06	91
18	2	1	1	2	3	4	48	7882.60	31	05	91
19	2	3	1	4	3	1	58	8779.00	03	06	91
20	2	2	2	1	3	4	60	5822.68	31	05	91
21	1	2	2	3	4	3	39	4004.80	03	06	91
22	2	1	1	2	3	3	40	5886.40	05	06	90

If some data were missing, you would just leave that cell empty. There are no empty cells in the salesq data, but if respondent number 5 had failed to indicate their sex, for example, you would just skip over that cell when entering the data. It would contain a full-stop, which is the *'system-missing'* value. This is the value that SPSS inserts into any empty cell in a column that contains data. It allows the program to keep track of the occupied cells- even those that are left with no data being entered have some content. (The notion of the *system-missing* value is explained in section 5.3.)

18.2 Correcting data

If you need to make corrections to any of the cell entries, simply move the cursor to that cell (most easily done by clicking on it), type in the correct numbers and press ↵ or an arrow movement key.

If you want to alter one number in a long numerical entry, click on the relevant cell. The cell contents are reproduced in the line below the title bar of the window; click at an appropriate position in this cell editor line, and you can edit the entry. To insert it in the sheet, press ↵ or use the mouse to select another cell in the sheet.

Copying or moving data in the sheet

To copy or move cells, select them using the click/drag technique and while they are highlighted select Edit from the menu bar of the Application window. If you are copying the cells (so they are repeated elsewhere), click on Copy. If you are moving the cells from one place to another, click on Cut. Then move the cursor to the point where you want the cells to be repeated or inserted, click to select that cell(s) and select from the menu bar Edit /Paste. (You can paste the copied or cut cells to an area outside the current spreadsheet, but any empty cells that result will be filled with the system-missing value.)

Inserting rows or columns in the sheet

Rows can be inserted into a sheet by selecting a cell in the row below the one where you want a row inserted and then using from the menu bar Data /Insert Case. A column is inserted by selecting a cell in the column to the right of where you want one inserted, and then choosing from the menu bar Data /Insert Variable.

Deleting rows (cases) or columns (variables)

Click on the case number on the left side of the row, or on the variable name at the top of the column and from the menu bar choose Edit/Clear.

18.3 Moving around in the spreadsheet

With a large sheet, you will want to be able to move around it rapidly. The Home key takes you to the first cell in a row, End to the last cell in a row, Ctrl+up arrow to the first row of a column, Ctrl+down arrow to the last row of a column. Page Up and

Page Down scroll up or down one window-height, and Ctrl+Page Up or Ctrl+Page Down scroll one window left or right.

To go to a particular variable

Select Utilities /Variables from the Application window menu, highlight the variable in the list presented in the box then revealed, and click on the Go To and Close buttons.

To go to any particular row

Select Data /Go To Case. Enter the case number in the text box, and click on OK and Close. Note that the case number is the number of the row, *$casenum* (see section 5.3), not any identification number that you may have entered as a variable. If you want to find the row of data for a particular respondent, use the procedure described in the next paragraph.

To go to a particular value on a variable or to a particular respondent

Select a cell in the column containing scores on the variable, and select Edit /Search for Data from the menu bar. You can then enter the value to be searched for in the text box of the Search for Data dialogue box, and click on the Search Forward or Search Backward buttons. (Clicking on Cancel will remove the dialogue box after the search has been made.) This technique can be used to find a particular respondent, so long as you have given each a unique identification number (id), as I recommend you to do. You can put the cursor at the top of the column containing the id numbers (with Ctrl+up arrow), and then select Edit /Search for Data. If you put the id number of the respondent you want in the Search text box and click on Select Forward, the row for that respondent will be found in the Data Editor.

Exercise 18.2: Save the data

Save the file as salesq.sav, following the procedure described in section 18.9 below.

18.4 Assigning names and labels to variables and values

Variable names

Variable names are used by SPSS to refer to the variables (columns) when it is processing the data. Left to itself, SPSS names the variables (columns) as var00001, var00002 and so on, which is not at all informative when you are looking at the table. So you need to insert meaningful names into the column headings.

When deciding on a variable name, it is sensible to use one that reminds you of what the variable actually is. So you would call sex 'sex', and age 'age'. But variable names must start with a letter, can't be longer than 8 characters, can't contain a blank space between characters, mustn't end in a full stop (although one can be enclosed by characters), mustn't use punctuation characters such as ! or *. Also, names can only be used once. If you had, for example, people's salary at two different times, you would have to name them salary1 and salary2 (or similar) to avoid using one name for two variables. Note that case is ignored, so SALARY, salary and Salary are all the same to SPSS and can't be used together in one set of variable names.

It is important to distinguish between variable names, variable labels and value labels. The variable name is used by SPSS when identifying which variables it is to analyse. Variable labels are added to the output to explain what the variable is. Value labels are added to the output to explain what a particular score on a variable denotes.

Variable labels

When you look at the results of an analysis, you may easily forget what the variable name means: what is salary1 or salary2, for example? It is helpful if the printout gives a more explanatory label than just the variable name, and these can be added at the same time as you assign variable names. Variable labels can be up to 120 characters, can contain any characters or spaces, and the case will be retained: if you type SALARY in December this is exactly what will be used as the label.

Value labels

Value labels are added to the output to explain what the values (scores) represent. If the respondent's sex has been coded such that a value of 1 represents male and 2 represents female, it is helpful when reading the output to have this extra information.

Assigning variable names and variable labels

To name the variable and/or assign a variable label, click on one of the cells in the column containing the data on that variable and from the menu bar of the Application window select Data /Define Variable. Clicking on this entry yields a dialogue box (Figure 18.1), with the cursor already positioned in the text box marked Variable Name. Type in the new name of the variable.

To assign a variable label, click on the Labels button in the bottom area of the Define Variable Dialogue Box, the area entitled Change Settings. This will reveal another dialogue box, headed Define Labels (Figure 18.2). Type the label into the text box to the right of Variable Label:, and click on the Continue button. This will return you to the Define Variable box, and the label will be shown on the relevant line of the centre part of the box, the area marked as Variable Description. Click on OK, and the name and label will be assigned. The column containing the data on that variable will now be headed with the variable name you assigned.

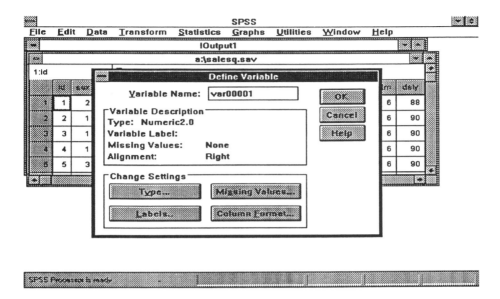

Fig 18.1 The Define Variable dialogue box.

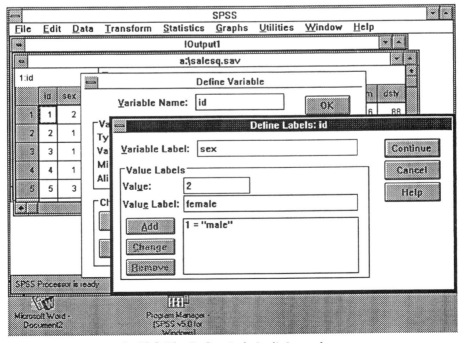

Fig 18.2 The Define Labels dialogue box.

Assigning value labels

To give labels to each value (score) on a variable, you use the Define Labels box (Figure 18.2), obtained from the Define Variable box as explained above. Move the pointer so it is in the Value text window, click the mouse to anchor the cursor, and type in the value. Then use a similar technique to type the label into the Value Label text box and click on the Add button. To insert the value label male for the score of 1 on sex, you would type 1 into the Value box and male into the Value Label box, then click on the Add button. The result, 1="male" appears in the list box to the right of the Add button.

If you need to change one of the labels, click on the label in the list that is shown, enter the new label in the Value Label box and click on the Change button. You delete a label by clicking on it in the list box, and then click on the Remove button.

Exercise 18.3

Assign names to each of the variables in salesq, using the names shown just above the first row of numbers in Table 18.1: id, sex, empl, att1 and so on. Assign variable labels: Employer to empl, Customer visits to cust, Start day to dstd, Start month to dstm and Start year to dsty. Assign value labels to sex: 1 represents male and 2 represents female. Finally, assign value labels to area: 1 represents North, 2 represents South.

18.5 Missing values

The idea of encoding no response to a variable as a separate number was described in section 5.3. You inform SPSS of the missing value for a variable through the Define Variable box, which is obtained by selecting Data/Define Variable from the Application window menu bar. When presented with the Define Variable dialogue box, click on the Missing Values button. This exposes the Define Missing Values box, and you can enter up to three different values each of which will be classed as missing (ie not a genuine data value). Having a number of different missing values can be useful: you may have one number to represent 'no response given', another to represent 'response was "Don't Know"', another to represent 'response was "Undecided"'. You will, of course, have had to encode these responses with the relevant numbers when you enter the data in the data editor. (You can also have a range of numbers defined as missing values or a range plus a single discrete value.)

To define a particular number as a missing value, type it into one of the Discrete missing values boxes and click on Continue.

Exercise 18.4

Using the technique described above, tell SPSS for Windows that a score of 3 on sex is a missing value (i.e. means that the respondent's sex is unknown).

18.6 Setting the column width of a variable

When you have selected Data /Define Variable from the menu, and obtained the Define Variable dialogue box, the Variable Description area provides further information about the variable. Type shows whether it is a numeric variable (i.e. numbers only), a date variable, a string variable (meaning it consists of letters or letters and numbers rather than just numbers), or one of a range of other types. It also indicates the width of the variable as it is displayed in the spreadsheet.

In Figure 18.1 the variable has a width of 8.2: this means the numbers displayed in this column can be up to 8 characters wide, including the decimal point, and there are 2 decimal places allowed. So the largest number which could be shown in this variable column is 99999.99. Until you change the settings, the variable is numeric and its width is set at 8 with 2 decimal places. This default setting is altered by clicking on the Type button in the Change Settings area of the Define Variable dialogue box. If you do alter the variable's column width, the altered settings are lost when you leave SPSS: they are not saved when you save the file.

It is important to appreciate that the width settings only control the width as displayed on the screen, and not the way the variable is stored in the program, where numeric variables are 40 characters wide with up to 16 decimal places. So although you may type in a number like 44.444, the sheet may if you have reset the column width, only show 44.44; but in carrying out calculations the program uses the full number, with (in this example) three decimal places.

The Alignment entry in the Variable Description area of the Define Variable box tells you how the entries in the column will be aligned; for numeric variables, the conventional setting is right aligned. It can be changed to left aligned or centred by selecting the Column Format button from the bottom of the box and clicking the relevant radio button in the Define Column Format dialogue box.

18.7 Defining the type of variable

This book assumes the use of numeric data, although string variables which use letters can be dealt with by SPSS. Dates in SPSS for Windows are a particular type of variable, but until you have had some experience it is better to leave the date information in salesq as numeric data. The issue of dates is dealt with in section 29.9.

18.8 Using templates for defining a number of variables

You may have a large number of variables for which you wish to assign the same value labels, missing values, column width, alignment specification or some combination of these features. It is tedious to go through the process of defining these attributes for each one, and you can use a template to do it for you. You create a template from Data /Templates... in the Application window menu bar, which exposes a Template dialogue box. Clicking on the Define button allows you to access Define Template buttons, and from them you can enter the settings you want. You can then save the template by clicking on the Add button. In the Template dialogue box you can give your specification a particular name or have it as the default template.

Having specified a template, you will want to apply it to a number of variables. When in the Data Editor, select the variables to which the template is to be applied by dragging along the row so that entries in the appropriate variables are highlighted. Then click on Data/ Templates... and select which attributes of the template you wish to apply by clicking on the relevant items from the list provided in the Apply area of the box. You can apply any combination of Type, Value Labels, Missing values, Column format specifications. Then click on the OK button, and the highlighted variables in the Data Editor will have the designated template attributes applied to them.

Exercise 18.5

Make any adjustments you wish to the variable names, column widths, value labels features of the data in salesq and then save it again.

18.9 Saving the data file

Saving the data file for the first time

Once you have entered the data, the first thing to do is to save it so that if anything goes wrong later you have a copy you can use. In most cases you will want to save the file on a floppy disk, so make sure your formatted disk is inserted into drive A. To save the file on the floppy disk, follow these steps:

❑ Check that the Data Editor is the active window, with the title bar in colour or darkened

❑ From the Application window menu bar, select File /Save As

❑ (If you use Save Data, the data file will be stored on the hard disk under the name Newdata.sav. This is rarely what is required!)

❑ You will be presented with the Save As Data File dialogue box. This offers many options that as a beginner you will not need, but there are 5 things you must do:

❑ Type in the name which you want the file to be called (for example, salesq.sav). Remember that the main part of the name cannot exceed 8 characters and must not contain any spaces, full-stops, commas.

❑ In the field headed Directories, click on [-A-]; this means the file will be stored on the floppy disk.

❑ The bottom half of the dialogue box lists a number of file formats: check that the round (radio) button next to SPSS is marked (with a dark centre). If any other one is marked, move the cursor so it is over the button to the left of SPSS and click the mouse. Note that you want SPSS and not SPSS/PC+ or any of the other alternatives.

❑ Move the pointer so it is over the button marked OK at the upper right, and click.

❑ The data file will then be stored on your floppy disk, with the name SALESQ.SAV (If you typed in as the filename MYDAT, the file will be MYDAT.SAV, of course.) The name will now appear in the Title bar of the Data Editor (spreadsheet) window.

❑ If you think you made a mistake, just repeat the steps given above, checking that you are making the right selections at each point.

Saving the data file for the second time

When you are working on a data file and have saved it once, or are working on a file that you have retrieved from disk, you can save the file under the same name as it already has by simply selecting File /Save from the Application window menu bar. The version you are now saving will over-write the previous one. If you want to keep the old version and the current one, use File /Save As (as described above), and type in a different name from the current one. For example, suppose you have made some changes to SALESQ.SAV and want to keep both the original and the altered versions; you would save the current version under a new name by typing in a name such as SALESQ2, and the file will then be saved as SALESQ2.SAV.

18.10 Retrieving data files

Retrieving a .SAV data file

To retrieve a data file from your floppy disk, select from the Application window menu bar File / Open /Data. You will be presented with the Open Data File dialogue box. Assuming the data file you want is on the floppy disk and has been saved previously by SPSS, double click on [-A-] in the Directories box. All the files on drive A, the floppy disk, ending with the .SAV extension will be listed in the Files box. Click on the name of the file you want to retrieve, and it will appear in the Name box at the top of the dialogue box. Having checked that this box contains the name of the file you want, click on the OK button on the right hand side of the dialogue box. The file will then be put into the Data Editor (spreadsheet) window, and its name will be the title of that window. (The Open Data File dialogue box indicates that you can retrieve files saved in other formats, but this facility is not covered here as it is likely to confuse the beginner.)

Retrieving a data file with a filename extension other than .SAV

If the data file had a filename extension other than .SAV, you need to replace the .SAV in the Name text box with the appropriate extension. For example, you may have a .sys file that you saved in SPSS/PC+, with the filename extension .SYS (Suppose the file is called PROJDAT.SYS) The easiest method of retrieving such a file is to replace the .SAV in the Name box with * . * as the * is a wild card symbol and means 'any letters'. When the Open Data File dialogue box is opened, the insertion point is in the Name box, so just type in a * . *, and double-click on [-A-] in the Directories box. All the files on the floppy disk will be listed in the Files box, and you can use the scroll bars to scroll down the list. When PROJDAT.SYS is visible, click on it and it will appear in the Name box. Then click on the OK button.

When you are faced with the Open Data File dialogue box, you will see that you can import files from other packages, such as Excel, dBase, Lotus 1-2-3. If you need this facility, it should be simple to use once you understand how to open files.

18.11 Finding out what is on your disk

Select File / Open /Data from the Application window, replace .SAV in the Name text box with * . *, and double click on [-A-] in the Directories list. All the files on the floppy will be listed in the File list, and you can scroll down it using the scroll bar.

18.12 Turning grid lines on or off

If you do not want the grid lines separating the cells in the Data Editor spreadsheet, turn them off by selecting Utilities from the menu: the dialogue box offers the appropriate option.

19

SPSS for Windows: Running the analysis

19.1 Using the menus to analyse the data

Once you have a data file open (an active Data Editor spreadsheet) and have decided which analyses you require, you are ready to run SPSS. Most of the analyses can be obtained by selecting from the menus in the Application window. (A summary of the menu structure is provided in Appendix C.)

Clicking on the Application window Statistics menu reveals a drop-down menu with some or all of these options:

Summarize
Compare Means
ANOVA Models
Correlate
Regression
Classify
Data Reduction
Scale
Nonparametric Tests
Multiple Response

Each entry has an arrowhead to show that there is another menu which can be obtained by clicking on the entry or by pressing the key of the underlined letter.

The Summarize entry, for example, has a submenu containing these entries:

Frequencies...
Descriptives...
Explore...
Crosstabs...
List Cases...
Report Summaries in Rows...

The ... indicates that if you select that entry, a dialogue box will be revealed in which you enter more details about the analysis you want.

Exercise 19.1

We want to find out for the data in the data file salesq the number of males and females and the number of people from each area i.e. we want to know how many cases there are for each level of the variable sex and for each level of the variable area. This information is obtained using the Frequencies procedure. So click on Frequencies, and a Dialogue Box (Figure 19.1) will appear.

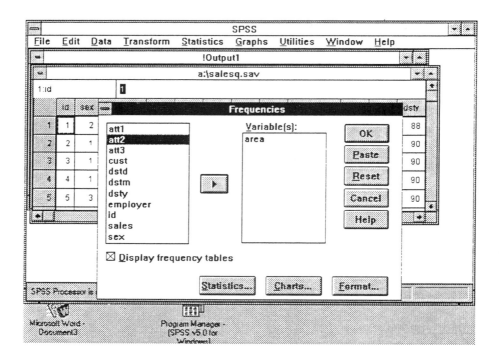

Fig 19.1. The dialogue box for Frequencies

Dialogue Boxes for the statistical procedures have a common format. In the left-hand box, which has no title but is known as the source variable list, there is a list of the variables in the Data File; the variable names are those which are given at the top of the columns in the Data Editor, so will be var00001, var00002 etc unless you have assigned variable names.

You have to tell SPSS which variables you want analysed, and the way to do this is to select each variable by clicking on its name, which will then be highlighted. Then click on the button marked with a right-pointing arrow, and the variable(s) will appear in the right-hand box, the one headed Variable(s). Select whichever variables you want analysing in this way. If you want to select a number of variables, you can use the drag method of selecting a set in one movement; pressing on the arrow button will transfer the names of all the variables in the set to the Variables box.

If you make a mistake, and have selected a variable you do not want analysing, you remove it from the Variable(s) box by clicking on it; the arrow in the arrow button will become a left-pointing one, and clicking on that will remove the highlighted variable from the list and return it to the left-hand box.

In our example, you click on sex in the left-hand box and then on the right-pointing arrow; then click on area in the left-hand box and on the right-pointing arrow again. The variable names sex and area will appear in the Variables(s) box.

Now click on the OK button at the top right of the Dialogue Box. (For the moment ignore the other buttons down the right hand side and along the bottom of the dialogue box.) The FREQUENCIES procedure will run, and a message to this effect will appear in the status bar of the Application window. The results will appear in the output window, !Output1. It is a simple as that!

The result of running this example is shown in Fig 14.3. The table shows the frequency of males, females and sex unknown (missing), corresponding to values 1, 2 and 3 on the variable sex. It also shows the frequency of each level (1 and 2) on the variable area. You can scroll the output, using the scroll bars on the righthand side of the Output window.

Exercise 19.2

Now try a second example, to obtain the mean and standard deviation of the number of customer visits (cust) for the data in salesq. Means can also be obtained via the Frequencies procedure, so select the Statistics menu from the Application window, then the Frequencies entry from the submenu. It will still have sex and area listed in the Variable(s) box. Remove them by clicking on them and pressing the left-pointing arrow. Select cust from the source variable list, and click on the right-pointing area so that cust appears in the Variable(s) box.

To obtain the means using Frequencies, you need to request them by clicking on the Command button labelled Statistics... at the bottom left of the dialogue box. When you click on this button, another dialogue box is revealed (Fig 19.2). This is where you indicate the statistics you want: click on the word Mean in the area labelled Central Tendency, and on the words Std. deviation in the area labelled Dispersion. As you click on these, the small squares next to the words will have a cross put into them to show they have been selected. If you click on the wrong thing, just click on wrongly-selected item and the cross will be removed from its indicator square to show it is not selected. (Clicking the Cancel button will cancel all the selections you have made and take you back up one level, to the Frequencies dialogue box.) Now click on Continue in the upper right of the dialogue box, and you will be returned to the Frequencies dialogue box; click on the OK button, and

the Frequencies procedure will run, the results again appearing in the !Output1
window.

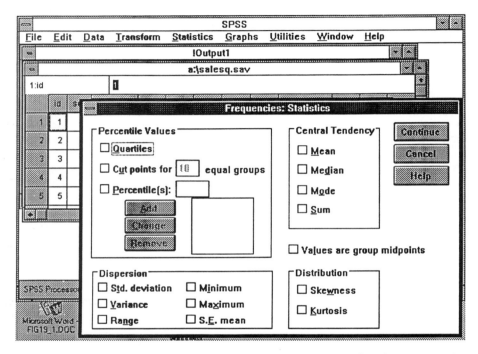

Fig 19.2. The dialogue box for indicating the statistics required under Frequencies

19.2 The output window buttons

Pausing the output

When output is generated, it scrolls through the output window, but clicking on the
Pause button in the output window menu bar will suspend the scrolling. To return to
scrolling, click on the Scroll button.

Rounding numbers in the output

The Round button has the effect of rounding the numbers in a selected area,
according to the specification you have previously set using Edit /Round from the
menu. (You can enter the number of decimal places you want in a text window.) To
operate this facility, you must select an area of the output file using the click/drag
procedure, and then click on Round. (If you click on the Truncate button, numbers
will be cut but not rounded, so 4.7 would become 4.)

The output window's menu bar has a Glossary button; clicking on this opens access to a Help facility, described in chapter 20.

19.3 Sending the output to a different output window

When SPSS for Windows starts, it always creates an output window entitled !Output, and the results of any analysis will be put in that window. You can open another output window, by selecting File /New /SPSS Output... A number of output windows can be visible simultaneously, but only one of them, known as the designated window, can receive output. To make an output window the designated window, click on the ! in the icon bar which forms the second line of the window. Any fresh output that you generate will be appended to the bottom of the file in the currently-designated output window.

19.4 Saving and retrieving an output file

Saving the output file

As you have seen the output is displayed in an output window. By default, this will be saved on the hard disk when you leave SPSS, with the name OUTPUT1.LST. It is almost always more convenient to save it on a floppy:

❑ Check that the output window is active

❑ Select File/Save As... from the Application window menu bar. (One option from the File menu is Save SPSS Output, but you only use this if you want the file stored on the hard disk with the name OUTPUT1.SAV.)

The dialogue box you will see is similar to that for saving the data file. Type the name of the file into the Name box, ensuring that it has the extension .LST

❑ Click on [-A-] in the Directories list

❑ Click on the OK button.

Saving a previously saved output file after editing it

Any changes you make to an output file you have retrieved from disk will be lost unless you save the file:

❑ Ensure the window is active

❑ Select File from the Application window

To save the current version of the file, overwriting previous ones, select Save SPSS Output, and the new version will be saved on the same drive from which it was retrieved.

To save the current version while keeping the previous one,

❑ Select Save As..., which will present the Save As !Output dialogue box. Type in a new name for the output file; remember it must not be more than 8 characters and must not contain a blank space.

❑ Check that the name has the .LST extension, or add it by typing it in.

❑ Click on [-A-] in the Directories field so the file is saved on the floppy disk

❑ Click on the OK button.

Saving a part of the output file

If you want to save just a portion of the text output file, highlight the area to be saved, using the click/drag procedure. Then go through the steps explained above for saving an output file. You will be asked to confirm that you want to save only the marked area; click on Yes to do so. If you click on No, the whole file will be saved.

Retrieving an output file from the floppy disk

If you have saved a .LST file that you want to examine, print or edit, it has to be opened in an output window. To do this:

❑ Select from the Application window menu bar File/Open/ SPSS Output. The Open Output dialogue box will be presented.

❑ If the file you want is on your floppy disk, click on [-A-] in the Directories box; all files with the .LST filename extension will be listed in the Files box on the left hand side. If necessary, you can scroll down the list

❑ Click on the name of the file you want, so that its name appears in the Name text box

❑ Click on the OK button. The file you have retrieved will be displayed in an output window.

19.5 Editing the contents of the Output window

When the output window contains text, it can be edited in a manner similar to using a word processor. The cursor can be moved around with the keyboard arrow keys, or by clicking with the mouse. To insert new material, click the mouse cursor at the point where you want to begin, and start typing. To overwrite the existing text, the procedure is the same except that the Insert mode must be off: press the Ins key on the keyboard, and the cursor will change to a black rectangle. To return to Insert mode, just press the Ins key again.

Deleting a single character is achieved using the –Del (back-space) key on the keyboard to delete the character to the left of the cursor, or the Delete key which deletes one character to the right.

A block of text can be marked with the click/drag procedure, and the marked block can then be copied or deleted (transferred to the Clipboard), and pasted in elsewhere in the document. When you have marked the block of text, select Edit from the menu bar of the Application window. To delete the marked block, click on Cut. To make a copy of the marked block, click on Copy. To insert a copy of the marked block, move the cursor to the point where you want it inserted, and then select Edit and click on Paste.

You can carry out a Search/Replace procedure by selecting Edit/Search or Edit/Replace from the application window.

19.6 Syntax files

Users of earlier versions of SPSS will be familiar with the notion of a command file, where one stores the commands which tell the package the analyses to perform as well as informing it about the data file to be used in the analyses. SPSS for Windows, by allowing on-screen selection of analyses, means that on many occasions such files are not necessary. But not every one of the finer options can be selected from the screen menus, and it is frequently useful to have the commands one is using saved separately so that one can re-run an analysis, for example, after making some alteration to the data, without having to make all the on-screen selections again.

To do this, one needs to create a Syntax File. A second major benefit of syntax files is that one can write the SPSS commands using a normal word processor, save them in text file form, import them into a syntax file and run it: so one can do the preparatory work even on a machine that does not have SPSS installed!

19.7 Entering commands in a syntax file

If you are selecting items from the on-screen menus, as described in section 18.5, you can paste the commands into a syntax window by using the Paste button in the dialogue box for the procedure you have selected; this has the effect of putting the commands into a syntax file window, initially entitled !Syntax1, which can be saved and edited if there any alterations to make. If no syntax file is open the first time you use Paste, one is automatically opened to receive the commands you are pasting. Subsequent uses of Paste add the current commands to the file, appending them to the existing contents of the syntax file. If you want to start pasting into a new syntax window, you need to open a new one and make it the designated syntax window. (See below for instructions on how to do this.)

To enter the names of variables in the commands in the Syntax file, you can readily type them in. Or you can use the Variables dialogue box which is obtained from the

Utilities/Variables menu of the Application window. This displays a dialogue box and you can select a variable from the list in the left-hand side of the box. Information about the variable appears in the right-hand window. If one clicks on the Paste button at the bottom of the window, the highlighted variable name is pasted into the Syntax file at the point where the cursor was located. This is rather laborious and most users will probably find this method not worth the effort.

19.8 Running the commands in a syntax file

The benefit of a syntax file is that you can run all or some of the commands it contains directly, without having to go through the process of making menu selections again. An example of a syntax file, containing a series of commands, is shown in Fig 19.3. One identifies the commands to run be selecting them with the click/drag procedure (or from the keyboard by holding down shift and using the up/down arrow keys), so they are highlighted, and then clicking on the Run button in the window's icon bar. If you want to run all the commands, the whole file can be selected using the Application window's Edit /Select All option; then click on Run in the Syntax File window. To run just one command, put the cursor anywhere in the line containing the command and click on Run.

```
SORT CASES BY sex .
SPLIT FILE
 BY sex .
T-TEST
 GROUPS=employer(1 3)
 /MISSING=ANALYSIS
 /VARIABLES=att2
 /CRITERIA=CIN(.95) .
SORT CASES BY area sex .
SPLIT FILE
 BY area sex .
T-TEST
 GROUPS=employer(1 3)
 /MISSING=ANALYSIS
 /VARIABLES=cust
 /CRITERIA=CIN(.95) .
```

Fig 19.3. Example of a syntax file

Exercise 19.3

Check that you can create a syntax file by repeating the steps involved in obtaining the Frequencies analysis of Exercise 19.1, but when you have filled in the

Frequencies dialogue box, do not press OK but click on Paste. You should obtain the !Syntax1 window shown in Fig 19.3.

Try running these commands by selecting the whole file and then clicking on the Run button in the syntax window.

Assuming this is successful, try editing the syntax file so that you obtain a Frequencies analysis of the data on the variable att1. To do this, make sure the syntax window is the active one, move the cursor (using the mouse) so it is to the right of the words sex area and click the mouse to anchor the insertion point. Use the backspace Delete key to delete these words and type in att1 in their place. Then select the whole file by selecting Edit /Select All from the Application window menus, and click on the Run button in the Syntax window. SPSS should then run the commands, and give you the results of applying the frequencies procedure to the variable att1 in the !Output1 window.

19.9 Opening another syntax file

As explained above, the first time you use a Paste button, a syntax file is opened automatically. But you can open a new (empty) one or open an existing one that has previously been saved. To open a new one, select File /New /SPSS Syntax from the Application window menu.

To open an existing syntax file, select File /Open /SPSS Syntax. A dialogue box will appear, showing files with the .SPS filename extension. If the file is on the floppy disk, you will need to click on [-A-] in the Directories list, so that the files on the floppy are shown in the list of files. Click on the name of the file you want to open, check that its name appears in the Name text box, and click on the OK button.

You can have more than one syntax window open at one time, but as with output files only one can be the 'designated' window to which commands are pasted, and from which commands can be run. You can make any syntax window the designated one by clicking on the ! icon in its icon bar.

19.10 Loading a text file into a syntax window

You can load a set of commands prepared outside SPSS and saved as a text file into a syntax file. Assume the text file is stored on a floppy disk which is in drive A. In SPSS, select from the Application window menu bar File/ New/ SPSS Syntax. When the dialogue box appears, type in the name of the file in the File text box, click on [-A-] in the Directories box and click on OK.

19.11 Editing the text in a syntax window

You can edit the contents of a syntax window just like any other text file, and type straight into it. This is beneficial to those who are familiar with the command structure of SPSS; if you have already written command files in SPSS/PC+, you will be able to write syntax files. But if you are not experienced with SPSS, be careful when trying to create commands directly. The syntax of commands is not simple, and there are a number of rules you must follow. For example, all command lines must start on a new line, and must end in a full-stop (period).

Subcommands are separated (usually) by /. You will see many examples of these command lines in the sections of this book devoted to SPSS/PC+.

19.12 The Syntax button in a syntax file window: Help on syntax

If you have a procedure command line in a syntax file, and the cursor is on that line, clicking on the Syntax button will open a Help window. The SPSS for Windows Help facility is very comprehensive, and is summarised in chapter 20. But the beginner should be warned that sometimes the help that appears when one presses the Syntax button in a syntax window consists of pages from the SPSS technical manuals and may be incomprehensible to a non-expert. So do try using the facility, but do not be depressed if the result is not very helpful!

SPSS for Windows: Printing files; Help facilities; modifying screen displays

20.1 Printing output, data and syntax files

You will certainly want to print your output files, and probably data files and syntax files as well. The procedures are basically the same, whichever file you want to print. First, ensure you have a printer connected, that it is properly configured for use by Windows, is loaded with paper and is on-line. (You may need local advice to do this, depending on your level of expertise.)

Printing the whole file

❏ Check the window to be printed is the active window

❏ Select File /Print... from the Application window menu bar

❏ The Print dialogue box will appear, with the name of the file to be printed in the Title bar. By default, one copy of the whole file will be printed. To print more than one copy, type in the number required in the Copies box.

❏ Click on OK

Printing part of the file

Before selecting the File/Print menu, highlight the area to be printed using the click/drag technique. Then select File/Print from the Application window menu bar. When the Print dialogue box appears, the Selection radio button will be selected: click on OK.

20.2 Altering page size for printing

You may find, after trying a print-out, that you need to alter the page size: if the printer is assuming a page 11 inches deep, and you have A4 paper, for example, you need to set the paper length. Or you may not want page breaks at all, just one continuous printing. To change the setting, select Edit /Preferences /Output to obtain the relevant dialogue box. You change the page size by altering the settings in the Page Size area at the bottom of the box. If you select Infinite, the output will print as a continuous 'page', with no page breaks. To set the size for A4 paper, you should set the length of Custom to 70 (the number of lines on an A4 sheet).

20.3 Help facilities

SPSS for Windows has very extensive Help facilities, which can be thought of as having two parts. The major one is concerned with using the package and the second part (the Glossary) is concerned with explaining the statistical terminology that appears in the output. Help is best studied by practising with it. The summary given here is just intended to get you started and explain how to access help and what some of the buttons in the help screens do. Help is a separate application, winhelp, installed with SPSS for Windows but placed in the Windows directory on the hard disk. If the Help system fails to operate, you need to reinstall SPSS for Windows.

20.4 On-screen help on how to use SPSS for Windows

Getting to and leaving Help

Selecting Help from the menu bar of the Application window or by clicking on the Help button in the dialogue boxes opens a Help window, in which information about the operation of SPSS is displayed. (Pressing the F1 key on the keyboard will also open Help.) The information presented will be relevant to that part of the package you were in when you requested help. So clicking on the Help button in the Frequencies dialogue box will present information about the Frequencies command, whereas the Help menu of the Application window enters the help files from the beginning. You can also access help information about the menu commands of the Application window by pressing Shift+F1.

Help is displayed in a hypertext form: key words are shown underlined and in a different colour, and by clicking on them, a fuller explanation of their meaning is shown.

You close the Help window in the usual windows way by double-clicking on the close box in the left corner of the title bar.

Moving around in the help file

The menu bar of the help window contains these entries:

Contents   Search   Back   History   < >

To see a list of the help topics, click on Contents. You can then move to one of the topics by clicking on it.

If you want an explanation of a particular word, select Search; this asks you to enter a word, and will show an index of topics. You can select a topic and if you press the Go To button the help information will be displayed.

To see the help page that you have just been looking at, select Back which displays the previously viewed page of help.

To obtain a list of the help pages you have viewed previously so you can return to any one of them by double-clicking on its name, click the History button.

<< shows the previous page in the help file. This may not be the one you last looked at.

>> shows the next page in the help file.

20.5 Saving, editing, copying parts of Help

The Help window has a main menu bar of

File Edit Bookmark Help

so you can save the help window's contents as a file, edit it, insert a bookmark to allow you to get back to a particular point, print parts of which you want a hard copy, copy parts of the Help information to another file or ask for help on help!

You can copy some of the help information to another window, or to another application outside SPSS, such as a Windows word processor. This is achieved by selecting Edit /Copy... from the help window menu bar, which opens a dialogue box. You then select the text to be copied (using the click/drag technique) and click on the Copy button. The text you had highlighted is copied to the Windows clipboard. If you make another window active by clicking in it, you can paste the help information into it: click at the point where you want the text inserted, and then select Edit/Paste from the Application window menu bar.

Edit /Copy pastes the copy of the help information to the Windows clipboard, so you could close SPSS for Windows, open another Windows application, such as Word for Windows or Windows Write, and then use Edit /Paste to paste the help information into a Word for Windows or Write file.

20.6 On-screen help on statistical terms

You may come across statistical terms in the output of your analyses which you do not understand or have temporarily forgotten. You can obtain an explanation of them by using the Glossary, which is accessed in two alternative ways. One method is to select Help /Glossary from the Application window menu. The other is to select the Glossary button from the output window. Either procedure will open the Glossary. You can scroll through the file (a tedious process unless you just want to browse), or you click on the Search button in the menu bar and enter the phrase for which you want an explanation.

20.7 Help with SPSS syntax

When you are using a syntax window, pressing the Syntax button will provide help information about the procedure on the current line of the syntax file. This can be highly complex, and is likely to be meaningful only to those who have a thorough understanding of SPSS commands. Nevertheless, you may find it valuable once you have developed some expertise with the package.

20.8 Modifying aspects of the data window

If you do not want the grid lines printed, you can remove them from the data editor window before you select File/Print. With the data editor active, select Utilities /Grid Lines from the Application Window menu and the dialogue box gives you the option of suppressing these lines.

If you have assigned value labels to the data so that, for example, a value of 1 in the variable sex has the label 'male' and value 2 has the label 'female', you can have these labels printed instead of the numbers when you print out the file. To do this, ensure the Data Editor is the active window, and select Utilities / Value Labels. Then print the file as explained above.

20.9 Modifying the source list of variables in dialogue boxes

It is possible to modify the variables shown in the source lists of the dialogue boxes, and the order in which they are listed. The variables are shown in the source lists of the dialogue boxes in alphabetical order. You can ask for them to be listed in the order in which they occur in the data file if you select Edit /Preferences and click on the File radio button. Note that if you do alter the display order, the alteration will not take effect until you open a data file.

When you have a very lengthy set of variables in the data file, it can be convenient to restrict those which are presented in the source list in the dialogue boxes. This can be done using Utilities /Define Sets: give the set a name, specify the variables to be included in a set, and then click the Add Set button to create it. To have this newly created set used in the dialogue boxes, select Utilities /Use Sets, enter the name of the new set in the Sets in Use list and remove from the list the ALLVARIABLES entry.

You can change the order in which variables are listed in the target lists by clicking on the name of the variable to be moved and then clicking on the control box in the top left of the dialogue box menu bar: options to Move Selection Up and Move Selection Down will be offered.

20.10 Modifying aspects of the output

Adding a title to each page of the output file

SPSS puts a heading at each page of the output file. You can add to or replace the headings by selecting Utilities /Output Page Title which produces a box allowing you to type in the page title and page subtitle you want. This allows you to use a heading which indicates what the content of the output file is, and is especially useful if you are sharing a printer as you can have you own name put on the pages of your output. Note that your title and subtitle can contain either inverted commas or apostrophes, not both.

Suppressing copies of commands from the output file

The output obtained when you run a statistical procedure includes a statement of the commands that were run, as well as any error messages that were generated, statements about the times that procedures took, and page headings. While these are useful while you are still checking the package is doing what you want, and when you are interpreting the results, they may be useless clutter in the output file if you want to print the output and pass it to someone else to show them the results.

It is strongly recommended that you leave these items in your output file while you are developing an analysis, so you can readily see which commands produced which parts of the output. But to produce a 'clean' output file, you may want to suppress these components of the output. To do this, select Edit /Preferences, which will reveal the Preferences dialogue box. Click on the Output button on the botline, and another dialogue box is shown. By clicking on the items in the Display area (upper left), you can suppress the listing in the output file of Commands, Errors and warnings, Page headers and Resource messages. If these are deselected, the cross in the square box to the left of each entry will be removed. When the settings are as you want them, click on Continue.

20.11 Changing fonts and type style

The facility for altering screen fonts is available by selecting from the Application window Utilities /Fonts. The dialogue box allows you to specify the typeface, type size, and whether you want bold or italic or both. When you have made the appropriate selections, click on the OK button.

21

Taking a preliminary look at the data

This chapter explains how to obtain outputs which allow you to check the system is reading the data file correctly and which provide an overall impression of the data.

Before proceeding with detailed statistical investigation, it is worth having a rough overview of the data to reveal any peculiarities or possible errors in the data file. LIST and EXAMINE (called EXPLORE in SPSS for Windows) are two procedures which allow you to do this.

21.1 Introductory comments for SPSS/PC+ users

If you have not yet done so, read chapter 16 about the use of .SYS files. Since these are much easier to deal with, they will be used from now on. The first line of the command files illustrating the various procedures is simply:

```
GET /FILE 'a:exl.sys'.
```

This retrieves the data from exdat, together with the data description. If the procedure commands follow immediately after the GET /FILE instruction, the output will be sent to the file SPSS.LIS in the SPSS subdirectory on drive C. To have the output sent to another file (fn.lis) on the floppy disk (drive A), the first two lines of the command files needed to follow the examples shown in these chapters should be:

```
GET /FILE 'a:exl.sys'.
SET /LISTING 'a:fn.lis'.
```

21.2 Introductory comments for SPSS for Windows users

If you have completed the example exercises described in chapter 17-19, you will be familiar with the techniques used to get SPSS for Windows to carry out an analysis:

❑ With a data file active, select the appropriate menu (eg Statistics) from the menu bar of the SPSS window, which reveals a drop-down menu

❑ Select the appropriate entry (Summarize, Compare Means etc) from the drop-down menu

❏ Select the appropriate entry from the next submenu (eg Frequencies, Descriptives etc)

❏ When presented with a dialogue box for the procedure you are requesting, specify the variables to be analysed

❏ Click on OK.

The procedure runs (the name of the procedure appears in the status bar at the bottom of the SPSS window while this is happening), and the output appears in the !Output window.

Once you have learned how to use the various Dialogue box options, the procedure should be straight-forward. To alter any of the choices you made in the Dialogue box, you merely have to get back to it by working through the menu selection process, and then you can change the choices you made and run the procedure again. Alternatively, if you have pasted the commands into a syntax file you can edit the commands in the file and then run them, as described in chapter 19.

The Windows interface means that the user can drive the system with much less insight into the way SPSS is structured than was needed by a user of version 3 or 4. It also means that because the menu and selection processes have so much in common whichever procedure you are using, a detailed explanation of how to obtain each procedure should be unnecessary. The user needs to know which of the various procedures to use to obtain a particular result, and how they are found in the menu system. Chapter 8 and section 40.2 are intended to provide a simple guide which will allow you to answer these questions.

In the following chapters, the procedures needed to obtain particular analyses, the answers to specific questions about the data, are described. The first parts explain which procedure is needed, and then there is an explanation of how SPSS/PC+ users obtain it, with illustrations of the output and an explanation in the text of what they show. This is followed by an explanation of how the procedure is obtained using SPSS for Windows. The outputs from SPSS/PC+ and SPSS for Windows are frequently the same, and so you should refer back to the Figures specified to see what a procedure provides. Where SPSS for Windows' output is notably different from that obtained with SPSS/PC+, separate illustrations are provided. The outputs illustrated all apply to the file of data described earlier, which for SPSS for Windows users is referred to as salesq.

21.3 LIST in SPSS/PC+

To find LIST from the main Menu, select analyze data, go right, select reports and tables, and go right again.

This procedure gives a simple listing of the data, and was mentioned in chapter 14; an illustration of the output is given in Fig 14.1. Usually it is the first procedure, so that the data can be checked against the original records and you can ensure that the data file has an accurate copy of the figures. It is obviously pointless to proceed with further analysis until you are confident the data is encoded accurately and is being read correctly by the system. To obtain a listing of the data for all the variables in the data file, the command is:

```
LIST.
```

To have a list of a subset of the variables use:

```
LIST /VARIABLES variable-name1 variable-name2.
```

So to obtain a listing of the values for the exdat variables age and employer, and send the output to ex.lis on the floppy disk, the commands are:

```
GET /FILE 'a:ex1.sys'.
SET /LISTING 'a:ex.lis'.
LIST /VARIABLES age employer.
```

To list the first 10 cases in the data file, use:

```
LIST /CASES FROM 1 TO 10.
```

LIST is particularly useful after a RECODE or a SORT procedure (described in chapters 27 and 28), to confirm they have done what was intended.

21.4 EXAMINE in SPSS/PC+

To find EXAMINE, *select* analyze data *from the main menu, go right, select* descriptive statistics *and go right again.*

The EXAMINE procedure provides summary statistics (mean, standard deviation, range, minimum and maximum etc.) and graphical displays of data which will reveal impossible values (such as a mistaken coding of a value of 5 for sex in exdat), outlying values, unexpected gaps etc. It also gives a histogram of the data, stem-leaf plots, boxplots, and tests to see whether data is normally distributed.

The line for this procedure is:

```
EXAMINE /VARIABLES variable-name.
```

To have the procedure applied to the variable cust in exdat, the command lines are:

```
GET /FILE 'a:ex1.sys'.
SET /LISTING 'a:ex.lis'.
EXAMINE /VARIABLES cust.
```

```
        CUST
Valid cases: 22.0    Missing cases: .0    Percent missing: .0

Mean     50.818 Std Err    3.6269  Min   28.000  Skewness    .6051
Median   44.500 Variance 289.3939  Max   83.000  S E Skew    .4910
5%Trim   50.308 Std Dev   17.0116  Range 55.000  Kurtosis -1.0005
                                   IQR   30.000  S E Kurt    .9528
```

```
        CUST
Frequency    Stem &  Leaf

    1.00     2  .  8
    6.00     3  .  036899
    7.00     4  .  0123688
    1.00     5  .  8
    2.00     6  .  08
    4.00     7  .  1269
    1.00     8  .  3

Stem width:   10
Each leaf:       1 case(s)
```

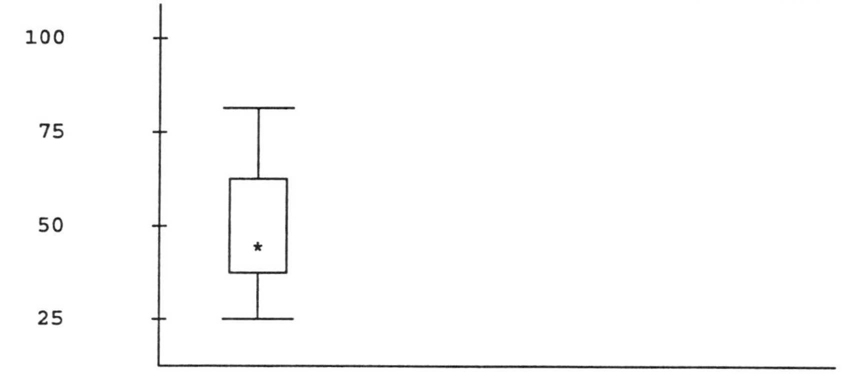

```
Variables     CUST
N of Cases       22.00
    Symbol Key:    *  - Median   (O) - Outlier   (E) - Extreme
```

Fig 21.1 Output from the command EXAMINE /VARIABLE cust. Stem-leaf and boxplots are explained in section 31.4.

This provides a listing of the summary statistics of the scores on the variable named, as shown in Fig 21.1. The printout shows a range of statistics including the mean, median, standard error, variance, standard deviation, minimum, maximum, range, interquartile range (IQR), and indices of skew. The 5%Trim figure is the mean of the scores when the most extreme 10% of the scores are omitted from the calculation: the highest 5% of scores and the lowest 5% of scores are both deleted before this mean is calculated. The trimmed mean can be a useful indicator of the 'average', less influenced by one or two extreme, outlying scores than the simple arithmetic mean.

The figure for skewness indicates how non-symmetric the distribution is. A positive value on kurtosis indicates that the distribution of the scores has heavier tails than a normal distribution curve. The values for both skewness and kurtosis will be close to zero if the distribution is normally distributed. The stem-leaf plot and boxplot are explained in chapter 31.

To get a list of the most extreme values of the variable, use:

`EXAMINE /VARIABLES variable-name /STATISTICS ALL.`

The printout then shows the five smallest and five largest scores on the variable, together with the case number of those scores. The case number is the number assigned to each case by the system when it reads the data file; the first case is number 1, the second number 2 and so on. The data file exdat includes ids (identification numbers), which are for this particular set of data the same as the case number, since they count up from 1 in regular sequence. But many data files do not do this: the ids may not be in sequence. You can tell EXAMINE to use the id numbers by having `/ID variable-name` in the command, replacing `variable-name` with the actual name of the variable to be used.

To obtain the EXAMINE statistics and plots for one variable according to the level of another variable, the command is:

`EXAMINE /VARIABLES variable1 BY variable2.`

So to examine the scores on cust for each employer, use:

`EXAMINE /VARIABLES cust BY employer.`

The printout shows the scores on `cust` for each employer. Part of the output from this command is shown in Fig 21.2. (The statistics for the complete set of scores on cust and the stem and leaf and boxplots have been deleted.)

```
      CUST
By  EMPLOYER  1

Valid cases:    8.0   Missing cases:   .0   Percent missing: .0

Mean     41.2500  Std Err    2.0420  Min   30.00  Skewness  -.8298
Median   41.5000  Variance  33.3571  Max   48.00  S E Skew   .7521
5% Trim  41.5000  Std Dev    5.7756  Range 18.00  Kurtosis  1.3531
                                     IQR    8.25  S E Kurt  1.4809
-------------------------------------------------------------------

      CUST
By  EMPLOYER  2

Valid cases:    8.0   Missing cases:   .0   Percent missing: .0

Mean     44.0000  Std Err    5.1409  Min   28.00  Skewness  1.0903
Median   39.0000  Variance 211.4286  Max   71.00  S E Skew   .7521
5% Trim  43.3889  Std Dev   14.5406  Range 43.00  Kurtosis   .3348
                                     IQR   22.75  S E Kurt  1.4809
-------------------------------------------------------------------

      CUST
By  EMPLOYER  3

Valid cases:    6.0   Missing cases:   .0   Percent missing: .0

Mean     72.6667  Std Err    3.6301  Min   58.00  Skewness  -.7947
Median   74.0000  Variance  79.0667  Max   83.00  S E Skew   .8452
5% Trim  72.9074  Std Dev    8.8919  Range 25.00  Kurtosis   .4550
                                     IQR   14.50  S E Kurt  1.7408
-------------------------------------------------------------------
```

Fig 21.2 Extracts of output from the command EXAMINE /VARIABLES cust BY employer.

A frequency table is obtained with this command:

`EXAMINE /VARIABLES variable-name /FREQUENCIES FROM (n) BY (b).`

Put one number for n and another for b in this line, to get a table showing the frequency of responses in bands of size b starting at n. For example,

`EXAMINE /VARIABLES cust /FREQUENCIES FROM (20) BY (10).`

gives a table in which the values of the scores on the variable cust are grouped into bands starting at 20 and containing a range of 10. The centre of the bands are therefore 25, 35, 45 etc and these are shown in the table (Fig 21.3) together with the frequency of scores in each band and the percentages.

```
CUST
                        Frequency Table
                        --------- -----
            Bin                                  Valid        Cum
          Center         Freq       Pct          Pct          Pct

      < 20
         25             1.00       4.55         4.55         4.55
         35             6.00      27.27        27.27        31.82
         45             7.00      31.82        31.82        63.64
         55             1.00       4.55         4.55        68.18
         65             2.00       9.09         9.09        77.27
         75             4.00      18.18        18.18        95.45
         85             1.00       4.55         4.55       100.00
-------------------------------------------------------------------
```

Fig 21.3 Extract of output from the command EXAMINE /VARIABLES cust
/FREQUENCIES FROM (20) BY (10).

To obtain a histogram, use:

```
EXAMINE /VARIABLES variable-name /PLOT HISTOGRAM.
```

which gives a histogram of the scores on the variable named. Histograms are explained further in chapter 31.

Exercise 21.1

Create the following command file, and save it as excom3:

```
GET /FILE 'a:ex1.sys'.
SET /LISTING 'a:ex3.lis'.
EXAMINE /VARIABLES cust.
EXAMINE /VARIABLES cust BY area /FREQUENCIES FROM (20) BY (10).
EXAMINE /VARIABLES area /PLOT HISTOGRAM.
```

Run this command file and examine the output to see the functions of the three EXAMINE lines. The output and comments on it are given in Appendix A.

21.5 LIST in SPSS for Windows

To obtain a listing of the data, select Statistics /Summarize /List Cases... The Dialogue box requires you to specify which variables should be listed. The box area entitled Cases to List lets you indicate whether you want all the cases listed (this is the default) or the first 10, 20 etc by selecting First through and then typing a number into the box. (If you ask for the first 20, these will be the first 20 rows of the data file spreadsheet.) You can have the case number included in the listing by selecting Number cases from the bottom of the Dialogue box; remember this is the number of the row in the sheet which the data occupies, not any identification number which you may have added as a variable (such as id in the salesq data file).

You can have every 5th, 20th etc row listed if you enter the appropriate number in the Interval text box.

When SPSS generates the output, it will try to provide a table such as Fig 14.1 in chapter 14. But if you have lengthy rows of data for each case, the scores will be given in a set of lines for each case. You can ask for just the first line to be shown, by making the appropriate choice in the Display area of the Dialogue box.

It is not possible, from the Menu system, to have the listing of cases starting anywhere except with case number 1. If you want to list cases starting with a higher number, such as listing cases 100 to 150, you have to paste the LIST command into a syntax file and then edit it so that it reads as follows:

LIST VARIABLES=ALL /CASES=FROM 100 TO 150.

You can specify the variables to be shown in the listing by naming them after VARIABLES=. So to have only sex and cust listed for cases 100 to 150, the command would be:

LIST VARIABLES=sex cust /CASES=FROM 100 TO 150.

21.6 EXPLORE in SPSS for Windows

The EXAMINE procedure of SPSS/PC+ is renamed EXPLORE in SPSS for Windows, and is obtained from the Statistics /Summarize /Explore... menu. The Dialogue box asks you to specify the variables to be analysed by adding them to the Dependent List text area. When you have specified the variables to be analysed, click on OK, and you will obtain a printout as shown in Fig 21.1.

You may wish the scores to be analysed separately for subgroups of cases, depending on their scores on one or more of the variables. For example, in salesq, suppose we want to Explore the scores on att1, att2 and att3 for men and women. Here sex is a factor variable, and we would need to have the name of this variable inserted into the Factor List text box. You can have a number of Factor variables; if we inserted sex and area into the Factor List, SPSS would Explore the scores of the variables listed in the Dependent List for each level of sex and then for each level of area.

From menus, you cannot ask for separate analyses of subgroups defined by combining scores on separate Factor variables: so you cannot get an analysis broken down into men from one area, men from the second area, women from the first area and women from the second area. To achieve this, you have to paste the command into a syntax file, and then edit it so that it separates the factor variables with the word BY. If we wanted the scores on att1, att2 and att3 to be analysed for each sex subdivided by area, the syntax file command would have to read:

EXAMINE VARIABLES=att1 att2 att3 BY sex BY area.

When EXPLORE provides details on particular cases from the data file, it labels them according to their sequence in the file (the number of the row they occupy in the spreadsheet). If you enter a variable name in the text box marked Label cases by:, the data on that variable is used in labelling the cases. So you could, for example, have cases labelled by an identification number which you had added to the data file. In salesq, the variable id is an identification number for each respondent.

Explore will exclude from the analysis any case that has data missing on any of the variables to be explored. You can alter this by selecting the Options button; the box revealed lets you choose Exclude cases pairwise, which means that every case that has data for the variable being Explored will be included in the analysis of that variable. So the number of cases Explored for different variables will fluctuate: a case that has missing data on the variable sex will not be included in the analysis of sex, but if the same case does have data for the variable area then it will be included when that variable is Explored.

If you have cases where there is no data on the variables that make up the Factor List, these cases can be made into a separate category or group of respondents by selecting the Report Values option. Their scores on the variables being Explored will be then be reported.

The Explore dialogue box allows you refine the analysis. From the Display area of the box, you can ask for the output to show statistics, plots (box and stem-leaf plots) or both, which is the default option.

If you want to obtain particular statistics, you click on the Statistics button. The box presented allows you a number of options. You can request maximum-likelihood estimators of location such as Huber's M-estimator (described in the SPSS for Windows manual). Selecting Outliers will display the cases with the 5 largest and 5 smallest values.

Percentiles and group frequency tables are also available.

The Plots button opens a dialogue box in which you can specify the characteristics of the boxplots or suppress it completely, and ask for a stem-and-leaf plot as well as a histogram. The box plot options are Factor levels together, which is used for comparing subgroups of respondents, and Dependents together which is used to compare the scores of one set of respondents on a number of variables. Stem and leaf and boxplots are explained in section 31.4.

When plots are selected, the output is sent to the Chart Carousel, (see section 32.6).

Do subgroups show homogeneity of variance?

If you select the Plots button from the Explore dialogue box, the section entitled Spread vs. Level with Levene Test allows you to request plots of the spread of scores against the level of the scores, and to test whether the subsets of scores show homogeneity of variance. Imagine we wanted to know whether the variability of the scores of men and women on sales was equal: the Levene test is one method of investigating this. You can obtain this test by having at least one Factor List variable and then selecting the Plot button from Explore's dialogue box, and choosing Untransformed. (If subgroups of respondents show unequal variances on the variables being compared, you may wish to apply a transformation to the raw data. There are options for applying various transformations to the data, or leaving it untransformed.) As well as the Levene test, this will give a graph of the median score of each subgroup (on the factor variable) versus the interquartile range. This permits one to see how variability varies with average level.

Are the scores normally distributed?

The Normality plots with tests button permits you to obtain a graph of the data plotted in such a way that it would be a straight line if the data were normally distributed. If the data is not normally distributed, the points will differ from the straight line, and the amount by which they differ is itself plotted as a detrended normal plot. If the data were normally distributed, the detrended plot would be a horizontal line passing through 0. These plots allow you judge visually whether the data is normally distributed. Tests of whether a set of data is normally distributed are the Lilliefors test and the Shapiro-Wilks test (when the number of scores is less than 50), and these are calculated and the probability values shown when you ask for Normal plots with tests. A low significance value means that the scores are not normally distributed, but with large sets of data non-perfect normal distribution is almost certain to occur and so the interpretation of these tests should be treated cautiously: the visual displays indicate how non-normal the distribution is.

21.7 Know what you want to find out; beware of means of nominal data

SPSS for Windows in particular offers the facility for obtaining plots and test statistics which may be unfamiliar to you. Do be very wary of obtaining analyses which you do not understand. If you have never heard of Lilliefors, you will only confuse yourself by being presented with it. As always, you should approach the data and the computer with clear ideas about what you want to know, and ask for the procedures which will provide results that you can interpret.

There is another point worth bearing in mind. SPSS will happily give the mean of a discrete, nominal variable, and this may be meaningless. There are examples in the scientific literature of eminent researchers making this mistake and reporting that the mean score on sex was 1.5. With categorical data such as sex, where respondents are 1, 2 or 3 (representing sex unknown), the mean of the scores is literally nonsense. But SPSS/PC+ does not know that; it only knows there is a set of figures, so it does not object when it is asked for the mean even if it is not appropriate to do so. It is the user's responsibility to look at the results of the analyses intelligently!

How many respondents gave a particular answer? Frequency data

Probably the first question you ask of your data is: how many people gave each alternative response to a particular question? The answer is obtained using the FREQUENCIES command. If you want cross-tabulations, showing how many people with a particular score on one variable obtained a particular score on another variable, the procedure needed is CROSSTABS.

22.1 FREQUENCIES in SPSS/PC+

To find FREQUENCIES *command in the menus, select* analyze data, *go right, select* descriptive statistics, *go right again.* FREQUENCIES *is the first entry in the submenu that is then revealed. Go right again to reveal the lengthy submenu.*

In SPSS/PC+, the format for a basic Frequencies command is:

```
FREQUENCIES /VARIABLES variable-name.
```

In exdat, for example, one may want to know how many respondents were from each employer, so the command file would be:

```
GET /FILE 'a:ex1.sys'.
SET /LISTING 'a:fn.lis'.
FREQUENCIES /VARIABLES employer.
```

The /VARIABLES section tells SPSS/PC+ which variables are to be analysed. An example of the FREQUENCIES procedure was included in excom2, and the output (stored in ex2.lis) is shown in Figure 14.3 in chapter 14.

The program analyses a number of variables one after the other if they are listed like this:

```
FREQUENCIES /VARIABLES variable1 variable2 variable3.
```

The order of the variables does not have to match the order in the DATA LIST line. When using FREQUENCIES to analyse a number of variables that are specified one after the other in the DATA LIST line, there is a short form of referring to them. Rather than using /VARIABLES sex employer area, you can use:

```
FREQUENCIES /VARIABLES sex TO area.
```

This tells SPSS/PC+ to apply the frequencies command to all the variables listed successively in the DATA LIST line starting with sex and continuing as far as area.

In Figure 14.3, the labels for the different values of sex have been included in the table: the output indicates that 1 on sex denotes male, 2 denotes female. This is the result of having put the VALUE LABELS command into the original command file, excom2.

In the tables obtained by FREQUENCIES, one can obtain some summary statistics: mean, standard deviation, maximum value and minimum value are shown, if one uses:

```
FREQUENCIES /VARIABLES variable-name /STATISTICS.
```

To obtain other statistics, select the /STATISTICS option from the submenu, and specify which statistics are required from the list presented in the submenu. For example:

```
FREQUENCIES /VARIABLES variable-name /STATISTICS ALL.
```

gives additional statistics such as median, mode, variance, sum and measures of skew.

If some of the data is missing, in that some cases do not have data for the variable being analysed, or if one of the data values has been defined as indicating missing data using the MISSING VALUES command, the table shows the frequencies of these missing values. But these are not included in the calculation of percentages, nor in the calculation of summary statistics such as the mean.

The table presents the values of the variable in ascending order. For a descending order, use the /FORMAT DVALUE command like this:

```
FREQUENCIES /VARIABLES variable-name /FORMAT DVALUE.
```

Alternatively, the table can give the most frequent values first if one uses /FORMAT AFREQ. The least frequent values come first with /FORMAT DFREQ. These subcommands, DVALUE, AFREQ and DFREQ can be typed in: when /FORMAT has been pasted into the line, obtain a typing window with Alt+T and type in the subcommand you want.

There may be occasions when you want the summary statistics but not the table. This is achieved by using:

```
FREQUENCIES /VARIABLES variable-name /FORMAT NOTABLE /STATISTICS.
```

Histograms and barcharts of the responses can be obtained from the FREQUENCIES command; these are described in chapter 31.

Exercise 22.1

Create the following command file, and save it as excom4:

```
GET /FILE 'a:ex1.sys'.
SET /LISTING 'a:ex4.lis'.
FREQUENCIES /VARIABLES sex employer.
```

```
FREQUENCIES /VARIABLES employer /FORMAT DVALUE.
FREQUENCIES /VARIABLES cust /FORMAT NOTABLE /STATISTICS ALL.
```

Run this command file and examine the output to see the functions of the FREQUENCIES procedure. The output is shown in Appendix A.

22.2 FREQUENCIES in SPSS for Windows

Obtain the frequencies procedure by selecting Statistics /Summarize /Frequencies... A detailed description is given in chapter 19.1 and 19.2.

22.3 How many times did a respondent give a particular answer? COUNT in SPSS for Windows

You may wish to know how often a respondent used a particular response category. For example, in salesq, how often did the respondents use the response 3 on the attitude questions? This kind of question can be answered in SPSS for Windows by using the Count procedure, obtained from the Transform /Count Occurrences... menu. COUNT creates a new variable, and the dialogue box asks you enter a name for this in the Target Variable text box. You then specify the variables to be analysed in the usual way, and click on the Define Values button which opens another box in which you indicate the value or range of values to be counted. To count how many times the response 3 was given to att1, att2 and att3 in salesq, you would enter these variables into the Variables list, enter a name such as num3 for the new variable, and put a label such as Number of 3 responses on att questions in the Target Label text box. Then click Define Values, and in the Value text box you would enter 3 and click on the Add button, and then on Continue which takes you back to the Count Occurrences box. Clicking on OK runs the procedure, and the new variable is added to the data in the Data Editor.

It is possible to perform COUNT on specified cases, such as only those which have a score of 1 on sex. This is achieved by selecting the If... button, and entering requirements in the If Cases dialogue box. The way to use this If Cases box is covered in section 29.4.

22.4 How is one variable related to another? Producing 2-dimensional tables: CROSSTABS in SPSS/PC+

To find CROSSTABS in the Menu, select analyze data, go right, select desstatistics and go right again. The submenu includes CROSSTABS.

You often want to examine how scores on two (or more) variable are related; for example, in exdat, what is the relationship between sex and employer? This requires a two-dimensional table showing the number of people of each sex who are employed by each employer. Tables like this are obtained using CROSSTABS:

```
CROSSTABS /TABLES variable1 BY variable2.
```

To obtain the table of sex by employer for exdat, the line is:

```
GET /FILE 'a:exl.sys'.
SET /LISTING 'a:ex.lis'.
CROSSTABS /TABLES= sex BY employer.
```

This command line gives the table shown in Fig 22.1. The first-named variable (sex) forms the rows, and the second one forms the columns. (So the table can be turned round by reversing the order in which the variables are specified.) The figures in the cells of the table are the number of cases (e.g. in exdat, four males worked for employer 1). Row and columns totals are provided, and are also expressed as a percentage of the overall total of cases.

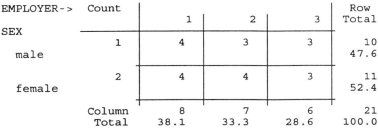

```
Crosstabulation:      SEX
                  By EMPLOYER

EMPLOYER->  Count                                         Row
                       1  |    2  |    3  | Total
SEX
          1         4  |    3  |    3  |     10
   male                                         47.6

          2         4  |    4  |    3  |     11
   female                                       52.4

          Column    8       7       6        21
          Total   38.1    33.3    28.6     100.0

Number of Missing Observations  =        1
```

Fig 22.1 Output from the command CROSSTABS /TABLES sex BY employer.

Note that in Fig 22.1, the total is 21 and one missing observation is shown; this is because the original data had one case where sex was coded as 3, indicating the sex of that respondent was unknown. Consequently there are only 21 cases that can be used in the sex by employer table.

You may want a further breakdown of the figures, with separate tables of variable1 by variable2 for each level of variable3; for example, suppose we want a sex by employer table, like that shown in Fig 22.1 but for each area group separately. This is achieved by:

```
CROSSTABS /TABLES= variable1 BY variable2 BY variable3.
```

For example:

```
CROSSTABS /TABLES= sex BY employer BY area.
```

'Area' here is referred to as a control variable, and one can have up to 8 of them (so the line contains the word BY nine times!)

It is often helpful to have the frequencies expressed as percentages as well as the actual frequencies themselves. To have the frequencies as percentages of the total number of cases included in the table, use /CELLS= TOTAL as in this line:

```
CROSSTABS /TABLES employer BY sex /CELLS= TOTAL.
```

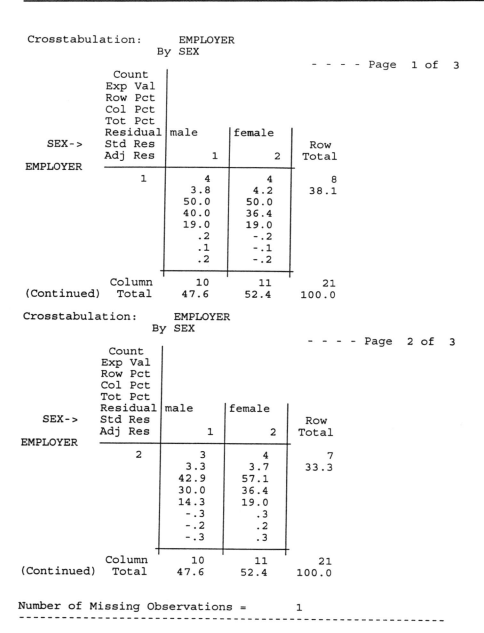

```
Crosstabulation:        EMPLOYER
                     By SEX
                                           - - - - Page  1 of  3
                  Count
                  Exp Val
                  Row Pct
                  Col Pct
                  Tot Pct
                  Residual|male    |female  |
      SEX->       Std Res |        |        |  Row
                  Adj Res |      1 |      2 |  Total
 EMPLOYER                 |--------|--------|
                  1       |      4 |      4 |      8
                          |    3.8 |    4.2 |   38.1
                          |   50.0 |   50.0 |
                          |   40.0 |   36.4 |
                          |   19.0 |   19.0 |
                          |     .2 |    -.2 |
                          |     .1 |    -.1 |
                          |     .2 |    -.2 |
                          |--------|--------|
                  Column        10       11       21
 (Continued)      Total       47.6     52.4    100.0


Crosstabulation:        EMPLOYER
                     By SEX
                                           - - - - Page  2 of  3
                  Count
                  Exp Val
                  Row Pct
                  Col Pct
                  Tot Pct
                  Residual|male    |female  |
      SEX->       Std Res |        |        |  Row
                  Adj Res |      1 |      2 |  Total
 EMPLOYER                 |--------|--------|
                  2       |      3 |      4 |      7
                          |    3.3 |    3.7 |   33.3
                          |   42.9 |   57.1 |
                          |   30.0 |   36.4 |
                          |   14.3 |   19.0 |
                          |    -.3 |     .3 |
                          |    -.2 |     .2 |
                          |    -.3 |     .3 |
                          |--------|--------|
                  Column        10       11       21
 (Continued)      Total       47.6     52.4    100.0


Number of Missing Observations =        1
```

Fig 22.2 Extract of output from the command CROSSTABS /TABLES employer BY sex /CELLS= TOTAL ROW COLUMN.

NOTE: The table for employer 3 has been deleted from this illustration.

The /CELLS= subcommand allows you a number of options. Fig 22.2 shows the actual frequency of cases in each cell, the expected value if there were no relationship between the two variables tabulated, the frequencies as a percentage of the total in the row, as a percentage of the total in the column, and as percentage of the overall total. There are also figures for residual, std res and adj res which are associated with the chi-square test and are unlikely to be needed. (Residual is the difference between the observed frequency and the expected frequency.) The top left cell of the table has a list which indicates what each of the figures in the cells in the main body of the table is.

22.5 Chi-square in SPSS/PC+

To apply the chi-square test, it is necessary to use CROSSTABS /STATISTICS CHISQ. *To find* CROSSTABS *in the Menu, select* analyze data, *go right, select* descriptive statistics *and go right again. The submenu includes* CROSSTABS. *Go right again for a submenu including* /TABLES *and* /STATISTICS

The chi-square test is used when respondents have been allocated to categories on two variables (e.g. sex, area). The test compares the number of cases falling into each cell of the table with the frequency that would be expected if there were no association between the two variables that form the table.

To obtain a chi-square test, use the CROSSTABS procedure with the /STATISTICS CHISQ option, which yields the chi-square test or the Fisher exact test if that is needed by the data in a 2 x 2 table:

CROSSTABS /TABLES= variable1 BY variable2 /STATISTICS= CHISQ.

(If you are using version 3 of SPSS/PC+, the subcommand is STATISTICS 1, as the submenu uses code numbers rather than names for the statistical tests you can request.) Fig 22.3 shows the output from these commands:

```
GET /FILE 'a:ex1.sys'.
SET /LISTING 'a:ex.lis'.
CROSSTABS /TABLES sex BY area /STATISTICS= CHISQ.
```

The frequency table, showing the number of cases in each cell of the table, is followed by the value of chi-square (labelled Pearson), the degrees of freedom (D.F.), and the probability (Significance). (The concept of statistical significance and the principles of the chi-square test are summarised in Appendix B.) If the Significance value is equal to or less than .05, you can conclude that the chi-square test indicates that there is a significant association between the two variables.

The output also gives you the figures for Likelihood Ratio chi-square and the Mantel-Haenszel chi-square test, which tests whether there is a linear relationship between the row and column variables. It is only applicable to ordinal data, and should not be used if the data is nominal.

The chi-square test is only valid if the expected frequencies for the cells in the table are sufficiently large: no cell should have an expected frequency less than 1 and fewer than 20% of the cells should have an expected frequency of less than 5. Below the table, the printout indicates the Minimum Expected Frequency and the number of cells with an expected frequency of less than 5 (Cells with E.F.<5). These figures indicate whether the chi-square test can validly be used on the data in the table.

With 2 x 2 tables, a different formula for chi-square is used which incorporates a correction for continuity. Fig 22.3 shows the chi-square values with and without this correction: the second of the two values (.48125 in Fig 22.3) is the one to use. If N is less than 20 in a 2 x 2 table, the Fisher Exact test should be used, rather than chi-square: SPSS does this automatically if any cell has expected value less than 5.

If the test is not valid, you must either alter the data table, amalgamating categories to remove cells with small expected frequencies, or collect more data. Fig 22.3 shows that the chi-square test is not valid on this table, as more than 20% of cells have an expected frequency smaller than 5; since it would not be meaningful to amalgamate groups, it would be necessary to collect more data in order to test the hypothesis that there is a tendency for sex to be related to area of work.

Exercise 22.2

Create the following command file, and save it as excom5:

```
GET /FILE 'a:ex1.sys'.
SET /LISTING 'a:ex5.lis'.
CROSSTABS /TABLES= area BY employer /CELLS= TOTAL.
CROSSTABS /TABLES= sex BY employer /STATISTICS= CHISQ.
CROSSTABS /TABLES= sex BY employer BY area.
```

Run this command file and examine the output to see what these CROSSTABS lines achieve. The output is illustrated in Appendix A.

22.6 CROSSTABS and chi-square in SPSS for Windows

You often want to examine how scores on two (or more) variable are related; for example, in salesq, what is the relationship between sex and employer? This requires a two-dimensional table showing the number of people of each sex who are employed by each employer. Tables like this are obtained using CROSSTABS, which is obtained by selecting Statistics /Summarize /Crosstabs... The Dialogue box asks you to enter a variable to form the rows of the table and a variable to form the columns from the variable list. If you insert more than one variable into the Row(s) or Column(s) boxes, you will obtain a set of cross-tabulations.

You may want a further breakdown of the figures, with separate tables of variable1 by variable2 for each level of variable3; for example, suppose we want a sex by employer table, like that shown in Fig 22.1 but for each area group separately. The variable area is referred to as control variable, and you have to enter it in the box under the heading Layer 1 of 1. You can have further control variables by clicking on the Next button.

The contents of the CROSSTABS table are set by clicking on the Cells button, which opens a box in which you can ask for Expected frequencies, and for the observed frequencies to be expressed as percentages of the row, column and/or total number of cases in the table.

If you wish to have the table organised in descending order of variable scores, or to obtain an index of the tables you are requesting, these can be set by using the Format button in the Crosstabs dialogue box.

The chi-square test is used when respondents have been allocated to categories on two variables (e.g. sex, area). The test compares the number of cases falling into each cell of the table with the frequency that would be expected if there were no association between the two variables that form the table. Chi-square and other tests of association such as the contingency coefficient, and also correlations are available from the Statistics button of the Crosstabs box. Take care in requesting statistics: ensure you understand which ones you want, and avoid the temptation to ask for ones you have never heard of! They are all explained in the SPSS for Windows User's Guide. The output of the chi-square test is shown in Fig 22.3, and explained in section 22.5.

```
SEX   by   AREA

                     AREA          Page 1 of 1
           Count
           Tot Pct  North    South
                                     Row
                       1        2    Total
SEX       -----------------------------
            1        3        7      10
   male            14.3     33.3    47.6
          -----------------------------
            2        6        5      11
  female          28.6     23.8    52.4
          -----------------------------
          Column    9       12      21
           Total  42.9     57.1   100.0

Chi-Square                Value      DF       Significance
-----------------         ---------- ----     ------------

Pearson                   1.28864     1         .25630
Continuity Correction      .48125     1         .48786
Likelihood Ratio          1.30665     1         .25300
Mantel-Haenszel test for  1.22727     1         .26794
     linear association
Fisher's Exact Test:
   One-Tail                                     .24494
   Two-Tail                                     .38700

Minimum Expected Frequency -      4.286
Cells with Expected Frequency < 5 -      2 OF     4 ( 50.0%)


Number of Missing Observations:   1
```

Fig 22.3 Output from the SPSS/PC+command CROSSTABS /TABLES sex BY area /STATISTICS= CHISQ and the SPSS for Windows chi-square test.

23

What is the average score?
Measures of central tendency and dispersion

If you want the mean score and standard deviation of all the respondents on one or more of the variables, you use the EXAMINE, FREQUENCIES or DESCRIPTIVES procedures. To obtain the medians, you need the DESCRIPTIVES procedure. Note carefully that you do not use the MEANS procedure to obtain the means of all respondents on a variable. MEANS is used when you require the means of subgroups of respondents, such as the mean of males and then separately the means of females.

Note also that when carrying out parametrical statistical tests, such as the t-test, the output will give the means and variances of the data, so there is no need to obtain them using a separate procedure.

23.1 Totals, means and standard deviations in SPSS/PC+

To find DESCRIPTIVES *command in the menus, select* analyze data, *go right, select* descriptive statistics, *go right again.* DESCRIPTIVES *is in the submenu that is then revealed. Go right again to see the submenu showing the alternatives available.*

This procedure provides summary statistics (such as mean and standard deviation) of scores on a variables, but does not give median or mode. It does not provide the frequency table that the FREQUENCIES procedure provides. Particular statistics can be requested, but it is simpler to use ALL like this:

```
DESCRIPTIVES /VARIABLES variable-name /STATISTICS ALL.
```

To obtain the means standard deviation of scores on a variable, use one of the following:

```
EXAMINE /VARIABLES variable-name.
FREQUENCIES /VARIABLES variable-name /STATISTICS ALL.
DESCRIPTIVES /VARIABLES variable-name /STATISTICS ALL.
```

The total of a set of scores is provided by FREQUENCIES and DESCRIPTIVES commands, but not be EXAMINE. EXAMINE is covered in chapter 21, FREQUENCIES in chapter 22.

To obtain a barchart or histogram (explained in chapter 31) use:

```
FREQUENCIES /VARIABLES variable-name /BARCHART.
FREQUENCIES /VARIABLES variable-name /HISTOGRAM.
```

23.2 Medians in SPSS/PC+

To find the median of a set of scores, use the FREQUENCIES procedure:

```
FREQUENCIES /VARIABLES variable-name /STATISTICS ALL.
```

This command file would give the median score on sales in exdat:

```
GET /FILE 'a:ex1.sys'.
SET /LISTING 'a:ex.lis'.
FREQUENCIES /VARIABLES sales /STATISTICS ALL.
```

23.3 Finding the means of subgroups of respondents: MEANS in SPSS/PC+

To find MEANS, *select* analyze data, *go right, select* descriptive statistics *and go right again. The submenu revealed includes* MEANS *as one entry.*

We frequently want to know the scores of subgroups from the data; for example, in exdat, assume we want the mean scores on sales for males and females. There are a number of ways of obtaining this information, but one of the easiest is to use the MEANS procedure. The general form of the command is:

```
MEANS /TABLES variable1 BY variable2.
```

For example, the output shown in Fig 23.1 shows the mean sales for each of the two sex groups. It was produced by these commands:

```
GET /FILE 'a:ex1.sys'.
SET /LISTING 'a:ex.lis'.
MEANS /TABLES sales BY sex.
```

Observe that the respondent whose sex is unknown, who was given a sex score of 3 (missing value) is not included in the table, and is shown as the missing case at the end of the printout.

```
Summaries of    SALES
By levels of    SEX

Variable        Value  Label           Mean      Std Dev    Cases

For Entire Population                  5831.9205  2377.9699     21

SEX              1     male            5950.6370  2772.4555     10
SEX              2     female          5723.9964  2089.1906     11

   Total Cases =       22
Missing Cases =        1 OR   4.5 PCT.
--------------------------------------------------------------------
```

Fig 23.1 Output from the command MEANS /TABLES sales BY sex._

If you wanted the mean scores on sales for the separate sex groups and then for the separate area groups, the command would be:

```
MEANS /TABLES sales BY sex area.
```

To have the output show the sum of scores for each group, use OPTIONS 6, and to obtain the variances OPTIONS 12:

```
MEANS /TABLES sales BY sex /OPTIONS 6 8 12.
```

There is often a problem here, and the program will stop, complaining that the table is too wide. Overcome this by including 8 in the /OPTION list as shown above. (It needs to be typed in, as it is not included in the /OPTIONS submenu unless you are using Extended menus.) It has the effect of suppressing the printing of the variable labels, and so makes the table narrower.

Exercise 23.1

Create the following command file, and save it as excom6:

```
GET /FILE 'a:ex1.sys'.
SET /LISTING 'a:ex6.lis'.
MEANS /TABLES sales BY sex area.
MEANS /TABLES sales BY sex/ OPTIONS 6 8 12.
```

Run this command file and examine the output to see how to obtain the means of subgroups of cases. The results are shown in Appendix A.

23.4 Measures of central tendency and dispersion in SPSS for Windows

To obtain the mean, sum and standard deviation of all respondents on any of the variables in the data file, you can use Frequencies, Examine or the descriptives procedure which is accessed via the Statistics /Summarize menu. You specify the variables to be analysed in the usual SPSS for Windows manner. To obtain mean and standard deviation, you can just click on OK, but if you want sum, variance, range, standard error and indices of kurtosis or skew, you have to select the Options button and then specify the statistics you want. You can have the means listed in alphabetic order of the variable names by selecting the Name display order in the Descriptives: Options box.

The median and mode are obtained if you use the Frequencies procedure, click on Statistics button, and check the appropriate boxes.

23.5 Obtaining z-scores in SPSS for Windows

The descriptives procedure is used to obtain z scores for any variable, by selecting the Save standardized values as variables option in the Descriptives dialogue box.

This option creates a new variable which is added to the data file, and is named as z+the first 7 letters of the variable name.

This z-score facility will exclude any cases that have a missing value score on the variable being analysed. If you wanted to exclude from the analysis any case that had a missing value on any of the variables for which you are obtaining z-scores, you have to paste the command into a syntax file and then insert into the command line a /MISSING LISTWISE subcommand.

23.6 Finding the means of subgroups of respondents in SPSS for Windows

To obtain the means of subgroups of respondents, you need the Means procedure, which is in the Statistics /Compare Means menu. Let us suppose you want the means scores of males and females on the sales variable in the salesq data file. Having selected Statistics /Compare Means for the Application window menu, you would insert the dependent variable (sales) in the Dependent List text box of the Means dialogue box, and then insert sex into the Independent List text box, and click on OK. Output from Means is shown In Fig 23.1.

The Means dialogue box has another area initially indicating Layer 1 of 1, which is rather intriguing. This allows you to subdivide the respondents into further subgroups. If you wanted to find the means scores of males and females from each area on the sales variable, you would have sales as the Dependent List variable, sex as the Independent List variable and use area as the Layer variable. Having inserted sex into the Independent List box, you would click on the Next button and then insert area in the Independent List box.

The Options button lets you request an analysis of variance to compare the means on the dependent variable(s) of the subgroups defined by the variable on the first layer of the independent variable list. So if you have used sales as the dependent variable and sex as the independent variable, selecting the ANOVA table and eta button will give you a one-way analysis of variance on the sales scores of the subgroups of the sex variable (ie males and females). According to the User Guide, eta is appropriate if the dependent variable is measured on an interval scale, and the independent variable is nominal or ordinal. Eta squared can be interpreted as the proportion of the total variability in the dependent variable that can be accounted for by knowing the values of the independent variable.

Parametric statistical tests

24.1 Introduction

This chapter describes the commands needed to obtain the commoner parametric statistical tests, which are used to compare sets of scores when one can make certain assumptions about the data. These assumptions are given in Appendix B; you have to be able to assume the data has been measured on an interval scale (rather than a nominal or rank scale), is normally distributed, and the subgroups of data have equal variance. If these assumptions cannot be made, one should use non-parametric analyses, which are covered in chapter 26.

Note that the examples shown here use the names of the variables in the exdat/salesq file; if you are applying the commands to a set of data with different variable names, you must of course use those variable names.

To compare two sets of scores, use the t-test. When comparing the scores of the same respondents on two variables, one needs the within-subjects (paired) t-test. The paired t-test would be used, for example, to compare the scores of the respondents on att1 and att2, to discover whether the mean response to att1 was significantly different from the mean response to att2. To compare the scores of two groups of different subjects on one variable, it is necessary to use the between-subjects or independent t-test. For example, to compare the sales figures of the males and females in exdat you require a between-subjects (independent) t-test.

To compare the mean scores of three or more groups of respondents on a particular variable, use the one-way analysis of variance. It involves calculating the F-ratio, the ratio of the variance arising from the difference between the groups to the variance arising within the groups.

To compare the scores of respondents who can be divided according to two independent variables, use the two-way analysis of variance. For example, in exdat we have scores on sales for respondents who are divided by sex and divided by area. Both these are between-subjects factors, since any one person is either male or female and works either in the North or in the South. Suppose we want to compare the sales scores of males and females, and of those working in the North with those working in the South, and also want to see whether there is an interaction between sex and area.

(For example, do men do better on sales than women when they working in the North but not when they are working in the South?) This analysis is obtained using the ANOVA procedure.

Note that ANOVA is only applicable when both the independent variables are between-subjects. This means that on each variable taken separately any individual respondent can only be in one of the groups. For example, sex is a between-subjects variable since any individual must be one or the other, and cannot be both.

Some variables are within-subjects, which means that any individual can appear in both groups. For example, suppose one measured the blood-pressure of male and female respondents before and after exercise. Sex would be a between-subjects variable, but blood-pressure would be a within-subjects factor, as the same people were measured twice. If the data involves a within-subjects factor, a repeated measures analysis of variance is required. This is obtained using the MANOVA procedure, which is not covered in this book, as it is only provided in optional additional modules of SPSS.

24.2 Within-subjects (paired) t-test in SPSS/PC+

To find T-TEST *in the menu, select* analyze data, *go right, select* compare group means *and go right again.*

The general form of the command for a within-subjects t-test is:

T-TEST /PAIRS variable1 variable2.

where the two variables named are the ones to be compared.

You can obtain a set of t-tests by naming more variables after the /PAIRS subcommand. To have t-tests comparing variable1 and variable2, variable2 and variable3, variable1 and variable3, use:

T-TEST /PAIRS variable1 variable2 variable3.

Fig 24.1 shows the output from the command:

T-TEST /PAIRS att1 att2.

After the means, standard deviations and standard errors of the scores on each variable, it provides the difference between the means, the correlation between the two sets of scores and the significance (probability) of the correlation, the t-value, degrees of freedom and the two-tailed probability of that t-value having arisen by chance. Note that if the probability level is .0000, this indicates the value is highly significant: the probability is less than .0001. Fig 24.1 shows that there is a significant difference between the scores on att1 and att2, as the probability level is less than .05.

```
Paired samples t-test:    ATT1
                          ATT2

Variable     Number                  Standard     Standard
           of Cases      Mean       Deviation       Error

ATT1           22        2.5455       1.101         .235
ATT2           22        3.0909        .921         .196


(Difference) Standard Standard | 2-Tail   |  t   Degrees of   2-Tail
    Mean     Deviation  Error  |Corr Prob |Value  Freedom      Prob.

  -.5455       .800     .171   |.700  .000|3.20    21           .004
-------------------------------------------------------------------
```

Fig 24.1 Output from the command T-TEST /PAIRS att1 att2.

24.3 Between-subjects (independent) t-test in SPSS/PC+

To find T-TEST *in the menu, select* analyze data, *go right, select* compare group means *and go right again.*

The general form of the command for the between-subjects or independent t-test is:

T-TEST /GROUPS variable1(x,y) /VARIABLES variable2.

After /GROUPS, you must specify the variable used to identify the two groups to be compared, and state the value of the groups' codes on this variable. The variable named after /VARIABLE specifies the scores which are t-tested.

Using the data in exdat, the line below compares the scores on sales of the groups from employers 1 and 3:

T-TEST /GROUPS employer(1,3) /VARIABLES sales.

The output from this command is shown in Fig 24.2. Below the summary statistics for each group, it gives an F value and two alternative values of t. If the probability associated with F is less than .05, use the t value for the separate variance estimate, otherwise the t value for the pooled variance estimate is the one to take. Fig 24.3 indicates that there is a significant difference between the sales of respondents from employers 1 and 3, as the probability value is less than .05. Observe that the table defines the two employers as group 1 and group 2, but the top of the output states that group 1 is employer 1 and group 2 is employer 3.

```
Independent samples of  EMPLOYER

Group 1:  EMPLOYER  EQ 1          Group 2:  EMPLOYER  EQ 3

t-test for:  SALES

                    Number              Standard      Standard
                   of Cases     Mean    Deviation      Error

        Group 1       8      5333.2313  2761.360      976.288
        Group 2       6      8207.4150   925.178      377.702

           |Pooled Variance Estimate|Separate Variance Estimate

   F    2-Tail|  t  Degrees of 2-Tail |  t   Degrees of  2-Tail
 Value  Prob. |Value  Freedom   Prob. |Value   Freedom    Prob.

 8.91   .028  |-2.43    12      .032  |-2.75    8.97      .023
 ----------------------------------------------------------------
```

Fig 24.2 Output from the command T-TEST /GROUPS employer(1,3) /VARIABLES sales.

Exercise 24.1

Create the following command file, and save it as `excom7`:

```
GET /FILE 'a:ex1.sys'.
SET /LISTING 'a:ex7.lis'.
T-TEST /PAIRS att1 att3.
T-TEST /GROUPS employer(1,2) /VARIABLES sales.
```

Run this command file to compare the respondents' scores on att1 and att3, and to compare the sales data for employers 1 and 2. The output is similar to Figures 24.1 and 24.2.

24.2 One-way analysis of variance in SPSS/PC+

To find MEANS, *select* analyze data, *go right, select* descriptive statistics *and go right again. The submenu revealed includes* MEANS *as one entry.*

To find ONEWAY *in the menu, select* analyze data, *go right, select* compare group means *and go right again.*

The one-way analysis of variance can be obtained using either of these commands:

```
MEANS /TABLES variable1 BY variable2 /STATISTICS 1.
ONEWAY /VARIABLES variable1 BY variable2(a,b).
```

ONEWAY allows you to compare pairs of sets of scores, with the range tests, and is probably the more useful procedure. When using ONEWAY, after BY one must state the independent variable and specify its maximum and minimum values in the brackets.

To compare the mean score on the variable cust (number of customers visited) of the respondents from each of the three employers in the exdat file, the relevant command file is either of the following:

```
GET /FILE 'a:exl.sys'.
SET /LISTING 'a:ex.lis'.
MEANS /TABLES cust BY employer /STATISTICS 1.

GET /FILE 'a:exl.sys'.
SET /LISTING 'a:ex.lis'.
ONEWAY /VARIABLES cust BY employer(1,3).
```

With ONEWAY, to obtain the mean, standard deviation and other summary statistics of each group being compared, you need to use the /STATISTICS subcommand:

```
ONEWAY /VARIABLES variable1 BY variable2(a,b) /STATISTICS 1.
```

Fig 24.3 illustrates the result of this subcommand. Tests of homogeneity of variance are provided if one uses /STATISTICS 3. The two requests can be combined with:

```
ONEWAY /VARIABLES variable1 BY variable2(a,b) /STATISTICS 1 3.
```

The first section of Fig 24.3 is the usual analysis of variance table, showing the degrees of freedom, sum of squares, mean square between groups and within groups. The F ratio is the between groups mean square divided by the within groups mean square. The probability associated with F is given in the final column: if it is less than 0.05, this shows there is a significant difference between the groups being compared.

The second section of Fig 24.3 was produced by incorporating /STATISTICS 1 in the procedure command. It provides summary statistics for the groups being compared; as can be seen, the mean for group 1 (those respondents employed by employer 1) is 41.25, the standard deviation is 5.7756, the standard error is 2.0420. The 95% confidence limits for the mean are followed by the minimum and maximum scores on cust for this group of respondents. (Standard error and confidence limits are explained in Appendix B).

If the one-way analysis of variance shows a significant difference between the three (or more) groups, it does not specify where this difference lies. For example, the results of the analysis of variance on the cust scores shows there is a difference between the employers in terms of how many customers were visited (Fig 24.3 shows F=17.8773; p=0.0000 indicates the F value is highly significant). But is there a significant difference between employers 1 and 2, between 1 and 3, between 2 and 3? These questions are answered using Scheffe, Duncan or Tukey tests, which can be requested in the ONEWAY command with the subcommand /RANGES as in these examples:

```
ONEWAY /VARIABLES cust BY employer(1,3) /RANGES SCHEFFE.

ONEWAY /VARIABLES cust BY employer(1,3) /RANGES DUNCAN.

ONEWAY /VARIABLES cust BY employer(1,3) /RANGES TUKEY.
```

The output from ONEWAY with /RANGES SCHEFFE is illustrated in Fig 24.3. The cust scores in exdat were subjected to an analysis of variance, summary statistics were requested, and the Scheffe test conducted with these commands:

```
GET /FILE 'a:exl.sys'.
SET /LISTING 'a:ex.lis'.
ONEWAY /VARIABLES cust BY employer(1,3) /RANGES SCHEFFE /STATISTICS 1.
```

The final section of the output indicates, with the asterisks, that group 3 (i.e. employer 3) is significantly different from both group 1 and group 2. The absence of asterisks shows that groups 1 and 2 do not differ from each other.

```
         - - - - - - - - - O N E W A Y - - - - - - - - - -
    Variable   CUST
By Variable    EMPLOYER
                             Analysis of Variance
                          Sum of          Mean          F
Source            D.F.     Squares        Squares     Ratio   Prob.
Between Groups      2     3968.4394      1984.2197   17.8773   .0000
Within Groups      19     2108.8333       110.9912
Total              21     6077.2727
-------------------------------------------------------------------
         - - - - - - - - - O N E W A Y - - - - - - - - - -
                       Standard   Standard
Group    Count  Mean   Deviation  Error   95 Pct Conf Int for Mean
Grp 1      8   41.2500   5.7756   2.0420   36.4215  To  46.0785
Grp 2      8   44.0000  14.5406   5.1409   31.8438  To  56.1562
Grp 3      6   72.6667   8.8919   3.6301   63.3353  To  81.9980
Total     22   50.8182  17.0116   3.6269   43.2757  To  58.3607

Group         Minimum       Maximum
Grp 1         30.0000       48.0000
Grp 2         28.0000       71.0000
Grp 3         58.0000       83.0000
Total         28.0000       83.0000
-------------------------------------------------------------------
         - - - - - - - - - O N E W A Y - - - - - - - - - -
    Variable   CUST
  By Variable  EMPLOYER

Multiple Range Test
Scheffe Procedure
Ranges for the   .050 level -
         3.75    3.75
The ranges above are table ranges.
The value actually compared with Mean(J)-Mean(I) is..
      7.4495 * Range * Sqrt(1/N(I) + 1/N(J))

(*) Denotes pairs of groups significantly different at the   .050 level
-------------------------------------------------------------------
         - - - - - - - - - O N E W A Y - - - - - - - - - -
    Variable   CUST
    (Continued)
                            G G G
                            r r r
                            p p p
      Mean        Group     1 2 3
     41.2500      Grp 1
     44.0000      Grp 2
     72.6667      Grp 3     * *
-------------------------------------------------------------------
```

Fig 24.3 Output from the command ONEWAY /VARIABLES cust BY employer(1,3)
/RANGES SCHEFFE /STATISTICS 1.

24.5 Two-way analysis of variance in SPSS/PC+

To find ANOVA *in the menu,* select analyze data, *go right, select* group means *and go right again.*

To obtain a two-way anovar with two independent variables that are between-subjects factors, the command is:

ANOVA /VARIABLES dependent_ve BY indep_vel(min,max) indep_ve2(min,max).

So the two-way analysis of variance comparing sales of males and females and of different geographical areas, is obtained with this command file:

GET /FILE 'a:ex.sys'.
SET /LISTING 'a:ex.lis'.
ANOVA /VARIABLES sales BY area(1,2) sex(1,2) /STATISTICS 3.

The /STATISTICS 3 gives the cell means for the dependent variable.

The output from this command is shown in Fig 24.4. The first part is the cell means, produced as a result of including the /STATISTICS 3 subcommand. It shows the overall mean score, the means for each category of area, for each category of sex and for each area/sex group. The numbers in brackets show the number of respondents upon which each mean is based. The analysis of variance table is then given; in this instance, none of the factors is significant as can be seen from the final column of Significance values of F: they are all larger than .05. The 1 case missing is the respondent from the original data file who had not indicated their sex, and was scored 3 (the missing value) on that variable.

24.6 Within-subjects (paired) t-test in SPSS for Windows

The dialogue box for the paired t-test is obtained by selecting Statistics /Compare Means /Paired-Samples T Test from the menus. You have to indicate the two variables to be compared by clicking on each of them; the first one will appear in the Current Selection Variable 1: area, and the second one will appear as Variable 2. To insert these into the Paired Variables list, click on the right-pointing arrow button: the two variables will then be shown as a linked pair. You can create further pairs in the same way.

Clicking on OK will produce an output as is shown in Fig 24.5, where the scores on att1 and att2 were compared. The top part of the output shows the means, standard deviations and standard errors of the score on the two variables and between these is the correlation between them (0.700 in this example). The significance of the correlation is provided: the value of .000 in Fig 24.5 indicates that the correlation is significant beyond the .001 level. The correlation is significant if the probability value is less than 0.05.

```
                    * * *   C E L L   M E A N S   * * *
            SALES
        BY AREA
            SEX

TOTAL POPULATION
    5831.92
   (      21)


AREA
          1              2
   6158.48     5587.00
   (      9)  (     12)


SEX
          1              2
   5950.64     5724.00
   (     10)  (     11)


          SEX
                     1              2
AREA     1    5321.34    6577.05
              (      3)  (      6)

         2    6220.33    4700.33
              (      7)  (      5)


            * * *   A N A L Y S I S   O F   V A R I A N C E   * * *
            SALES
        BY    AREA
            SEX
```

	Sum of Squares	DF	Mean Square	F	Signif of F
Source of Variation					
Main Effects	2430917.664	2	1215458.832	.204	.818
AREA	2161857.779	1	2161857.779	.362	.555
SEX	751285.695	1	751285.695	.126	.727
2-way Interactions	9141051.914	1	9141051.914	1.531	.233
AREA SEX	9141051.914	1	9141051.914	1.531	.233
Explained	11571969.578	3	3857323.193	.646	.596
Residual	101522846.164	17	5971932.127		
Total	113094815.742	20	5654740.787		

```
-----------------------------------------------------------------

    22 Cases were processed.
     1 Cases (  4.5 PCT) were missing.
```

Fig 24.4 Output from the command ANOVA /VARIABLES sales BY area(1,2) sex(1,2)
/STATISTICS 3.

You may recall that the paired t-test involves taking the difference between the two scores for each respondent and finding the mean of these difference scores. The bottom part of the output gives this mean difference, its standard deviation and standard error. The value of the t statistic is then shown, with its degrees of freedom (df) and its probability level (2-tail Sig): if the probability is less than .05 (in Fig 24.5 it is .004), you can conclude there was a statistically significant difference between the two sets of scores. The final line of the output shows the 95% confidence interval of the mean difference.

```
                 - - - t-tests for paired samples - - -
```

Variable	Number of pairs	Corr	2-tail Sig	Mean	SD	SE of Mean
ATT1				2.5455	1.101	.235
	22	.700	.000			
ATT2				3.0909	.921	.196

Paired Differences					
Mean	SD	SE of Mean	t-value	df	2-tail Sig
-.5455	.800	.171	-3.20	21	.004
95% CI (-.900, -.190)					

Fig 24.5 Output for a paired t-test in SPSS for Windows

Dealing with cases that have missing data

The Paired T Test procedure will exclude any case which has missing data on either of the variables in the pair being compared. This is referred to as Exclude cases analysis-by-analysis. If you are requesting a number of t-tests, the package will omit those cases which have missing data on the variables being analysed and do this separately for each test. You can ask the program to omit from all t-tests any cases which have missing values on any of the variables being analysed, known as Exclude cases listwise. This is obtained by clicking on the Options button in the Paired samples T-Test box and then selecting the alternative from the Missing Values area of the Options dialogue box.

The Options button of the T Test box also allows you to suppress the printing of the variable labels, and alter the confidence intervals shown by entering a number (such as 99 for the 99% interval) in the text box.

24.7 Between-subjects (independent) t-test in SPSS for Windows

The Dialogue box for the independent t-test is obtained by selecting Statistics

/Compare Means / Independent Samples T Test from the menu. The variables to be compared have to be inserted into the Tests Variable(s) text window. The variable used to divide the respondents into the two groups to be compared has to be inserted into the text window Grouping Variable, and you then have to click the Define Groups button, which opens a dialogue box. The normal procedure is to enter into the Group 1 and Group 2 windows the values on the grouping variable which define the two groups to be compared. So, for example, to compare the scores on sales for respondents of employer 1 with those for respondents on employer 3, you insert the variable employer in the Grouping Variable box of the Independent Samples T Test dialogue box, click on the Define Groups button and when presented with the Define Groups dialogue box enter 1 into the Group 1 window and 3 into the Group 2 window. Click on Continue to return to the T-Test box, and click on OK. The printout is shown in Fig 25.6.

The first section shows that the variable being tested was sales, and the scores being compared were those for the employer 1 and employer 3 groups. The mean score on sales for each group are shown, with the standard deviations and standard errors. The mean difference and the outcome of Levene's test for equality of variances are provided, and then t values, degrees of freedom, probability of t, standard errors for the difference and 95% confidence intervals (CI) for the difference are given. If the Levene test shows that the two groups had unequal variances (ie the probability value given is less than 0.05, as it is in Fig 24.6 where it is 0.045), you should use the t value for unequal variances (the final line of Fig 24.6). If the Levene test had a probability value greater than 0.05, you would be entitled to use the t value for equal variances (you would accept that the two groups had the same variance).

```
t-tests for independent samples of  EMPLOYER

                          Number
          Variable       of Cases    Mean         SD       SE of Mean
          -----------------------------------------------------------
          SALES
          EMPLOYER 1          8    5333.2313   2761.360      976.288
          EMPLOYER 3          6    8207.4150    925.178      377.702
          -----------------------------------------------------------

          Mean Difference = -2874.1837

          Levene's Test for Equality of Variances: F= 5.026  P= .045


          t-test for Equality of Means                    95%
Variances  t-value    df    2-Tail Sig    SE of Diff    CI for Diff
------------------------------------------------------------------------
Equal      -2.43      12      .032        1183.786   (-5454.10, -294.269)
Unequal    -2.75     8.97     .023        1046.804   (-5242.86, -505.504)
------------------------------------------------------------------------
```

Fig 24.6 Output for an independent t-test in SPSS for Windows

The Define Groups box has an option Cut point, and a text window which you enter a value into. This has the effect of dividing the cases into two groups, one with scores below the value of the Cut point and the other having scores above the Cut point.

Dealing with cases that have missing data

The T test procedure will exclude any case which has missing data on either the variable used to create the groups being compared or on the variable which is being subjected to the t test. This is referred to as Exclude cases analysis-by-analysis. If you are requesting a number of t-tests on a series of variables, the package will omit those cases which have missing data on the variable being analysed and do this separately for each test. You can ask the program to omit from all t-tests, any cases which have missing values on either the grouping variable or on any of the variables being t-tested. This is obtained by clicking on the Options button in the T Test box and then selecting the Exclude cases listwise alternative.

The Options button of the T Test box also allows you to suppress the printing of the variable labels.

24.8 One-way analysis of variance in SPSS for Windows

The dialogue box for the one-way analysis of variance is obtained by selecting Statistics /Compare Means /One-Way ANOVA from the menus. You specify the dependent variable, the scores to be compared, by entering it in the Dependent List box. The variable used to create the groups of respondents to be compared has to be entered in the Factor box, and the range of scores on this variable has to be specified. For example, to compare the sales data for respondents from the three employers in salesq, you have to put sales as the Dependent List variable, and employer as the Factor. But you also have to indicate that the values on the employer variable vary between 1 and 3, and this is done by clicking on the Define Range button. In the box that appears you would enter 1 in the Minimum box and 3 in the Maximum box. If you had a variable that had 5 values, rather than the 3 of the variable employer, then you would enter the appropriate minimum and maximum values in the boxes of the Define Range dialogue box.

You are likely to want the means, n and other statistics for each group of respondents being compared in the analysis of variance, and these are obtained by selecting Options from the One-Way ANOVA box and checking Descriptive in the Statistics area.

To test whether the groups being compared have equal variance, you can ask for the Levene statistic from the One-Way Options.

The analysis will exclude any case which has a missing value on the dependent of factor variables, or has a score on the factor variable which is outside the range specified with Define Range. If you are requesting a number of analyses, you can ask for any case that has missing values on any of the variables involved to be excluded from all analyses. This is done by clicking on the Options button and selecting the Exclude cases listwise option.

Analysis of variance can tell you that there is a difference between the means of the three or more groups of respondents, but it does not tell you just where the differences occur: is group 1 different from both group 2 and group 3, does group 2 differ from both group 1 and group 3? Questions like this are answered by comparing the means of the subgroups, and there are two types of procedure. One is referred to as *a priori* comparisons, and these are ones that were planned before the data was collected: you might, for example, have predicted that group 3 differs significantly from group 1 but not from group 2. *Post-hoc* tests, on the other hand, are comparisons suggested after you have examined the data.

A priori contrasts, including orthogonal contrasts, can be obtained in Oneway by clicking the Contrasts... button. How to use this is best explained with an example. Suppose we are comparing the scores on sales for the three employers in salesq, and had predicted that there would be a significant difference between the scores for employer 1 and the combined scores for employers 2 and 3. To test this prediction we would use linear contrasts: the coefficient for employer 1's data can be set at −1 and the coefficients for employers 2 and 3 each set to 0.5. The coefficient of 1 for group 1 is entered in the box marked Coefficient, and the Add button used to insert it into the list. The coefficient of 0.5 for group 2 is then entered in the Coefficient box and Add used to insert it in the list, and finally the coefficient for group 3 is inserted in the list by using the Add button. The order of the coefficients is crucial, as they are applied in sequence to the ascending order of values on the factor variable: the first coefficient is assigned to the lowest value, the second to the next-to-lowest value and so on. Coefficients can be removed or altered by highlighting them and using the Remove or Change buttons. Further sets of contrasts can be entered if you click on the Next button.

Post-hoc tests such as Duncan's test, Tukey's test, Scheffe's test (and others) are obtained if you click on the Post Hoc... button in the One-Way ANOVA box and select the tests you require from the list provided in the dialogue box which is presented.

You can ask for the trend components (linear, quadratic, cubic etc) via the Contrasts... button.

Fig 24.3 shows the output of the ONEWAY procedure, in which the scores on the variable cust were compared for the three employers, descriptive statistics were requested and a Scheffe post-hoc test was specified. This figure was obtained with SPSS/PC+, but the output from SPSS for Windows is very similar. It is explained in section 24.2.

24.9 Two-way analysis of variance in SPSS for Windows

Two-way analysis of variance is obtained by selecting Statistics /ANOVA Models /Simple Factorial from the menu. The dialogue box is similar to that for the One-Way ANOVA described above, but you have to enter at least two Factor variables in the box headed Factor(s) and define their ranges. You can enter variables in the Covariates box, if you wish to include an analysis of covariance.

Most beginners will use the default method of assessing the effects in the analysis of variance, referred to as the Unique method. There are alternatives, known as Hierarchical and Experimental methods, which can be specified through the Options button. Options also allows you to specify how Covariates are entered, but again this is a facility unlikely to be needed by the beginner. The manual provides an explanation of these more advanced features for those who feel they may need them.

Fig 24.4 shows the output of ANOVA where sales was the dependent variable, area and sex were the Factor variables, and the Hierarchical method was requested. The Means and counts (ie number of cases) for each subset of scores was requested by selecting them from the Options dialogue box. (They are not available if one asks for the Unique method to be used.) So Fig 24.4 provides the mean score on sales and the number of cases (in brackets) for all the cases analysed, for each of the areas (area = 1 and area = 2), for each of the sexes (sex = 1 and sex = 2) and then for each sex/area combination. For example, the mean score for those cases where sex = 1 (ie for the male respondents) is 5950.64 with an n of 10; the mean score for those cases where sex = 1 and area = 1 (corresponding to males from the North) is 5321.34 and the number of these cases is 3, shown in the brackets under the mean.

The familiar analysis of variance table lists the sources of variation, divided into main effects and interactions, and for each one there is the sum of squares, the degrees of freedom, the mean square (the sum of squares divided by the degrees of freedom), the value of F and the probability of F (Signif of F). If any value in this final column is smaller than 0.05, there is an effect significant at the .05 (5%) level.

Correlations and multiple regression

The correlation coefficient expresses the relationship between two variables as a number that can vary between −1 and +1. Multiple regression is a procedure in which you predict the score on a dependent variable from the scores on a number of independent variables (see Appendix B Section B10.5). Rank correlation in SPSS/PC+ is described in section 27.2. In SPSS for Windows it is provided automatically when one requests a parametric correlation.

25.1 Parametric (Pearson) correlation in SPSS/PC+

To find CORRELATIONS *in the menu, select* correlation and regression *and go right.*

To find the parametric correlation between two variables, use the command:

```
CORRELATIONS /VARIABLES variable1 variable2 /STATISTICS 1.
```

The /STATISTICS 1 tells SPSS/PC+ to print out the mean and standard deviation of the variables being correlated. It can be omitted.

To obtain all the correlations between three variables, list the variables like this:

```
CORRELATIONS /VARIABLES variable1 variable2 variable3.
```

The correlation between responses on att1 and att2 in exdat, shown in Fig 25.1, was found with:

```
GET /FILE 'a:ex1.sys'.
SET /LISTING 'a:ex.lis'.
CORRELATIONS /VARIABLES att1 att2 /STATISTICS 1.
```

The output gives the correlation and indicates, by asterisks, its significance level. As the last line indicates, * indicates the correlation is significant at the 0.01 level, and ** indicates significance at the .001 level.

```
Variable        Cases           Mean            Std Dev

ATT1            22              2.5455          1.1010
ATT2            22              3.0909           .921

Correlations:   ATT1            ATT2

    ATT1        1.0000          .7001**
    ATT2         .7001**        1.0000

N of cases:     22              1-tailed Signif:  * - .01  ** - .001

" . " is printed if a coefficient cannot be computed
-----------------------------------------------------------------
```

Fig 25.1 Output from the command CORRELATIONS /VARIABLES att1 att2
/STATISTICS 1.

25.2 Scattergrams in SPSS/PC+

To find PLOT *in the menu, select* graph data *from the main menu and go right.*

There are a number of ways of obtaining a scattergram, as described in sections 31.2 and 31.3. One method is to use:

`PLOT /PLOT variable1 WITH variable2.`

which produces a scattergram but does not yield the correlation coefficient.

The easiest procedure for obtaining both the correlation and the scattergram is to use:

`PLOT /FORMAT REGRESSION /PLOT variable1 WITH variable2.`

As an illustration, Fig 25.2 shows the output from:

`PLOT /FORMAT REGRESSION /PLOT att1 WITH att2.`

The scatterplot is given, and followed by the correlation, and statistics on the regression line (slope, intercept etc). The figures in the scatterplot indicate the number of cases occurring at that intersection of values on the two variables plotted.

The best-fitting straight line through the data points is obtained if one draws a line connecting the R characters on the left and right vertical axes.

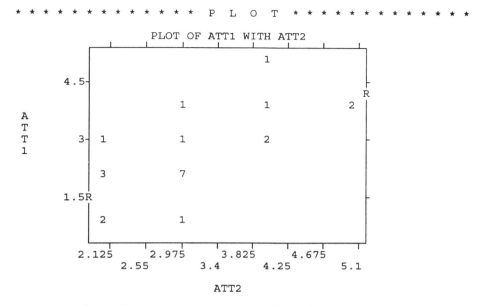

```
* * * * * * * * * * * * * *  P  L  O  T  * * * * * * * * * * * * * * *
                    PLOT OF ATT1 WITH ATT2
                                        1
        4.5                                                    ┤
                                                            R
  A                     1            1            2
  T
  T          3┤  1         1            2
  1
              3         7

        1.5R                                                  ┤

              2            1

         2.125      2.975       3.825       4.675
               2.55       3.4        4.25        5.1

                            ATT2
```

22 cases plotted. Regression statistics of ATT1 on ATT2:
Correlation   .70006 R Squared .49009 SE of Est .80559 Sig .0003
Intercept(SE) -.04082(.61438)   Slope(SE)   .83673(.19085)
----

*Fig 25.2 Output from the command PLOT /FORMAT REGRESSION /PLOT att1
WITH att2.*

Exercise 25.1

Create the following command file, and save it as excom8:

```
GET /FILE 'a:ex1.sys'.
SET /LISTING 'a:ex8.lis'.
CORRELATIONS /VARIABLES cust sales /STATISTICS 1.
PLOT /TITLE 'Customer visit against sales'
/PLOT cust WITH sales.
```

Run this command file and examine the output. The CORRELATIONS command
gives a table similar to Fig 25.1. The PLOT command produces a scatterplot similar
to Fig 25.2, but without the correlation statistics since the subcommand /FORMAT
REGRESSION is not included.

25.3 Multiple regression in SPSS/PC+

To find REGRESSION *in the menu, select* analyze data, *go right, select*
correlation and regression *and go right.* REGRESSION *is in the submenu.*

In exdat, we have the data on each person's sales. We can readily correlate the sales score with the scores on the other variables, such as number of customers visited, response to the att1 question and so on. The correlation between sales and customers visited is 0.7266 (exercise 25.1). The regression equation, which expresses the relationship between sales and cust as an equation can be obtained using the REGRESSION command like this:

`REGRESSION /VARIABLES sales cust /DEPENDENT sales /METHOD ENTER.`

In this procedure, you must name the variables, specify the one that is the dependent variable, and also specify the method to be used. In this simple example, with just one independent variable (cust), the subcommand shown above is sufficient.

In multiple regression, you use a number of independent variables to predict the dependent variable. For example, you can predict sales from cust (number of customers visited), since the correlation between these two variables is 0.7266, significant at the .001 level. But will the prediction be better if you also consider the person's response to the att1 question and the att2 questions? It is with this type of problem that multiple regression is concerned.

The techniques of multiple regression are more advanced than most beginners with SPSS/PC+ are likely to need. Consequently, the topic is not pursued here, other than demonstrating a comparatively simple example:

`REGRESSION /VARIABLES sales cust att1 att2 att3 /DEPENDENT sales /METHOD ENTER.`

This asks for multiple regression of sales, with the four variables cust, att1, att2 and att3 being used as independent (predictor) variables.

The output from this command is given in Fig 25.3. It shows the dependent variable is sales, and that the multiple regression method used was the one known as 'enter'. After listing the predictor variables that were entered into the equation, it gives the Multiple R (.73362 in Fig 25.3) which is the correlation between the predictor variables combined and the dependent variable. R squared indicates the proportion of the variability in the dependent variable which is accounted for by the multiple regression equation. The figure labelled 'Adjusted R square' is an estimate of R squared for the population (rather than the sample from which the data was obtained), and includes a correction for shrinkage.

The analysis of variance table shown in Fig 25.3 shows the sum of squares explained by the regression equation and the 'residual' sum of squares. The residual sum of squares is the variability in the dependent variable which is left unexplained by the regression equation. The F statistic is obtained by dividing the Mean Square regression by the Mean Square residual. If F is significant (the probability value shown is less than 0.05), one can assume there is a linear relationship between the predictor and the dependent variables and that the regression equation allows you to predict the dependent variable at greater than chance level.

The final part of Fig 25.3 lists the predictor variables and some statistics associated with each one. B is the regression coefficient for the variable. In the present example, we have a regression equation like this:

$$sales = w1(cust) + w2(att3) + w3(att2) + w4(att1)$$

The values of w1, w2 etc are regression coefficients and determine how much weight is given to each of the predictor variables; the last section of Fig 25.3 show the regression coefficients (B) for each predictor variable. It is important to realise that these B values do not show how important each predictor variable is; the relative importance is shown when the B values have been transformed into standard scores, when they are referred to as beta. These are given in Fig 17.3, and indicate that cust has much more influence on the dependent variable, sales, than do att1, att2 or att3.

```
     * * * *   M U L T I P L E   R E G R E S S I O N   * * * *
Listwise Deletion of Missing Data
Equation Number 1    Dependent Variable..   SALES
Beginning Block Number  1.  Method:  Enter

Equation Number 1    Dependent Variable..   SALES

Variable(s) Entered on Step Number
     1..    CUST
     2..    ATT3
     3..    ATT2
     4..    ATT1

Multiple R              .73362
R Square                .53820
Adjusted R Square       .42954
Standard Error     1755.50691

Analysis of Variance
                    DF      Sum of Squares       Mean Square
Regression           4      61058696.52776    15264674.13194
Residual            17      52390676.44811     3081804.49695

F =       4.95316       Signif F =   .0078
----------------------------------------------------------------
Equation Number 1    Dependent Variable..   SALES

----------------- Variables in the Equation -----------------
Variable            B        SE B        Beta        T   Sig T

CUST          94.08951    26.41230     .68864     3.562  .0024
ATT3         214.41919   521.54581     .10900      .411  .6861
ATT2        -186.74295   664.80260    -.07401     -.281  .7822
ATT1         188.65193   594.57453     .08936      .317  .7549
(Constant)   444.19126  4131.18896                 .108  .9156

End Block Number   1   All requested variables entered.
----------------------------------------------------------------
```

Fig 25.3 Output from the command REGRESSION /VARIABLES sales cust att1 att2 att3 /DEPENDENT sales /METHOD ENTER.

The final columns of this part of the output show T values and their probabilities (Sig T). These indicate whether the regression coefficients for each variable are greater than zero. In Fig 25.3, the T values for att1, att2 and att3 are not significant, so one would conclude that these variables do not predict sales. The T value for cust is significant (p = .0024), so this does predict sales.

The final row of the table, labelled (constant), refers to the intercept of the regression line. The T value indicates whether it is significantly different from zero.

A full explanation of the numerous regression procedure subcommands will be found in the SPSS manuals.

25.4 Parametric (Pearson) and rank correlation in SPSS for Windows

To obtain the correlation coefficient between two variables, select from the menus Statistics /Correlate /Bivariate. The variables to be analysed have to be inserted in the Variables list in the usual SPSS for Windows manner, and you can specify which correlation coefficients you require by checking the relevant alternatives in the Correlation Coefficients area of the dialogue box. You can ask for the correlation between all possible pairings of three or more variables simply by inserting all the variables into the Variables list.

Fig 25.4 illustrates the output from the correlation procedure with means and standard deviation requested from the Options button; the correlations requested were those between scores on att1 and att2 in the salesq file. The significance of a correlation is by default presented in the output using a two-tailed hypothesis. If you have predicted in advance the direction of the relationship between the variables, you are entitled to use a one-tailed hypothesis, and this can be requested in the Bivariate Correlations dialogue box. SPSS indicates, until you specify otherwise, whether a correlation is significant by printing asterisks: * indicates significant at the 0.05 level, and ** significant at the 0.01 level. If you want the actual significance levels to be displayed in the printout, check the Display actual significance level box in the Bivariate Correlations window. This was done in order to obtain the display illustrated in Fig 25.4.

The first part of the printout in Figure 25.4 shows the n, means and standard deviations for the two variables. The matrix shows the correlation coefficients: each variable correlates with itself 1.00, and in this example att1 and att2 are correlated 0.7001. The number of cases involved and the probability of the correlation having arisen by chance are given under the correlation coefficient.

You may well want the mean and standard deviations of the scores on the variables being correlated to be shown in the printout, and this can be achieved if you select the Options button and check the Means and standard deviations box.

You may want to obtain the correlations between all the variables in one list and all the variables in a second list. To do this, you have to Paste the correlation command into a syntax file, and then edit the command line so that the two list of variables are separated with the word BY.

```
Variable        Cases           Mean          Std Dev
ATT1              22           2.5455          1.1010
ATT2              22           3.0909           .9211

         - -  Correlation Coefficients  - -

                ATT1            ATT2
ATT1           1.0000           .7001
             (    22)         (    22)
             P=  .            P=  .000

ATT2            .7001          1.0000
             (    22)         (    22)
             P=  .000         P=  .

(Coefficient / (Cases) / 2-tailed Significance)

 " . " is printed if a coefficient cannot be computed
```

Fig 25.4 Output from the correlation procedure in SPSS for Windows

Missing values in bivariate correlations

The correlations procedure will exclude any case which has missing data on either of the variables being correlated. This is referred to as Exclude cases pairwise. If you are requesting a number of correlations, with three or more variable entered in the Variables list, you can ask SPSS to exclude from all the analyses any case that has a missing value on any of the variables: this is Exclude cases listwise, and is available via the Options button.

Scattergrams

The graphing and charting facilities of SPSS for Windows are so extensive that they are covered separately in chapter 32. Section 32.4 deals with scattergrams.

25.5 Partial correlation in SPSS for Windows

The correlation between two variables may arise because both are correlated with a third variable. Partial correlation is a technique which allows you to examine the correlation between two variables when the effect of other variable(s) has been partialled out. Partial correlation analysis is obtained from the Statistics /Correlate /Partial menu. You enter into the Variables list the two variables to be correlated, and into the Controlling for: list the control variables, the ones whose influence on the correlation between the two variables is to be partialled out.

To obtain the means and standard deviations on each variable, and/or a matrix showing the zero-order correlations between all the variables, you ask for them via the Options button. (A zero-order correlation is the usual correlation, with no partialling out for the effects of a control variable.)

Fig 25.5 illustrates the output from the Partial Correlations procedure. In this example, the correlation between sales and att3 was examined, with cust as the control variable. The first part of the output shows the means and standard deviations of each variable, and then the correlations are shown with the number of cases used in their calculation and their probability values.

```
Variable Mean Standard Dev Cases
SALES 5859.6232 2324.2958 22
ATT3 3.4091 1.1816 22
CUST 50.8182 17.0116 22


- - P A R T I A L C O R R E L A T I O N C O E F F I C I E N T S - -

Controlling for.. CUST

SALES ATT3
SALES 1.0000 .1184
( 0) ( 19)
P= . P= .609

ATT3 .1184 1.0000
( 19) ( 0)
P= .609 P= .

(Coefficient / (D.F.) / 2-tailed Significance)
'' . '' is printed if a coefficient cannot be computed
```

Fig 25.5 Output from the partial correlation procedure in SPSS for Windows

25.6 Multiple regression in SPSS for Windows

Multiple regression is obtained by selecting Statistics /Regression /Linear from the menus, which open the Linear Regression dialogue box. You must enter the dependent variable in the Dependent box, and the predictor variables in the Independent box using the normal procedure of clicking on the variables in the source list and then on the appropriate arrow button. You can specify the regression method to be used from Enter, Stepwise, Remove, Backward or Forward. Enter is the default method, and enters all the variables in one step. Stepwise examines each variable for entry or removal, Backward enters all the variables and then removes them one at a time depending on a removal criterion, Forward enters variables one at a time, and Remove means that variables in the block are removed in one step. (These methods are described in the manual, but the beginner is unlikely to need them: here, as always, only use statistics that you understand.) It is possible to specify one method for one block of variables and another method for another block; to do this, you have to create a second block of predictor variables by clicking on the Next button and then enter the predictor variables for this set. To move between the blocks of variables, use the Previous and Next buttons.

Various statistics can be requested from the Statistics button; when this is clicked, a dialogue box is revealed allowing various options to be requested. If you select Descriptives, the output will include the means and standard deviations of the variables being analysed as well as a correlation matrix.

Figure 25.3 shows the major section of the output from a simple multiple regression, in which sales was the dependent variable, and cust, att1, att2 and att3 were used as predictor (independent) variables.

The Plots button will allow you to obtain a scatterplot of the dependent variable (Dependnt in the source variable list) with standardized predicted values or one of a number of other predicted or residual variables which are calculated by the regression procedure. These newly calculated variables can be saved from the Save button and its associated dialogue box.

The Options button permits you to alter the criteria used when the stepwise, forward or backward methods are used, by inserting your own values for F or for the probability of F. You can also force the suppression of a constant term in the regression equation, by deselecting the Include constant in equation option.

The WLS button in the Linear Regression dialogue box allows you to obtain a weighted least-squares model, and is explained in the Manual (p. 351).

Missing values in multiple regression

The program will exclude from the analysis any case that has a missing value on any of the variables being analysed; this is referred to as Exclude cases listwise. You can have any missing values replaced with the mean of the scores on that variable, or you can ask the program to calculate correlations for all cases which have no missing value for the two variables being correlated (Exclude cases pairwise). These alternative treatments for missing values are obtained from the Options button of the Linear Regression dialogue box.

26

Non-parametric analyses

Non-parametric tests are used when the data does not lend itself to parametric statistical analysis, because it is rank data, or is skewed, or the groups show unequal variance. A wide range on non-parametric tests are available in the NPAR procedure. In this chapter only the more commonly used ones are considered, but others will be found in the same menu as those described here. A description of these tests will be found in Appendix B.

26.1 Finding the non-parametric tests in the menus

In SPSS/PC+

To find the non-parametric analyses, select analyze data *from the main menu, go right and select* other *from the submenu; go right again and select* NPAR *from the submenu. Go right: the submenu allows you to select the non-parametric test you want.*

In SPSS for Windows

All the nonparametric tests except the independent sample chi-square (the chi-square most familiar to most users) and rank correlation, are obtained from the Statistics /Nonparametric Tests menu.

26.2 Chi-square for two or more independent samples in SPSS/PC+

This chi-square is not located in the NPAR section, but is found under FREQUENCIES.

If the data is nominal, and the numbers act merely as labels for the various conditions (as when 1 is used to denote male and 2 to denote female), the analysis will depend on frequency counts, tables of cross-tabulations, chi-square. The method for obtaining chi-square for two or more samples was covered in chapter 22; just to recapitulate, to obtain a chi-square on the data for variable1 (e.g. sex) and variable2 (e.g. area), the command needed is:

`CROSSTABS /TABLES sex BY area /STATISTICS CHISQ.`

The output from this command is shown in Fig 22.3.

26.3 One-sample chi-square in SPSS/PC+

To find this test in the menu, see 26.1 above.

The one-sample chi-square test is used to test a hypothesis such as 'Suicide rate varies significantly from month to month'. If the hypothesis is false, the suicide rate will be the same for every one of the twelve months. The one-sample chi-square compares observed suicide rates per month with what would be expected if the rate were equal for all months. To take an example from exdat, you could test the hypothesis that the number of respondents from the three employers is significantly different from what would be expected if each had contributed an equal number of respondents to the pool. The result is shown in Fig 26.1, which was produced with this command file:

```
GET /FILE 'a:exl.sys'.
SET /LISTING 'a:ex.lis'.
NPAR TESTS /CHISQUARE employer.
```

The categories of employer are listed, with the number of cases for each (cases observed). The expected frequencies which would occur if all employers had had an equal number of cases is shown in the column headed Expected. The Residual column shows the difference between the observed and the expected values. The final lines show the value of chi-square, the degrees of freedom (df) and the probability level. In this example, chi-square is not significant, as the probability (0.834) is larger than .05.

```
- - - - - Chi-square Test

    EMPLOYER
                 Cases
    Category  Observed  Expected  Residual
           1        8      7.33       .67
           2        8      7.33       .67
           3        6      7.33     -1.33
                   --
    Total          22

        Chi-Square              D.F.        Significance
             .364                 2              .834
----------------------------------------------------------------
```

Fig 26.1 Output from the command NPAR TESTS /CHISQUARE employer.

26.4 Two matched groups: Wilcoxon test in SPSS/PC+

To find this test in the menu, see 26.1 above.

This test is used to compare the scores of one group of subjects on two variables (a within-subjects comparison), or to compare the scores of two matched groups of respondents on a variable. For example, we may wish to test whether the scores of our exdat respondents on the att1 variable are different from their scores on att2. To use the Wilcoxon test, the command line needed is:

`NPAR TESTS /WILCOXON variable1 variable2.`

For our problem, the line is:

`NPAR TESTS /WILCOXON att1 att2.`

The result of this command is shown in Fig 26.2. The Wilcoxon test involves taking the difference between the scores on the two variables for each respondent, and ranking these difference scores disregarding sign. The sign of the difference is then assigned to the rank values, and these signed ranks can be summed. The printout shows how many cases had att2 score less than (Lt) att1 scores, how many had att2 greater than (Gt) att1, and how many were tied (ie the scores on att1 and att2 were the same). It gives also the mean rank for those situations where the scores were not tied. The test yields a z value, and this together with the relevant probability level is provided in the output. In this instance, probability is less than .05, so you can conclude there is a significant difference between the scores on att1 and att2.

```
- - - - - Wilcoxon Matched-pairs Signed-ranks Test

      ATT1
with ATT2
     Mean Rank      Cases
        8.50           3    - Ranks  (ATT2 Lt ATT1)
        9.11          14    + Ranks  (ATT2 Gt ATT1)
                       5      Ties   (ATT2 Eq ATT1)
                      --
                      22     Total

        Z =   -2.4142            2-tailed P =   .0158
------------------------------------------------------------
```

Fig 26.2 Output from the command NPAR TESTS /WILCOXON att1 att2.

26.5 Three or more matched groups: Friedman test in SPSS/PC+

To find this test in the menu, see 26.1 above.

The Friedman test is used to compare the scores on a particular variable of three or more matched groups. The relevant command line is:

`NPAR TESTS /FRIEDMAN variable1 variable2 variable3.`

To compare the scores of the exdat respondents on att1, att2 and att3, the Friedman test is required since there are three conditions, and a within-subjects comparison:

`NPAR TESTS /FRIEDMAN att1 att2 att3.`

The result of this command is shown in Fig 26.3. The Friedman test ranks the scores on the variables for each respondent separately, and calculates the mean of these rank score for each variable. These means are shown in the printout, with a chi-square statistic, degrees of freedom and significance (probability) level. In Fig 26.3, the significance value is less than .05 and so you would conclude there is a significant difference between the scores on the three variables.

```
- - - - - Friedman Two-way ANOVA

    Mean Rank     Variable
         1.55     ATT1
         2.14     ATT2
         2.32     ATT3

         Cases           Chi-Square          D.F.     Significance
          22               7.1818              2           .0276
-----------------------------------------------------------------
```

Fig 26.3 Output from the command NPAR TESTS /FRIEDMAN att1 att2 att3.

26.6 Two independent groups: Mann-Whitney in SPSS/PC+

To find this test in the menu, see 26.1 above.

Mann-Whitney is used for comparing two independent groups on a specified variable. The general form of the command is:

`NPAR TESTS /MANN-WHITNEY variable1 BY variable2(x,y).`

In the Mann-Whitney command, you use BY variable2 (x,y) to form two groups based on their scores (x and y) on the variable named as variable2.

For example, to compare the sales of respondents from employer 1 and employer 3, in exdat, the command is:

`NPAR TESTS /MANN-WHITNEY sales BY employer(1,3).`

The result of this command is shown in Fig 26.4. Note that the comparison is between those respondents employed by employer 1 and those employed by employer 3. In the Mann-Whitney, the scores on the variable from the two groups are ranked together. The average rank of each group is shown in the table, as are a value for U and a value for z with the associated two-tailed probability. In this example, the probability is less than .05, and you conclude that there is a significant difference between sales for employers 1 and 3.

The Mann-Whitney procedure also carries out the Wilcoxon Rank Sum test, and the output shows the value of W and its associated probability.

```
- - - - - Mann-Whitney U - Wilcoxon Rank Sum W Test

      SALES
   by EMPLOYER
      Mean Rank      Cases
          5.38          8   EMPLOYER = 1
         10.33          6   EMPLOYER = 3
                        --
                        14   Total

                             EXACT            Corrected for Ties
        U            W     2-tailed P           Z       2-tailed P
       7.0         62.0      .0293           -2.1947      .0282
```

Fig 26.4 Output of the command NPAR TESTS /MANN-WHITNEY sales BY
employer(1,3).

26.7 Three or more independent groups: Kruskal-Wallis in SPSS/PC+

To find this test in the menu, see 26.1 above.

This test is used when three or more independent groups are to be compared. The relevant command is:

NPAR TESTS /KRUSKAL-WALLIS variable1 BY variable2(x,z).

In the Kruskal-Wallis test, you use BY variable2(x,z) to form three or more groups based on their scores on the variable named as variable2. For example, BY employer(1,3) tells SPSS/PC+ to compare the scores on variable1 of the three employer groups whose minimum code number is 1 and maximum code number is 3.

In exdat, for example, to compare the groups from the three different employers in terms of customer visits (cust), the command is:

NPAR TESTS /KRUSKAL-WALLIS cust BY employer(1,3).

The result of this command is shown in Fig 26.5. The data on customer visits has been ranked, and the mean rank for each employer is given in the table. Two chi-square values are shown below the table, the second one having been corrected for tied ranks. Probability values are provided, so in Fig 26.5 one can see that there is a significant difference between the customer visits of the three employers, as the probability value (.0040) is less than .05.

```
- - - - - Kruskal-Wallis 1-way ANOVA

CUST customers visited
by EMPLOYER
Mean Rank Cases
9.00 8 EMPLOYER = 1
8.38 8 EMPLOYER = 2
19.00 6 EMPLOYER = 3
--
22 Total

Corrected for Ties
CASES Chi-Square Significance Chi-Square Significance
22 11.0425 .0040 11.0550 .0040
------------------------------------------------------------------
```

Fig 26.5 Output from the command NPAR TESTS /KRUSKAL-WALLIS cust BY employer(1,3).

26.8 Nonparametric tests in SPSS for Windows

All the nonparametric tests except the chi-square test for independent samples (see section 22.6) and rank correlation (see section 25.4) are obtained from the Statistics /Nonparametric Tests menu. Each test has its own dialogue box, in which you must specify the variables to be analysed in the conventional SPSS for Windows manner of selecting the variable name from the source list and clicking on the arrow button. Not all the tests available will be described here, as once you are familiar with the way the system operates and how to use the Help facility, there should be little difficulty in making appropriate decisions for specifying the test you want.

Obtaining the mean, standard deviation, lowest and highest scores and number of cases

The various tests allow you to obtain these statistics on the variables being analysed by selecting the Options button and then, in the Statistics area of the dialogue box that appears, select Descriptive.

Missing values in nonparametric tests

The Options button of the dialogue box for each test allows you to specify how missing values should be treated. The default is Exclude cases test-by-test, which means that where you have requested a number of tests to be done, as each test is carried out any cases that have missing values on the variable being analysed are excluded. The alternative is Exclude cases listwise: if this is selected, cases with a missing value on any of the variables inserted into the Test Variable List box are excluded from all analyses.

26.9 One-sample chi-square in SPSS for Windows

The one-sample chi-square test is used to test a hypothesis such as 'Suicide rate varies significantly from month to month'. If the hypothesis is false, the suicide rate will be the same for every one of the twelve months. The one-sample chi-square compares observed suicide rates per month with what would be expected if the rate were equal for all months.

To run this test, you select Statistics /Nonparametric Tests /Chi-square, and this opens the appropriate dialogue box. Insert a variable into the Test Variable List box. By default, each value of score on the variable generates its own category, but you can specify the range of values to be used by stating the lower and upper values. In this way you could exclude cases which had a score outside the range you specify.

Fig 26.1 shows the results of applying a one-sample chi-square on the employer variable in salesq, to see whether the number of respondents from each employer differs from what would be expected if each employer had an equal number.

SPSS will assume that you are comparing the observed distribution with an expected distribution in which the cases are spread equally across the categories. This can be altered, using the Values area in the Expected values part of the dialogue box. So you can compare the observed distribution of suicides with that expected if January had twice as many suicides as August, and all other months had an equal rate mid-way between the January and August ones. The way to achieve this is to enter a value for each category in the Values text box and click on Add. You must enter the values in the order corresponding to the ascending order of the categories for the variable being tested.

26.10 Two matched groups: Wilcoxon test in SPSS for Windows

This test, used for comparing two related sets of scores, is available from the Statistics /Nonparametric Tests /2 Related Samples menu. You have to indicate the two variables to be compared by clicking on each of them; the first one will appear in the Current Selections Variable 1: area, and the second one will appear as Variable 2. To insert these into the Paired Variables list, click on the right-pointing arrow button: the two variables will then be shown as a linked pair. You can create further pairs in the same way. Fig 26.2 shows the output for a Wilcoxon test to compare the scores on att1 and att2 of the respondents in salesq.

26.11 Three or more matched groups: Friedman test in SPSS for Windows

This test compares more than two related sets of scores and is available from the Statistics /Nonparametric Tests /K Related Samples menu. Specify the variables to be compared with the usual SPSS for Windows method of clicking on the variable names and then on the right-pointing arrow. The output is shown in Fig 26.3, the test having been used to compare the scores on att1, att2 and att3.

26.12 Two independent groups: Mann-Whitney in SPSS for Windows

The Mann-Whitney compares the scores on a specified variable of two independent groups. It is in the group of tests accessed by selecting Statistics /Nonparametric Tests /2 Independent Samples from the menu. In addition to specifying the variable to be analysed, you must indicate the variable to be used to create the two groups of respondents whose score are to be compared. This is done by inserting the variable name in the Grouping Variable box and then you have to specify which groups you need by clicking on the Define Groups button. Suppose we want to compare the scores on sales of the respondents in salesq from the employers 1 and 3. Enter the variable name employer into the Grouping variable box, click the define Groups button, and then enter 1 into the box labelled Group 1 and 3 into the box labelled Group 2. Fig 26.4 shows the result of using the Mann-Whitney to compare scores on sales for respondents of employer 1 and employer 3.

26.13 Three or more independent groups: Kruskal-Wallis in SPSS for Windows

Kruskal-Wallis is used to compare the scores on a variable of more than two independent groups. It is found under Statistics /Nonparametric Tests /K Independent Samples. As with the Mann-Whitney, you have to specify a Grouping Variable by selecting a variable from the source list and inserting it in the Grouping variable box. You then have to define the range of the grouping variable by clicking on the Define Range button which opens a dialogue box in which you enter the values corresponding to the lowest and highest scores on the grouping variable. For example, to compare the scores on cust for the respondents of the three employers in the salesq set of data, remember that the employers were coded as 1, 2 or 3. So in the Several Independent Samples: Define Range box, you would enter 1 as the Minimum and 3 as the Maximum. The result of this procedure is shown in Fig 26.5.

27

Ranking and sorting the data

27.1 Ranking in SPSS/PC+

To find RANK *in the menu, select* modify data or files, *go right, from the submenu select* modify data values *and go right again.*

To have the scores on a variable ranked, with the lowest score having a rank of 1, the appropriate command is:

`RANK variable-name.`

To have the scores ranked in descending order, so that the highest score has the rank of 1, select order from the RANK submenu, and select (D) so the line is:

`RANK variable-name (D).`

If the (D) subcommand is included, all the variables named before that order will be ranked in descending order. To have one variable ranked in ascending order and another in descending order, make this clear by using:

`RANK variable1 (A) variable2 (D).`

Here variable 1 will be in ascending order, because it is followed by (A), and variable 2 will be in descending order.

To rank the data on sales in exdat, you would use:

`RANK sales.`

RANK creates a new variable, which by default has the name of the variable being ranked preceded by R. So when sales are ranked, you obtain a new variable called rsales. This variable name must be used if you wish to list or analyse the ranked values, so to LIST the results of the RANK sales command, the command is:

`LIST id rsales.`

The result is shown in Fig 27.1. The first section shows that the variable sales has been ranked, and the new variable created by the ranking is rsales. Its label is rank of sales. The output then shows the rsales scores for each respondent.

```
From         New
variable     variable   Label
--------     --------    -----
 SALES        RSALES    RANK of SALES

ID     RSALES
 1      4.000
 2     10.000
 3     22.000
 4     18.000
 5     14.000
 6     15.000
 7      6.000
 8      5.000
 9     11.000
10     17.000
11      9.000
12      1.000
13     21.000
14      2.000
15      8.000
16     20.000
17      3.000
18     16.000
19     19.000
20     12.000
21      7.000
22     13.000

Number of cases read =   22    Number of cases listed =   22
------------------------------------------------------------
```

Fig 27.1 Output from the commands RANK sales. and LIST id rsales.

You can specify a new variable name for the ranked data, so that it has a name other than (in this example) rsales. This is achieved with:

RANK variable /RANK INTO newname.

There are a number of options on how to assign ranks to tied values. Unless you specify otherwise, using the /TIES subcommand, tied values will be given the mean rank value of the scores.

The basic RANK command ranks the whole set of scores on the variables named. You frequently need the ranking of scores within subgroups; for example, one may require the data for males and females to be ranked separately. This is achieved using the command:

RANK variable1 BY variable2.

To rank the sales figures of the males separately from the ranking of the females' sales figures in exdat, one needs this command:

RANK sales BY sex.

The output in Fig 27.2 shows the ranking of sales for men and women separately. To have all the males' data appear before the females', the SORT command (described in section 27.5) was used. The table was produced with the LIST command; note that the variable listed was rsales, the new variable created when sales was ranked. The complete set of procedure commands was:

```
RANK sales by sex.
SORT sex.
LIST id sex rsales.
```

```
ID  SEX     RSALES
 2   1       5.000
 3   1      10.000
 4   1       8.000
 8   1       3.000
 9   1       6.000
10   1       7.000
12   1       1.000
13   1       9.000
17   1       2.000
21   1       4.000
 1   2       2.000
 6   2       8.000
 7   2       3.000
11   2       5.000
14   2       1.000
15   2       4.000
16   2      11.000
18   2       9.000
19   2      10.000
20   2       6.000
22   2       7.000
 5   3       1.000
```

```
Number of cases read =  22    Number of cases listed =  22
```

Fig 27.2 Extract of output from the commands RANK sales BY sex.; SORT sex.; LIST id sex rsales.

You may wish to rank a variable twice in one program run. For example, in Exercise 27.1, cust is ranked overall and then ranked again by employer. The first ranking will create the variable named rcust; the second time cust is ranked, another default name will be created (ran001), but it is more informative to specify the name for the ranked cust scores on the second rank command using the RANK.../RANK INTO subcommand. Exercise 27.1 includes this naming procedure to illustrate how the process operates.

27.2 Rank correlation in SPSS/PC+

To obtain a rank correlation between two variables, it is necessary to rank the variables and then use the CORRELATIONS command (chapter 25) as in this example, which calculates the rank correlation between cust (number of customers visited) and sales:

```
RANK cust sales.
CORRELATIONS /VARIABLES rcust rsales.
```

Note that the correlation command uses the names of the ranked variables, rcust and rsales.

Exercise 27.1

Create the following command file, and save it as excom9:

```
GET /FILE 'a:ex1.sys'.
SET /LISTING 'a:ex9.lis'.
RANK cust sales.
CORRELATIONS /VARIABLES rcust rsales.
RANK cust BY employer /RANK INTO rnkbyem.
SORT employer
LIST id employer rnkbyem.
```

Run this file to find the rank correlation between customer visits and sales and to obtain a list of ranked customer visits for each employer. The output is shown in Appendix A.

27.3 Ranking in SPSS for Windows

Select Transform /Rank Cases from the menu, and enter into the Variable(s) box the variables to be ranked. To have rank values assigned in ascending order, so the lowest score has a rank value of 1, you need do nothing, but if you want the scores ranked in descending order so the largest value has the rank of 1 then you select Largest value in the Assign Rank 1 to area of the Rank cases dialogue box.

The basic rank command ranks the whole set of scores on the variables specified. You frequently need the ranking of scores within subgroups; for example, one may require the data for males and females to be ranked separately. This is achieved by entering a variable name into the By box of the Rank cases dialogue box. So to have the scores of the males and females on sales ranked separately, you insert sales into the Variables box, sex into the By box and click on OK.

Rank creates a new variable, which by default has the name of the variable being ranked preceded by R. So when sales are ranked, you obtain a new variable called rsales which is added to the data in the Data Editor spreadsheet. The name of the new variable must be used if you wish to list or analyse the ranked values.

There are a number of options on how to assign ranks to tied values. Unless you specify otherwise, via the Ties button, tied values will be given the mean rank value of the scores. Alternative methods of ranking, unlikely to be used by the beginner, are available from the Rank Types button.

The output from ranking the sales scores of the salesq file is added to salesq in the Data Editor. The effect is similar to that shown in Figure 27.1. Figure 27.2 shows the outcome when the sales data is ranked separately for men and women, but in SPSS for Windows the result is added to the Data Editor spreadsheet.

27.4 Rank correlation in SPSS for Windows

Rank correlations are provided by the CORRELATIONS procedure, described in section 25.4.

27.5 Putting the cases in a different order: SORT in SPSS/PC+

To find SORT *in the menu select* modify data *or* files, *go right, select* manipulate files *and go right again.*

There are occasions when you may wish to sort the cases into a new order. For example, if you were analysing just the first 50 cases in a large data file, you might want those first 50 cases to be all males, or all of a given level of income or having some other feature. You can have the cases sorted into a specified order using the SORT command, which has the general form:

SORT variable-name.

In our data file, exdat, males (sex = 1) and females (sex = 2) are distributed throughout the data file. If we want all the males to be listed together, we can use:

SORT sex.

This sorts the cases according to their value on the sex variable, putting all the cases where sex = 1 (i.e. males) before the cases where sex = 2 (the females). If you wished all the females to come first, you would use:

SORT sex (D).

The (D) tells the program to sort in descending order (so 2 comes before 1).

You may want the cases sorted by two variables, eg by area and by sex. This is achieved by:

SORT variable1 variable2.

If the (D) order command is included in the line, all the variables named in the line before (D) are sorted in descending order, unless one specifies the use of ascending order with (A).

SORT area (A) sex (D).

tells the program to sort the variable area in ascending order, the variable sex in descending order.

Fig 27.3 shows the effects of running this command file:

```
GET /FILE 'a:exl.sys'.
SORT employer (A) BY sex (D).
LIST employer sex id.
```

As can be seen, it has re-ordered the cases in the file, sorting by ascending employer number and then putting all the females before the males.

```
EMPLOYER SEX ID

        1    2   1
        1    2   7
        1    2  18
        1    2  22
        1    1   3
        1    1   9
        1    1  12
        1    1  17
        2    3   5
        2    2  11
        2    2  14
        2    2  15
        2    2  20
        2    1   2
        2    1   8
        2    1  21
        3    2   6
        3    2  16
        3    2  19
        3    1   4
        3    1  10
        3    1  13

Number of cases read =    22    Number of cases listed =   22
-----------------------------------------------------------------
```

Fig 27.3 Output from the commands SORT employer (A) BY sex (D). and LIST employer sex id.

Sorting cases in this way is useful when preparing the data for printing out, as it groups together similar cases (such as all respondents of a given sex or age). It is often needed when using the REPORT command or when adding data files together.

27.6 Putting the cases in a different order: SORT in SPSS for Windows

The SORT procedure is used to sort the cases in the data file into a desired sequence. The procedure is obtained from the Data /Sort Cases... menu. Enter the variable(s) to be used for sorting the data into the Sort by box, and select ascending or descending Sort Order.

If you enter two variables in the Sort by box, the cases will be sorted first of all by the first one in the list and then by the second one in the list and so on. So if you wanted the data in salesq to be sorted so that all the males (sex = 1) from the North (area = 1) came first, followed by all the men from the South (area = 2), then all the women from the North and finally all the women from the South, you would put sex and area into the Sort by box.

When the cases have been sorted, they are shown in the new order in the Data Editor spreadsheet.

28

Modifying the data: Changing the way it is coded and grouped

This chapter explains how to change the way data is coded, so that for example all those respondents who scored over 40 on customer visits can be merged to form one group. It also explains how to rename variables and round numbers.

Sometimes you may want to code the data in a different way from that used when the data file was initially created. For example, the exdat file includes data on the number of customers visited. You may want to divide the respondents into just two groups: those who visited more than 40 customers, and those who visited less than 40. The RECODE procedure will do this for you.

Another common situation is when you want to reverse the scoring of one of the variables. For example, in the Sales Personnel Questionnaire, there were three questions asking respondents about their attitude to their job. Questions 5 and 6 (named as att1 and att2) have the responses coded so that 1 indicates the respondent is very satisfied and 5 indicates dissatisfaction. But for question 7 (att3), 1 indicates dissatisfaction and 5 indicates satisfaction. Suppose you wanted the scores on att3 to be scored in the opposite direction, so they are consistent with att1 and att2, with a low score meaning very satisfied and a high score (5) meaning very dissatisfied. This kind of alteration is easily made using the RECODE command.

28.1 RECODE in SPSS/PC+

Find RECODE *in the menu by selecting* modify data or files *from the main menu, going right, selecting the* modify data values *option and going right again.*

The general form of the RECODE command involves specifying the variable to be recoded, and then giving formulae to indicate which 'old' scores should be recoded as which 'new' scores. An example is probably the easiest way of explaining how RECODE operates. To modify the exdat data so that two groups are formed according to their standing on the cust scores, insert into the command file the following line:

This puts everyone with a customers visited score of 0 to 40 inclusive into group 1, everyone with a customers visited score of 41 or more into group 2. The expression HI means the highest score on the variable. The equivalent term for the lowest score is LO, so (0 THRU 40 = 1) could have been (LO THRU 40 = 1).

The second example involves modifying the scores on the att3 variable, the responses to question 7 in the Sales Personnel Questionnaire. We want a score of 5 to be changed to 1, a score of 4 to be changed to 2 and so on, so that the scores are the reverse of the way they were originally encoded. This can be achieved with this command:

```
RECODE att3 (5=1) (4=2) (2=4) (1=5) .
```

After stating the variable to be recoded, simple formulae indicate the existing value and the new value. In this example the previous value of 5 is transformed to 1, 4 becomes 2, 2 becomes 4 and 1 becomes 5. (It is not necessary to recode 3, since it stays as 3.)

If a number of variables are to be recoded, they can be put on a single line, separated by / as in this example:

```
RECODE cust (LO THRU 40 = 1) (41 THRU HI = 2) /att3 (5=1) (4=2) (2=4)
(1=5) .
```

So far we have just used RECODE for integers. With non-integers, (which have figures after the decimal point) the task is only slightly more difficult. Imagine you want to recode respondents' sales so that 0 to 3999.99 is a 3, 4000 to 7999.99 is a 2, and anything over 8000 is a 1. If you use RECODE sales (0 THRU 3999 =3) (4000 THRU 7999 =2) (8000 THRU HI = 1), a figure of 7999.50 would not be recoded because it falls between the limits specified; it is more than 7999 but less than 8000. The answer is to reverse the order in which the recoding is specified so the command is:

```
RECODE sales (8000 THRU HI = 1) (4000 THRU 8000 = 2) (LO THRU 4000 =3) .
```

You might imagine that this would cause problems, because the first instruction tells the program to recode 8000 as a 1 and the second one tells it to recode 8000 as 2. But any value given in a RECODE line is only operated upon once; so any values of 8000 will be recoded as 1 by the first instruction. When the program comes to the second instruction there will be no values of 8000 for it to find, but all values up to 8000 (including 7999.50) will be available to be recoded as 2.

RECODE only applies to the data when it has been brought into the active file. The original data file is not affected by running the RECODE command, so there is no risk of making permanent (and non-reversible) changes to the entries in the data file. To store a copy of the data to which the RECODE has been applied, carry out the recode, and then save a .SYS file, as explained in chapter 16.

Exercise 28.1

Create a command file, excom10, that will recode the scores on the sales variable in exdat to form two groups. Group 1 have sales of less than 7000, and group 2 have sales of 7000 or more. An example that will do this and list the results is given in Appendix A.

28.2 AUTORECODE in SPSS/PC+

Find AUTORECODE *in the menu by selecting* modify data or files *from the main menu, going right, select* modify data values *and go right again.*

This command is similar to RECODE, but it automatically recodes all the scores on a variable into consecutive integers. For example, the customers visited scores in exdat include a 28, a 29, a 30, a 33 and the largest figure is 83. Using AUTORECODE, the scores will be modified so that the lowest score is changed to 1, the second-lowest to 2, the third-lowest to 3 and so on. The command line for achieving this data modification is:

AUTORECODE /VARIABLES variable-name /INTO new-variable-name.

When the autorecoding takes place, a new variable is created; it has to be named in the /INTO section of the command. Adding the /PRINT subcommand gives a table showing the original scores and the autorecoded scores.

CUST Old Value	NEWCUST New Value	customers visited Value Label
28	1	28
30	2	30
33	3	33
36	4	36
38	5	38
39	6	39
40	7	40
41	8	41
42	9	42
43	10	43
46	11	46
48	12	48
58	13	58
60	14	60
68	15	68
71	16	71
72	17	72
76	18	76
79	19	79
83	20	83

Fig 28.1 Output from the command AUTORECODE /VARIABLES cust /INTO newcust /PRINT.

Fig 28.1 shows the effect of running this command file:

```
GET /FILE 'a:exl.sys'.
SET /LISTING 'a:ex.lis'.
AUTORECODE /VARIABLES cust /INTO newcust /PRINT.
```

The original scores on cust are shown in the Old Value column, the AUTORECODEd scores on newcust are shown in the second column. By default, the value labels on the new variable (newcust) are the original variable's values, as is shown in the third column of Fig 28.1. There are only 20 values of newcust, since the original 22 sets of data (Table 6.1) has only 20 different values of cust.

28.3 RECODE in SPSS for Windows

RECODE is obtained from the Transform /Recode/Into Same Variables or the Transform /Recode /Into Different Variables menus. If you choose Recode /Into Same Variables, the recoded values will replace the old values in the Data Editor. If you choose Recode /Into Different Variables, the recoded values make a new variable, which you have to give a name to, as described below.

You specify the variables to be recoded by entering them in the Variables list and then select the Old and New Values button. Specify the old value and the new value; for example, if you want a score of 5 to be recoded as a 1, 5 goes into the Old Value's Value box, and 1 into the New Value's Value box. You then click on the Add button.

You can specify a range of values. Suppose we wanted to recode the data so that two groups are formed according to their standing on the cust variable, with all cases where cust is 40 or less being given a new, recoded score of 1 and all those with a cust score of 41 or more having a recoded score of 2. You could define one range as 0 through 40 and assign it the new value of 1, click on Add, and then define the second range as 41 through highest, assign it a new value of 2 and click on Add.

You can ask for only certain cases to be recoded: if you wanted only the men's scores (sex = 1) recoded, for example, click on the If... button. This opens the If dialogue box which is explained in section 29.6.

Recode /Into Different Variables operates in a similar way to Recode /Into Same Variables, except that as the title suggests new variables are created to receive the recoded values. In order to ensure you do not lose the original data, this is probably the better option to select.

The procedure is similar to that for Recode /Into Same Variables. Specify the variables to be recoded by entering them in the Input Variable ->Output Variable box; you must then provide a name for the variable when it has been recoded, by typing in the new name in the Output Variable Name box and clicking on Change. When you have typed in the new name, click on the Change button and the new name will be inserted next to the old name in the Input Variable –>Output Variable list. Define the values to be recoded as for Recode /Same Variables, explained above.

When you have specified the old values to be recoded, you must decide how you want any unspecified values to be treated. If you do nothing, they will all be given the system missing value, which is rarely what is needed. To ensure that old values you do not want recoded are carried over into the new variable with the same values as before, make sure you select All other values in the Old and New Values dialogue box, and then select Copy old values in the New Value area of the box and finally press the Add button. The entry ELSE –> COPY appears in the list to show that all unspecified values will be carried over into the new variable.

When the recode is performed under the Recode /Into Different Variables procedure, the new variables are added to the spreadsheet in the Data Editor.

28.4 Automatic Recode in SPSS for Windows

This procedure is similar to Recode /Into Different Variables, but it automatically recodes all the scores on a variable into consecutive integers. For example, the customers visited scores in salesq include a 28, a 29, a 30, a 33 and the largest figure is 83. Using Transform /Automatic Recode, the scores will be modified so that the lowest score is changed to 1, the second-lowest to 2, the third-lowest to 3 and so on. The procedure creates a new variable for the recoded scores, and you must give it a new name by highlighting the variable you have entered in the Variable –> New Name list, typing the new name in the text box to the right of the New Name button, then clicking on that button.

28.5 Multiple responses in SPSS for Windows

Surveys often use questions with non-exclusive responses: suppose that instead of asking the people who completed the sales questionnaire described in chapter 7 which employer they worked for now, we asked them to indicate which of the employers they had ever worked for. We might find individuals who had worked for employer a only, others who had worked for a and b, others who had worked for b and c, and so on. There are alternative ways of dealing with such data. One method would be to have a variable for each employer and use a score of 1 to indicate 'yes' and 2 to indicate 'no'. This is referred to as the multiple dichotomy method.

The alternative method described in the SPSS Base System User's Guide is known as the multiple category method. Here one would have three variables, and the score on each one would indicate which employer had been mentioned. In our example, a score of 1 would represent Jones, 2 Smith and 3 Tomkins. So a respondent who had been employed by Jones and by Tomkins would score 1 on variable1, 3 on variable2 and have a missing value on variable3.

Whichever method one chose, the responses on the variables need to be combined either into a multiple dichotomy set or into a multiple category set. This is achieved by selecting from the menu Statistics /Multiple Response /Define Sets. The dialogue box allows you to specify the variables to be entered into a set. You have to indicate for each variable whether the scores are dichotomies (the scores represent yes or no) or whether the scores have more than 2 alternatives. The former is used for the multiple dichotomy method, the latter for the multiple category method. You have to enter a name for the set and Add it to the list, where the name you gave will be preceded with a $ sign.

The analysis of multiple response sets is achieved by selecting either Statistics / Multiple Response /Frequencies or Statistics / Multiple Response /Tables. Frequencies produces tables which show the number of respondents giving each possible response (ie each employer, in our example) collapsed across the variables in the set. The Tables subcommand is used to produce cross-tabulations, in which the responses are collapsed across the variables in the defined set and then tabulated against scores on another variable.

28.6 Changing names of variables in SPSS/PC+: MODIFY VARS

To find MODIFY VARS *in the menu, select* read or write data *and go right.*

There may be occasions when you want to alter the names of the variables in the file. There are two ways of doing this. One is to edit the DATA LIST FILE line of the original command file and replace the unwanted variable name with another. (If you are using a .SYS file, you will have to create a new one that includes the name change.) Alternatively, use MODIFY VARS like this:

MODIFY VARS /RENAME (variable1 = newname).

This will rename the variable variable1 as newname. The effect of MODIFY VARS is on the active file, not on the files saved on your disk, so is lost when you leave SPSS/PC+, unless you save a .SYS file.

28.7 Changing names of variables in SPSS for Windows

Changing the name of a variable in SPSS for Windows merely requires you to repeat the process of naming the variable (section 18.2), typing the new name into the Variable name text box of the Define Variable dialogue box.

28.8 Rounding numbers in SPSS/PC+

The data file contains columns of figures, some of which may be decimals. You can round the numbers to any required number of decimal places by marking the rectangle (see section 12.5), and then pressing F8 and selecting the Round entry from the minimenu. Type in the number of decimal places required and press ↵.

28.18 Rounding numbers in SPSS for Windows

To round the numbers in the output file, highlight the numbers and select Edit /Round from the menu; another box is opened and you can enter the details of how you want the numbers rounded. The Round button in the output window performs the same function.

29

Modifying the data: Calculating a 'new' score

This chapter explains how to calculate a new variable from the data; for example, from respondents' sales and the number of customers visited, you can create a new variable which is the average sales per customer visit by the COMPUTE procedure. It also explains how to deal with dates.

29.1 COMPUTE in SPSS/PC+

To find COMPUTE *in the menu, select* modify data or files, *go right, select* modify data values *and go right again.*

Often, you will want to calculate a new score from the data. This task is achieved with the COMPUTE command, which has the general form:

`COMPUTE newvariable = variable1+mathematical operator+variable2.`

For example, in the exdat file, there are scores on customers visited (cust) and on sales. To calculate the average sales per customer visited for each respondent, use compute as here:

`COMPUTE salcus = (sales)/(cust).`

This tells SPSS/PC+ to compute a new score for each case, the new score to be known as salcus. In this example, it is calculated by dividing sales by cust. The label for the new variable or score must be a new one, i.e. one not already used in the data file. And of course the equation must indicate how the new variable is calculated from existing variables.

In computing a new variable, one can use the usual arithmetic operators: + − * / and ** for exponentiation. (So cust**2 represents the square of cust.) One can also use the square root, the absolute value of a score, the value rounded to the nearest whole number, or the integer value of a non-integer. These and other transformations are obtained by selecting the instructions submenu from the COMPUTE menu, and then selecting the functions submenu.

The order in which the formula to the right of the = sign is evaluated follows the conventional rules. Exponentiation is performed first, then multiplication and division, then addition and subtraction. Use brackets to force calculation in the order required.

For example, the average score (avatt) of the responses to questions att1, att2 and att3 is computed by this command:

```
COMPUTE avatt = (att1 + att2 + att3)/3.
```

A different (and incorrect!) result would of course be given by

```
COMPUTE avatt = att1 + att2 +att3/3.
```

When the COMPUTE line has been inserted into the command file, the 'new' variable can be used in subsequent analyses. So you could go on with

```
FREQUENCIES /VARIABLES avatt.
```

29.2 Missing Values in COMPUTE in SPSS/PC+

To find VALUE ( ) *from the* COMPUTE *submenu, select* ~instructions *and go right, select* functions *and go right again.*

You will recall that you can specify that a particular value of a variable in the data file means that that data is missing; for example, 1 = male 2 = female and 3 = sex not known. Here 3 is the missing value for the sex variable. If any case has a missing value for the variables mentioned in the COMPUTE instruction, the new variable will not be calculated. So if you asked for

```
COMPUTE newval = sex + employer.
```

this would not be calculated for those cases where sex = 3. It is possible to over-ride this, however, by using

```
COMPUTE newval = VALUE(sex) + VALUE(employer).
```

When VALUE is applied, the values given to the variables named (sex, employer) are used to compute newval even if they are missing values (such as the score of 3 on sex).

29.3 Compute with IF in SPSS/PC+

To find IF *in the menu, select* modify data or files, *go right, select* modify data values *and go right again.* IF *is in the submenu then revealed.*

There are occasions when you may want to compute a variable only if some other condition is fulfilled. Again, this is readily accomplished:

```
IF (sales GT 7000) ok=1.
```

takes each case and checks to see whether sales is greater than (GT) 7000. If it is, a new variable (ok) is assigned the value of 1. Note that the expression before the = must be in brackets.

Use AND, OR, NOT to make the conditional more precise:

```
IF (sales GT 7000 AND sex EQ 1) manok=1.
```

gives the variable manok the value of 1 if sales is greater than 7000 and the respondent has a sex value of 1.

When evaluating the IF expression, NOT is evaluated first, AND is evaluated before OR.

After creating a new variable using COMPUTE or the conditional transformation IF, it can be given a variable label and value labels as with any other variable. But these commands must occur after the variables have been defined. For example:

```
COMPUTE salcus = (sales)/(cust).
VARIABLE LABELS salcus 'Average sales per customer visit'.
```

Note that the transformations that are carried out by the commands RECODE and COMPUTE only apply to the data when it has been brought into the active file and is being processed. The original data file (stored on the floppy) is not changed. To transform the data in ways described here and keep a file of the transformed data, it is necessary to save a system file as in this example:

```
GET /FILE 'a:ex1.sys'.
COMPUTE avatt = (att1 + att2 +att3)/3.
RECODE cust (LO THRU 40 = 1) (41 THRU HI = 2) /att3 (5=1) (4=2) (2=4)
(1=5).
SAVE /OUTFILE 'a:revex.sys'.
```

If this set of commands is run, the file revex.sys is saved on the floppy disk. Its contents are found using this series of commands:

```
GET /FILE 'a:revex.sys.'
SET /LISTING 'a:ex12.lis'.
LIST.
```

Exercise 28.1

Create a command file, excom11, to compute the new variable newv1, the sum of the scores on att1 and att2 and list the result. A command file that fulfils these requirements is shown in Appendix A.

29.4 COMPUTE in SPSS for Windows

Often, you will want to calculate a new score from the data. For example, in the salesq file, there are scores on customers visited (cust) and on sales. To calculate the average sales per customer visited for each respondent, you need to use Compute.

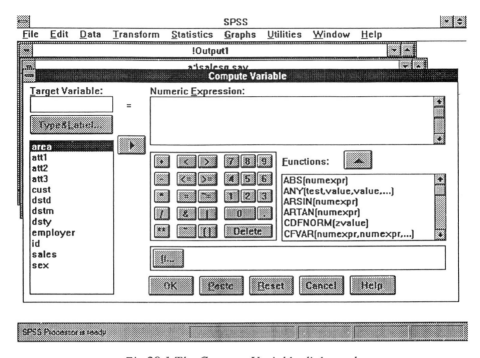

Fig 29.1 The Compute Variable dialogue box

Compute is found under the Transform menu. When selected, it opens a dialogue box entitled Compute Variable. Type a name for the variable you are computing into the Target Variable text box: the name must begin with a letter, must not be more than eight characters long, and must not contain a space. You can assign a label to the new variable name by selecting the Type&Label button from the dialogue box and responding to the box revealed.

The new variable will be calculated from some combination of the existing variables, linked by mathematical operators. For example, you might want to calculate a new variable, totatt, which is the total of the scores on att1, att2 and att3. The box headed Numeric Expression is where you indicate the formula that is used to calculate the new variable, and you select existing variables to enter into the formula by the usual process of clicking on their names in the left-hand list and then on the right-pointing arrow. Mathematical operators (the plus sign, multiplication sign etc) are entered into the formula by clicking on the appropriate button in the area which looks like a calculator key-pad. So the formula for calculating totatt is att1 + att2 + att3, and you enter this into the Numeric Expression box by clicking on att1 in the lefthand list and on the arrow, then on the + sign in the key-pad, then on att2 in the variable list and the right arrow etc.

When you have created the formula you want, click on the OK button at the bottom of the screen.

The key pad area allows you to use not only arithmetic operators in your formula, but also relational operators such as < and > as well as logical operators: the keypad has an & key to represent AND, a key with a vertical line (l)to represent OR, and a "~" key which represents NOT. (So the ~= key means Not Equal to.)

You will notice that a list appears under the label Functions, and this allows you access to a set of transformations and mathematical functions which you can use in the formula. For example, if you wanted to obtain the log of the scores on variable cust, you would enter a new variable name, logcust, and then scroll down the Functions list until the LG10 function was exposed. Click on that and then on the upward pointing arrow above the list of Functions. The function you selected will appear in the Numeric Expression list, with question marks to show that you still have to enter the arguments for the expression (ie the variables to be used when calculating the log, mean, square root or whatever you are asking for). Click on the first question mark in the expression in the Numeric Expression list, then click on the appropriate variable (cust, for example) in the variable list on the left of the dialogue box. The Numeric Expression will then read LG10[cust]. Clicking on OK will then run the compute procedure, and the new variable logcust will be added to the Data Editor.

The Functions list allows you to select a number of transformations and statistics expressions. You can obtain the absolute value of scores with ABS, the SQRT provides square roots, arcsines are provided by ARSIN, and there are many others. The statistical functions allow you to obtain the mean, sum, standard deviation, variance, minimum or maximum of a set of scores, but remember this refers to a set of scores obtained by each respondent. Suppose you want to obtain the average score on att1, att2 and att3 for each respondent: you would put a name for the new variable in the Target variable box and then from the Functions list select MEAN(numexpr,numexpr,..). It appears in the Numeric Expression window, and you then click on the names of the variables for which you want the mean by clicking on them in the variable list and then clicking on the right arrow. In this example, you would select att1, att2 and att3 so that the formula in the Numeric Expressions text box read MEAN(att1,att2,att3).

The earlier example of calculating the total of scores att1, att2 and att3 could be obtained more simply by using the function SUM(att1,att2,att3).

Once you are familiar with the operation of compute, you can use it to obtain a number of useful transformations of the scores. To round scores to the nearest integer, use the RND function; to simply delete the decimal part of a number use TRUNC.

The Functions list contains an entry ANY(test,value,value...), one of the Logical Functions. What this does is to check whether the scores for each respondent on a named variable (the one referred to as test) match a specified value. For example, ANY(year,90,91) will examine the data for each respondent to see whether the score on the variable year matches the values given- 90 or 91. If there is a match, the new variable is added to the Data Editor and a score of 1 is given.

29.5 Missing values in COMPUTE in SPSS for Windows

If you are using an arithmetic expression, such as att1+att2+att3, then any case which has a missing value on any of the variables included in the formula (in this example att1, att2, att3) will be classified as having a missing value on the new variable you are computing.

Statistical functions work differently: if you compute a new variable using the function MEAN(att1,att2,att3), then the new variable will have a missing value if the respondent has missing data on ALL of the variables in the expression. This could be misleading: you might ask for the mean of att1, att2 and att3 for a respondent who only has scores on att1 and att2. The mean that is given will be the mean of the two scores the respondent has, and you may be unaware that for this respondent the mean calculated is not the mean of three variables but only of two. You can prevent this happening by using MEAN.3(att1,att2,att3): before the opening bracket, put a decimal point and follow this with a number equal to the number of variables listed in the function. With this formulation, any case that has a missing value on any one of the variables named between the brackets will have a missing value assigned on the computed variable.

29.6 Compute with IF in SPSS for Windows

You may want to compute a new variable for just some cases in your data file, cases that meet certain criteria. For example, you might want to calculate the sum of att1, att2 and att3 only for people from the North area. To do this, you click on the If... button in the Compute variable dialogue box, and this opens another box entitled Compute Variables: If Cases. The structure of this box resembles the previous Compute Variables one, but you can specify the conditions to apply before the Compute procedure takes place. For example, to have the calculation of the totatt variable restricted to those cases where the response indicated they worked in the Northern area, you need the box in Compute Variables: If Cases to contain the expression area = 1.

The expression is created very much as the Numeric Expression in Compute Variables was obtained, by selecting variable names from the list, entering them into the box by clicking on the arrow button, and using the calculator key pad to obtain arithmetic or logical expressions and functions. Once the formula is entered in the box, click on the Include if cases satisfies condition: button, and then on the Continue button at the bottom of the box.

29.7 AGGREGATE in SPSS for Windows

You may wish to collapse data across a set of cases, and form a new 'case' which has scores which are derived from the collapsed data. As an example, you could collapse the scores for each of the sexes and have one case representing 'men' and a second case representing 'women'. (This procedure should be used only rarely and after some thought about whether it is justified. This example is merely to allow me to explain what Aggregate achieves.)

To obtain an aggregation, select Data /Aggregate from the menu. You have to specify in the Break Variable(s) box the variable to be used to identify the groups to be formed. In the example I am using, this would be sex. In the Aggregate Variable(s) box you enter the variables to be aggregated; SPSS will create a new variable. You have to indicate the function to be used in making the aggregation: do you want the aggregate score to be the mean of the individual cases or their sum or the percentage of cases falling between certain limits or some other function? The mean is used by default; if you want any other function, you have to select the Functions button and fill in the dialogue box.

The Aggregate procedure creates a new data file, aggr.sav in the current directory. If you want a different name or the file to saved elsewhere, click on the File button and complete the dialogue box.

29.8 Dealing with dates in SPSS/PC+: YRMODA

YRMODA *is deep in the menu system. To find it, start at the top-level main menu and select and go right at each of these points:* modify data or files, modify data values, COMPUTE, ~instructions, functions. *Scroll to the bottom of the submenu to find* YRMODA.

This function converts a date into the number of days since October 15, 1582. While this may appear at first sight somewhat useless, it does in fact allow one to calculate the interval between two dates, such as determining the age of a respondent from their date of birth. In exdat, we have the respondents' date of starting their job, recorded as dtsd (which gives the day), dstm (which gives the month) and dsty (which gives the year). Imagine that on June 1st, 1995 we want to calculate tenure, the time for which each respondent has been doing their job. How can we do it?

We need the difference (in years) between the date the respondent started the job and June 1st, 1995. Using the YRMODA function, the number representing June 1st, 1995 is YRMODA(1995,6,1), and that for the respondent's job-start date is given by YRMODA(dsty,dstm,dtsd). (Note that as the name suggests, YRMODA needs dates in the order year-month-day.) So we can find the difference in years with this command:

```
COMPUTE TENURE = (YRMODA(1995,6,1) - YRMODA(dsty,dstm,dtsd)) / 365.35.
```

The result of using this command is shown in Fig 29.2.

The data on tenure obtained with this command is only present in the active file, and is not stored on the floppy. To have a permanent copy of this data, save a .SYS file.

```
ID      TENURE
 1       7.00
 2       4.98
 3       4.98
 4       5.00
 5       4.98
 6       4.98
 7       5.00
 8       4.98
 9       4.98
10       4.98
11       4.98
12       5.00
13       3.99
14       3.99
15       3.99
16       4.00
17       3.99
18       4.00
19       3.99
20       4.00
22       4.99

Number of cases read =   22    Number of cases listed =   22
----------------------------------------------------------------
```

Fig 29.2 Output from the commands COMPUTE TENURE = (YRMODA(1995,6,1) – YRMODA(dsty,dstm,dtsd)) / 365.35. and LIST id tenure.

29.9 Dealing with dates in SPSS for Windows

As mentioned earlier, SPSS for Windows has a complex set of alternative methods for dealing with dates (and times). The YRMODA function described in the previous section can be used to express a time interval in days, but in SPSS for Windows it is not available from the menus: to use it you would have to type it into a syntax window.

You can define a variable in SPSS for Windows as having one of a number of alternative date formats, using the Define Variable procedure described in section 18.7. If you do define a variable as a date, European users will find the default date format is acceptable. You can then enter a date as day/month/year so that 4th June 1990 could be entered into the Data Editor as 4/06/90. If the data is listed, the default date form will print 4-June-90; if you used the European date format, the printout would be 4/6/90.

A variable defined as a date is stored as the number of seconds since midnight on October 14th 1582. To find the interval between two dates, they can be subtracted, and the result will be in seconds. You can convert it to days, hours and minutes by defining the resulting variable as having the DTIME format. But only the List and Report procedures will display the output in a date and time form: others will continue to express the interval in seconds.

In salesq, the dates were entered as three separate variables: dstd, dstm and dsty. So one could use the YRMODA function described in 29.8 to find a time interval. One could use the DATE.DMY(d,m,y) function to convert the three variables in salesq to a SPSS for Windows date format with this Compute command:

Compute beginday = DATE.DMY(dstd,dstm,dsty).

This will create a new variable (beginday), expressed in seconds, which can be used in other procedures.

Selecting subgroups for analysis

30.1 Selecting permanent subgroups in SPSS/PC+: SELECT IF

To find SELECT IF *in the menu, select* modify data or files, *go right, select* select or weight data *and go right again.*

You may wish to perform an analysis on a subset of the cases. If you want a subset to be selected for all subsequent analyses, use SELECT IF; but if you want a subset for just one analysis, use PROCESS IF, described in the next section.

You tell SPSS/PC+ to select only certain types of case for all subsequent analyses, use:

```
SELECT IF (variable-name+condition+score).
```

Using the data in exdat as an example, suppose you want to compare (using a t-test) the sales scores of men and women but only for those respondents who worked in the North of the country (area = 1). To select respondents from the North, ie who have an area score of 1, use:

```
SELECT IF (area EQ 1).
```

This command tells the program to select just those cases where the respondent reported working in area 1, and would have to be put before the line asking for the t-test. So the complete set of commands would be:

```
GET /FILE 'a:ex1.sys'.
SET /LISTING 'a:ex.lis'.
SELECT IF (area EQ 1).
T-TEST /GROUPS sex(1,2) /VARIABLES sales.
```

These condition operators can be used to select certain subgroups:

EQ or = mean equal to　　　　　　　NE or <> mean not equal to
GT or > mean greater than　　　　　LE or <= mean less than or equal to
LT or < mean less than　　　　　　 GE or >= mean more than or equal to

To get a subset of respondents who had any employer other than 1, use:

```
SELECT IF (employer NE 1).
```

Note that SELECT IF continues to operate for the rest of the run. For example, if we select just the females from the data file using SELECT IF (sex = 2), and do some analysis on the female's scores, we cannot then use SELECT IF (area = 2) to pick out everyone, male or female, from area 2. If we have SELECT IF (sex = 2) and then SELECT IF (area = 2), our selected group is now females of area 2. This might not be what is wanted. We may want to select just the females to do one analysis, and then select Southern area subjects of either sex for a second analysis. This can be done, but requires the use of PROCESS IF rather than SELECT IF.

30.2 Selecting temporary subgroups in SPSS/PC+: PROCESS IF

To find PROCESS IF *in the menu, select* modify data or files, *go right, select* select or weight data *and go right again.*

This command works just like SELECT IF except that it is only in effect for one following procedure. So one could analyse just the males and then just the females like this:

```
PROCESS IF (sex = 1).
CROSSTABS /TABLES employer BY area.
PROCESS IF (sex=2).
CROSSTABS /TABLES employer BY area.
```

If SELECT IF had been used in this example, it would not work. As you would have selected only the cases where sex = 1 in the first line, the third line would not be able to find any cases which matched the criterion of having sex = 2.

The example just given is not in practice the way you would normally obtain a CROSSTABS of employer by area for each sex separately; the simpler way of achieving that is to use:

```
CROSSTABS /TABLES employer BY area BY sex.
```

Exercise 30.1

Create a command file, excom12, which will show the mean score on att3 only for those respondents who scored '1' on att1, and then gives a frequency table of the responses on att2 only for respondents working in the South (area 2). A command file that does this is given in Appendix A.

30.3 Selecting a random sample of cases in SPSS/PC+: SAMPLE

To find SAMPLE *in the menu, select* modify data or files, *go right, select* select or weight data *and go right again.*

With very large data file, you may wish to select a sample of cases for analysis. To select a 10% random sample, use:

SAMPLE 0.10.

A 20% random sample is obtained by:

SAMPLE 0.20.

To obtain a specific number of cases (say 50) selected at random from a data file containing 500 cases, use:

SAMPLE 50 FROM 500.

To obtain a precise number of cases in the sample, you must give the total number of cases in the file after FROM. If you give a number that is larger than the actual number of cases in the data file, the number requested will be scaled proportionally. For example, the line above asked for 50 cases from 500, a 10% sample. If the file actually had only 400 cases, the SAMPLE command would yield 40 cases, still a 10% sample.

The SAMPLE command is like PROCESS IF in that it is only operative for one following procedure.

30.4 Selecting the first n cases in SPSS/PC+: N

To find N *in the menu, select* modify data or files, *go right, select* select or weight data *and go right again.*

To analyse just the first n cases in the data file use:

N 100.

which selects the first 100 cases. N 20 selects the first 20 cases, of course.

30.5 Selecting permanent subgroups in SPSS for Windows: SELECT CASES

You may frequently wish to perform an analysis on a subset of the cases. You tell SPSS for Windows to select only certain types of case by using: Data /Select Cases from the menu. This opens a dialogue box, which has a number of paths through it.

Suppose you want to compare (using a t-test) the sales scores of men and women but only for those respondents who worked in the North of the country (area = 1). To select respondents from the North, ie who have an area score of 1, click on the If... button, which opens another box, entitled Select Cases: If. This requires you to enter the variables to be used for selecting cases and mathematical or logical expressions. (It is described in section 29.6.) So for the example of selecting the cases where area = 1, you need to have this formula in the main text box of this dialogue box. Then click on Continue and when you are returned to the Select cases box click on OK.

Note that Select Cases continues to operate for the rest of the SPSS run. For example, if we select just the females from the data file using Select cases /If (sex = 2), and do some analysis on the female's scores, we cannot then use Select cases /If (area = 2) to pick out everyone, male or female, from area 2. If we have Select Cases /If (sex = 2) and then Select Cases /If (area = 2), our selected group is now females of area 2. This may not be what is wanted. We may want to select just the females to do one analysis, and then select Southern area subjects of either sex for a second analysis. This can be achieved using Split File.

Imagine you want to compare on the variable cust the scores of males from the North and the South and then compare the scores of the females from the North and the South. Select Cases will not do this, as once a subset of cases has been made, it is permanent: having selected males, you cannot gain access to the females. But it is possible using Split File.

30.6 Selecting temporary subgroups in SPSS for Windows: SPLIT FILE

If you want to analyse a series of subgroups of respondents, Split File allows you to do so. You would select Data /Split File, and in the box revealed select the Repeat analysis for each group button. Then select the variables to be used to divide the cases into subgroups and enter them in the Groups Based on text box. In our example, area and sex would need to be entered in this box.

There are some important aspects of this command to bear in mind. Once invoked, the Split File command continues to be operative throughout an SPSS run of commands (so it is like Select Cases), but you can turn it off by getting back to the Split File box and select the Analyze all cases button. So to analyse the men and then the women, and then carry out a further analysis on both sexes, you need to use Split File for the analysis of the two separate sex groups and then turn it off in order to have both sexes available for the next analysis.

When it is operating, Split File sorts the data in the data file so that it has all cases with the same value on the grouping variables in the correct sequence. (This is done automatically, but if the data is already sorted in the appropriate order, the sorting can be omitted by selecting the File is already sorted button.)

30.7 Selecting a random sample of cases in SPSS for Windows

With very large data file, you may wish to select a sample of cases for analysis. To select a 10% random sample, use from the menu Data /Select Cases; in the Select Cases dialogue box, select Random sample of cases and click on the Sample button. Another box is revealed and allows you to specify a percentage of the cases or an exact number of cases selected randomly from the data file.

30.8 Selecting the first n cases in SPSS for Windows

To analyse just the first n cases in the data file, you have to type the command into a Syntax file, with n being a integer:

N n.

This operates for the remainder of the SPSS run, so only the first n cases can be analysed by any subsequent procedures.

If you have entered an identification number as a variable (as has been done in salesq), you can achieve the same effect from the menus using the Select Cases technique, described above in 29.5. To analyse only the 10 cases with identification numbers below 11, select Data /Select Cases and then use If id<11.

31

Graphs in SPSS/PC+

31.1 Histograms and barcharts

To find FREQUENCIES *and* EXAMINE *in the menu, select* analyze data, go *select* descriptive statistics *and go right again.*

Histograms differ from barcharts in that a histogram will show an empty row where there is no data whereas Barchart leaves out any empty rows. Both histograms and barcharts are subcommands of the FREQUENCIES procedure:

```
FREQUENCIES /VARIABLES variable-name /HISTOGRAM.
FREQUENCIES /VARIABLES variable-name /BARCHART.
```

In exdat, dsty gives the year in which the respondents started their job. There is no case of anyone starting in 1989, but one person started in 1988, and the rest in 1990 or 1991. The histogram of this data is shown in Fig 31.1 and the barchart in Fig 31.2. As can be seen, the histogram has an empty row corresponding to year 89, while the barchart does not.

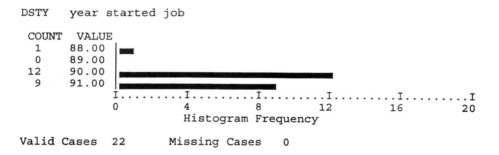

```
DSTY    year started job

  COUNT   VALUE
    1     88.00  |▬
    0     89.00  |
   12     90.00  |▬▬▬▬▬▬▬▬▬▬▬▬▬▬▬▬▬▬▬▬▬▬▬▬▬
    9     91.00  |▬▬▬▬▬▬▬▬▬▬▬▬▬▬▬▬
           I.........I.........I.........I.........I.........I
           0         4         8         12        16        20
                       Histogram Frequency

Valid Cases   22      Missing Cases   0
```

*Fig 31.1 Extract of output from the command FREQUENCIES /VARIABLES dsty
/HISTOGRAM.*

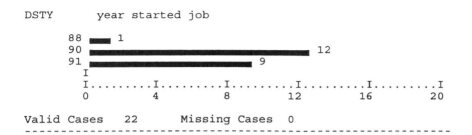

```
DSTY      year started job

     88 ██ 1
     90 ████████████████████████████ 12
     91 ████████████████████ 9
      I
      I.........I.........I.........I.........I.........I
      0         4         8        12        16        20

Valid Cases   22     Missing Cases  0
------------------------------------------------------------
```

Fig 31.2 Extract of output from the command FREQUENCIES /VARIABLES dsty /BARCHART.

The horizontal scale of histogram or barchart can be percentages rather than frequencies by using:

`FREQUENCIES /VARIABLES dsty /HISTOGRAM NTILES.`

It is also possible to obtain histograms from the EXAMINE command, covered in section 21.3, using:

`EXAMINE /VARIABLES variable-name /PLOT HISTOGRAM.`

31.2 Scattergrams

To find PLOT, *select* graph data *from the main menu and go right;* PLOT *is in the submenu.*

To obtain a simple bivariate scattergram, use PLOT/PLOT and indicate the two variables to be plotted:

`PLOT /PLOT variable1 WITH variable2.`

The first variable named is plotted on the vertical axis.

Specify labels for the two axes with:

`PLOT /VERTICAL 'vertical label' /HORIZONTAL 'horizontal label' /PLOT variable1 WITH variable2.`

Replace the phrases within inverted commas with whatever labels are required.

To specify a title for the graph, include /TITLE `Put the title here'`, so the complete line is:

`PLOT /TITLE 'Fig 1' /VERTICAL 'vertical label' /HORIZONTAL 'horizontal label' /PLOT variable1 WITH variable2.`

The size of the graph can be altered by specifying the lines down it will occupy (VSIZE) and its width in character spaces (HSIZE) as here:

`PLOT /VSIZE 30 /HSIZE 40 /PLOT variable1 WITH variable2.`

The graph shown in Fig 31.3 was obtained by combining these subcommands to form this line:

```
PLOT /TITLE 'Customers v Sales' /VERTICAL 'Customers visited' /HORIZONTAL
'Sales in month' /VSIZE 15 /HSIZE 30 /PLOT cust WITH sales.
```

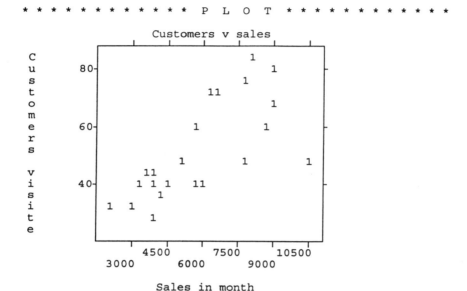

22 cases plotted.

Fig 31.3 Output from the command PLOT /TITLE 'Customers v Sales' /VERTICAL 'Customers visited' /HORIZONTAL 'Sales in month' /VSIZE 15 /HSIZE 30 /PLOT cust WITH sales.

31.3 Scatterplot with correlation coefficient

To find PLOT, *select* graph data *from the main menu and go right;* PLOT *is in the submenu.*

To find REGRESSION *in the menu, select* analyze data, *go right, select* correlation and regression *and go right again. The* SCATTERPLOT *subcommand is found by selecting* residual analysis *from the* REGRESSION *submenu and going right. Note that the main procedure* REGRESSION *is not to be confused with the* FORMAT REGRESSION *subcommand of the* PLOT *procedure.*

To obtain a scatterplot and measure of correlation, use either PLOT or REGRESSION.

The command using the PLOT procedure is:

```
PLOT /FORMAT REGRESSION /PLOT variable1 WITH variable2.
```

(It is not possible to obtain a scattergram from within a CORRELATIONS command line.)

Note that the final /PLOT subcommand must be the last entry in the PLOT line.

An example of this command is given in chapter 25 and the output shown in Figure 25.2.

If you are using the REGRESSION procedure, a number of plotting alternatives are available. A simple scatterplot of the standard score on variable1 and variable2 is obtained from:

```
REGRESSION /VARIABLES variable1 variable2 /DEPENDENT variable1 /METHOD
ENTER /SCATTERPLOT (variable1 variable2).
```

REGRESSION requires that the variables be stated, the dependent variable be specified, the regression method be given, as in the line shown. (More explanation of REGRESSION is provided in chapter 25.) Fig 31.4 shows the scatterplot result of using this series of commands:

```
GET /FILE 'a:exl.sys'.
REGRESSION /VARIABLES cust sales /DEPENDENT cust /METHOD ENTER
SCATTERPLOT (cust sales).
```

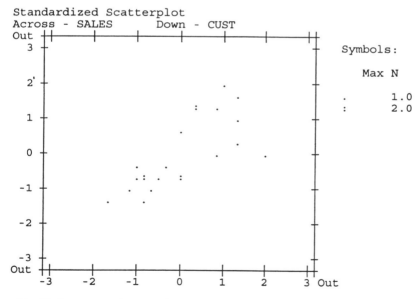

Fig 31.4 Extract of output from the command REGRESSION /VARIABLES cust sales /DEPENDENT cust /METHOD ENTER /SCATTERPLOT (cust sales).

31.4 Stem-leaf plots and boxplots

These are obtained with the EXAMINE procedure, described in chapter 21.

```
EXAMINE /VARIABLES variable1.
```

provides both types of diagram. A stem and leaf plot is similar to a histogram, but numbers indicate the actual values plotted.

Fig 31.5 shows a stem-leaf plot obtained with the commands:

```
GET /FILE 'a:ex1.sys'.
EXAMINE /VARIABLES cust.
```

```
Frequency    Stem & Leaf

    1.00        2 . 8
    6.00        3 . 036899
    7.00        4 . 0123688
    1.00        5 . 8
    2.00        6 . 08
    4.00        7 . 1269
    1.00        8 . 3

Stem width:    10
Each leaf:        1 case(s)
```

Fig 31.5 Stem-leaf plot from the command EXAMINE /VARIABLES cust.

The first column shows the number of scores in the band indicated by the stem. For example, the first line of Fig 31.5 shows there was one respondent who scored in the twenties on customers visited (the stem is 2). The actual score of this respondent was 28 (the leaf is 8, so the actual score is 2, the stem, and 8 the leaf).

A boxplot summarises the scores on a variable by displaying the median (as an asterisk), the 25th and 75th percentiles as the lower and upper edges of a box surrounding the median. The box length represents the interquartile range of the scores. Outliers are cases which are between 1.5 and 3 boxlengths from the edge of the box, and Extremes are more than 3 boxlengths away. Lines are drawn from the edge of the box to the largest and smallest values which are not outliers. An example is given in Fig 31.6, but for these scores there are no Outliers nor Extremes.

The boxplot allows you to make a number of 'eye-ball' judgements about the distribution of the scores. The median is the indicator of the central value, and the length of the box indicates the variability of the scores. If the median is not in the middle of the box, the distribution of scores is skewed.

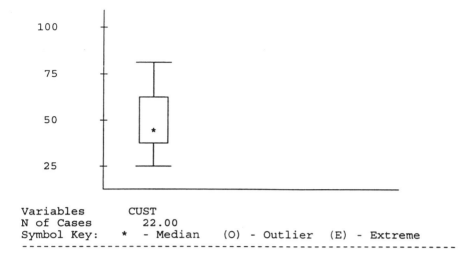

```
Variables      CUST
N of Cases      22.00
Symbol Key:   *  - Median   (O) - Outlier   (E) - Extreme
-------------------------------------------------------------
```

Fig 31.6 Boxplot of cust from the command EXAMINE /VARIABLES cust.

32

Graphs in SPSS for Windows

32.1 Histograms and barcharts from Frequencies; Box-plots from Explore

Histograms and barcharts of the distribution of the scores on variables in the data file can be obtained from the Statistics /Summarize /Frequencies menu, if you click on the Charts button. (The difference between a histogram and a barchart is that a histogram shows an empty space for a value having no cases, whereas a barchart does not. An example is shown in Figure 32.1.) You can ask for either type of display (but not both), ask for a normal curve to be superimposed on a histogram, have the axis labelled as actual frequencies or as percentages. Click on Continue and then on the OK button in the Frequencies dialogue box.

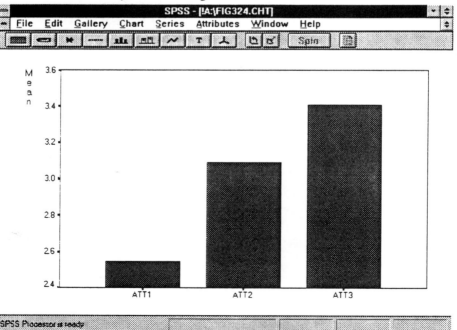

Fig 32.1 Example of barchart showing mean score on att1, att2 and att3

When the Frequencies /Charts or Explore /Plots procedure has run, click on the chart icon in the !Output1 window's icon bar. The Chart Carousel window will be opened, showing the chart of the results. Click on the Edit button of the Chart Carousel icon bar, and the chart will be shown in a window headed !Chart. The facilities available in the !Chart window are described in section 32.7 below. You can save the chart by with File /Save As or File /Chart (section 32.8), and print it with File /Print (section 32.10).

Stem-and-leaf plots, histograms, boxplots and spread by level plots can be obtained from the Statistics / Summarize /Explore /Plots menu: examples and an explanation of stem-and-leaf plots and boxplots are provided in section 32.2.

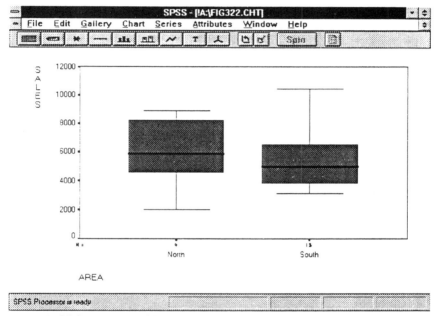

Fig 32.2 Example of boxplot of data from salesq: sales against area

Scattergrams and all other types of chart are obtained by using the Graphs menu of the SPSS window menu bar, not the Statistics menu.

32.2 Graphs, charts and scattergrams from the Graphs menu

The basic steps in creating a chart from the Graphs menu are straight-forward, but there are numerous alternatives in format. It would be tedious and unnecessary to describe them all here. Once the user is familiar with the basic steps, there should be little difficulty in investigating the other features available.

To create a chart via the Graphs menu, you must have a data file open in an active !Data Editor window. (To make it active, click in its menu bar or title bar.). Then click on Graphs in the SPSS window menu bar. You can select from the drop-down menu the type of chart you want to create: a barchart, line graph, area chart, pie chart, boxplot, scattergram or histogram. The system will guide you through a series of dialogue boxes in which you can specify how you want the chart drawn, the titles and legends to be put on it, the scales for the axes etc. The particular boxes presented to you depend on the choices you have made previously, so I shall only describe the general structure of the system here. Once you have understood the basic techniques, you will undoubtedly enjoy some hours investigating the many other options.

When you have indicated which type of chart you want, the first dialogue box has a Define button which takes you further into the system. But it also has an area entitled Data in Chart Are, with three alternatives. The headings offered are rather unclear, and the following explanation may be helpful.

If you want a chart showing the average score of subgroups of your respondents on one of the variables you measured, or if you want to show how many people obtained each score on one or more of the variables, you are asking for Summaries for groups of cases. This option can plot, for example, a barchart showing the number of males and females in the data set, or the average salary of the respondents in different years. This is the default option – the one that is active unless you select one of the others. Figure 32.3 provides an example.

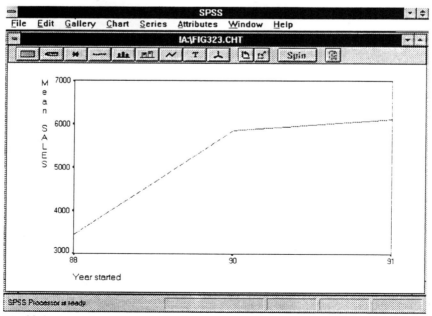

Fig 32.3 Example of linegraph of scores on sales versus year. Note: This graph was obtained by selecting the Summaries for groups of cases *option*

If you want to summarize more than one variable, such as the mean score on att1, att2 and att3, you select the Summaries of separate variables option. For example, selecting this option and plotting cust and salary can produce a chart in which the averages of these two variables are shown. The charts produced can be quite complex, as you can obtain summaries of a number of variables for subgroups of respondents. So you could have the average of cust and of salary for men and women from salesq plotted on one chart, as in Figure 32.4.

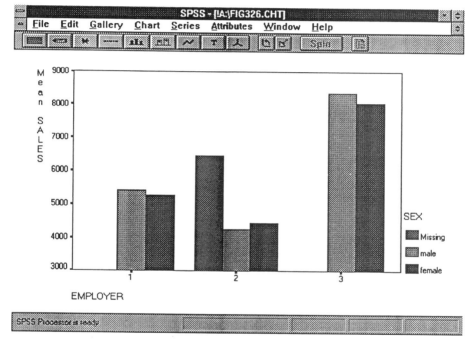

Fig 32.4 Example of histogram showing mean sales for each employer subdivided by sex.
Note: This graph was obtained with the Summaries of separate variables *option*

The third option is Values of individual cases. This means that the data on the selected variables are plotted for each respondent (or row of data). Respondent (case) is plotted along the horizontal axis of a bar chart with this option. An example is shown in Figure 32.5, which displays the values on the cust variable of salesq for each case. It is worth emphasising that this type of display is rarely useful, (although they are popular with many beginners).

If the Summaries for Groups of cases option has been selected from the Define chart dialogue box and the Define button is pressed, you are presented with another dialogue box allowing you to specify what the lines/bars represent. The options vary according to the type of chart you have chosen. By default, the chart shows the number of cases having a particular value on the variable being plotted, but you can ask instead for a plot which shows the % of cases, cumulative number or cumulative percentages. The Other summary function allows you to make further choices: Other is usually the mean of the data for the variable, but for stacked bar, stacked area and pie charts it is the sum.

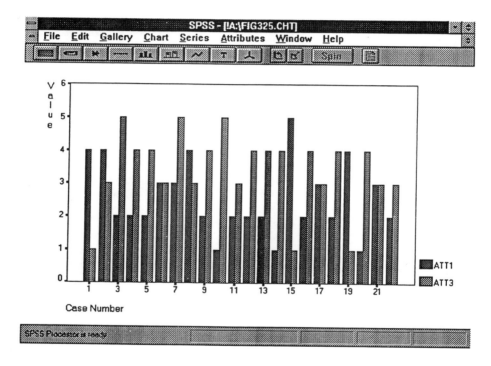

Fig 32.5 Example of barchart of scores on att1 and att3 for each respondent.
Note: This graph was obtained by selecting the Values of individual cases *option*

It is possible to have different Summary statistics, by selecting the variable and entering it in the Variable box of the Bars Represent area, then clicking on the Change Summary button. From the Summary Function dialogue box you can specify which of the alternatives you wish to be the summary statistics from those offered, which include median, mode, number of cases, standard deviation and others. You can also ask for a plot of the number or percentage falling above or below a particular value (which you enter into the Value text box), percentiles, even the percent or number of cases with values between and including a Low and High value which you enter into text boxes. As I have said, the range of possibilities is enormous, and experimentation is the best way to discover what they all do!

32.3 Creating a bar chart

From the SPSS window, select Graphs and then Bar... which opens the Bar Charts window. You can select a Simple, Clustered or Stacked barchart by selecting the appropriate icon. A Simple barchart represents each value on the variable being plotted as a bar, and the bars are equally spaced along the axis. In Clustered charts, some bars are clustered together. For example, one might want to plot the average scores of males and females on test1 and on test2, with the scores on test1 grouped (clustered together) and the scores on test2 clustered together (see Fig 32.4). A stacked barchart shows two or more variables in each bar.

For your first attempt, creating a bar chart of the area scores in salesq, check that Summaries for groups of cases is the selected option and then click on the Define button. This reveals the Define Simple Bar dialogue box.

You must identify the variables to be plotted: in the Define Simple Bar box, click in the list on the left of the box the variable to be plotted; in this example it is area. The variable has to be entered into the box marked Category Axis, and do this by clicking on the right-pointing arrow. Check that in the upper part of the window, labelled Bars represent, the N of cases option is selected. Then click on OK, and after a few seconds, the chart will be presented in the Chart Carousel.

You might like to try another, plotting the average salary of men and women. Make the data window active by clicking in its menu bar or scroll bar area, and repeat the procedure for making a simple bar graph, but when you get to the Define simple bar box, remove the variable area from the Category Axis by clicking on it and then clicking on the left-pointing arrow to its left. Put the variable sex in the Category Axis box, and then put the variable salary into the Variable box of the Bars Represent area of the dialogue box. Then click on the Other summary function button, and another box will allow you to select which summary statistic you want. The default is the mean, which is the one you want here, so click on Continue, which returns you to the Define Simple Bar box, and you can then click on OK. The chart will, after a short delay, appear in the Chart Carousel window.

32.4 Creating a scattergram

Selecting Graphs /Scatter invites you to indicate whether you want a simple scatterplot, an overlay in which multiple scatterplots are put into the same frame, a scatterplot matrix or a 3-dimensional plot. Initially, the Simple option is likely to be most useful. You may wonder what a scatterplot matrix is. Suppose you selected three variables and asked for this option, then you would obtain scatterplots for variable1 versus variable2, variable2 v variable3, and variable1 v variable3... and the same plots with the axes swapped so you also get variable2 versus variable1, variable3 v variable2, and variable 3 v variable1!

Having selected the type of scatterplot required, click on Define and this will produce a window in which you specify the variables to be plotted on each axis by selecting the variable from the list on the left and clicking the right-pointing arrow for the Y (vertical) axis and then repeat the procedure for the X (horizontal axis).

You can separate the plots for subgroups of respondents: for example, one could plot cust versus sales for all the respondents in salesq, but have the data for females indicated by a different marker from those used to plot males' data. This is achieved by entering sex as the variable in the Set Markers by text box.

If you want the regression line shown in the scatterplot, select Chart /Options from the menu and click on the Fit Options button. The linear regression line is the default, although quadratic and cubic can be selected instead. Click on Continue to return to the Scatterplot Options box, and then on OK.

You can swap the axes of the scatterplot if you select Chart /Series /Displayed.

Scatterplots in three dimensions require you to specify the three variables to be used as the axes. When the plot is presented, and put into a !Chart window, you can enjoy playing with it by rotating it around various axes if you select from the menus Attributes /3-D Rotation.

32.5 Displaying the chart

When the chart is first created, it is displayed in the Chart Carousel window. Click on the Edit button of the Chart Carousel icon bar, not the Edit menu of the SPSS window, and the chart will be shown in a window headed !Chart.

You will see that with the Chart Carousel window open, the menu bar of the SPSS window alters, and the entries become

File   Edit   Carousel   Window   Help

File allows you to save and print the charts in the carousel. To alter the typeface used in the charts and to have grid lines displayed, use Edit /Preferences from the menu bar. Carousel allows you to move between the charts in the carousel and to have a chart put into a chart editing window. These functions can also be accessed from the icons in the icon bar of the Chart Carousel window itself.

32.6 The Chart Carousel window

The chart carousel is like a magazine of slides for a slide projector. The magazine may be empty, or it may contain a set of charts stored singly as slides. The Chart Carousel window's menu bar has a number of entries. On the left-hand side is a drop-down list of the charts that are available at the present time: those which are currently in the magazine. If you click on the down-pointing arrow with the line underneath it, a list of the available charts will be revealed. You can click on any of the entries, and the name will then be pasted into the text window. Clicking on it will then put the named chart into the Carousel window.

If the carousel contains a number of charts, the menu bar's down arrow icon selects the next chart in the carousel and puts it into the window; the up arrow icon selects the previous chart in the carousel. If the carousel has only one chart in its magazine, these two buttons will be dimmed to indicate they are not available.

The Edit button in the carousel window menu bar is clicked if you want to alter the chart shown in the carousel window (as you almost certainly will). This puts the chart shown in the Chart Carousel into a Chart window, entitled !Chart. Only when a chart is in a !Chart window can it be edited.

The Discard button in the carousel window, as the name suggests, deletes the current chart.

The 'typed page' icon switches you to the output window, where the text output of the analyses are situated. If you inadvertently click on this icon, and want to return to the Chart Carousel, click on the chart icon in the text output window.

32.7 The !Chart window

Charts are inserted into a !Chart window by selecting the Edit button from the Chart Carousel menu bar. When the !Chart window is open, the SPSS window menu alters again and has the entries:

File   Edit   Gallery   Chart   Series   Attributes   Window   Help

These menus allow you to make numerous alterations to the chart in the !Chart window.

The icon bar of the !Chart window duplicates the commands available from the Attributes menu. By clicking on the icons you can, reading from left to right, set the pattern for filling enclosed areas, set the colours, specify the marker used to plot a point, set the thickness and style of lines, specify whether bars have a shadow or 3-d appearance, determine whether bars are labelled, decide how interpolated lines are drawn, vary the font and size of text used in the chart, apply 3-d rotation for a 3-d plot, swap axes, explode the slice of a pie chart, spin a 3-d plot and with the right-hand icon, switch to the output text window.

The facilities for editing charts are so numerous that it is best to learn by experimentation. How to achieve some of the effects you are most likely to need is described in section 32.11.

32.8 Saving a chart

You can save a chart either from the Chart Carousel or from the !Chart window. Charts are saved with the filename extension .CHT.

If you are in a !Chart window, select from the menu bar File /Save As. The name of the file may appear in the Files box, and you can then click on it so it appears in the Name box. The directory in which it will be saved is shown, and you can alter this by clicking on the required alternative in the Directories box: to save the file to the floppy disk, you need to click on [-A-] in the Directories box.

If the chart is in the Chart Carousel, it can be saved by selecting from the SPSS window menu bar the File /Save As options or the File /Save Chart option. When you have either clicked on a name from the list offered or entered a new name and indicated the directory or drive to save the file on, click on the Save Chart button at the bottom of the dialogue box to save the file.

The Save As: Chart Carousel dialogue box contains a Save All button. This allows you to save all the charts in the Chart Carousel: type a name of 5 or less characters. If you typed in 'name', all the charts will be saved as name1.cht, name2.cht etc.

32.9 Retrieving charts

You can retrieve a previously saved chart by using the File /Open options from the menu bar of the SPSS window. A drop-down menu asks you to indicate which type of file you want to open, and if you click on the chart file option a list of .CHT files will be offered. If your file is on your floppy disk, you will have to click on [-A-] in the Directories list to have the .CHT files from the floppy disk presented in the list of files available to be opened. Just click on the name of the file you want and then click on OK: the file will then be presented in a !Chart window. The title of the window will show the drive the file came from and the file name, such as !A:\PLOT1.CHT.

32.10 Printing charts

If the chart is in the Chart Carousel or a !Chart window, it can be printed by selecting File /Print from the SPSS menu bar. The Print Chart dialogue box is presented. By default, the Redraw image for printer facility is operative. This has the effect of redrawing the chart image so it corresponds to the fonts available in the printer.

32.11 Editing charts

There are numerous editing possibilities, once the chart is in an active chart window, and only some of them will be explained here: once the basics are understood, the user will learn most, and most enjoyably, by experimenting with the host of alternatives.

To use the editing facilities, you need to appreciate that a chart contains two kinds of object. 'Series objects' are the bars, lines and markers that represent the data. 'Chart objects' are the layout and labelling features. To modify an object, you either use the Series and Chart menus of the SPSS window, or you can double-click on the object you wish to modify. With either procedure, an appropriate dialogue box is then presented allowing you to specify the attributes of the object. For example, to change the way the bar in a barchart is filled with a pattern, double click on one of the bars. To change the label for the vertical axis, double click on the existing label.

With a chart window active, the menu bar of the SPSS window contains the menu titles:

File   Edit   Gallery   Chart   Series   Attributes   Window   Help

To alter the title of the chart, select Chart /Title from the SPSS window menu, and type text into the Title 1 and/or Title 2 text boxes; then click on OK.

To alter the title or labels of the horizontal axis, double click on the existing one, which is to the left and below the horizontal axis. This reveals the Category Axis box, and you can enter a different title. To alter the labels of the categories, click on the Labels button. In the Category Axis: Labels dialogue box you can click on the existing label, shown in a list in the label text area, and it will appear in the text box. You can then edit it and click on the Change button. When the labels have been altered, a click on the Continue button returns you to the Category Axis box and you click on OK.

To alter the title, scale or labels of the vertical axis, double click on the existing vertical axis title, and the Scale Axis box is exposed. It functions in a similar way to the Category Axis box used to modify the horizontal axis.

That part of the chart which indicates which variables are shown is known as the legend. Double clicking on the existing legend will reveal a Legend box allowing you to add a title to the legend, alter the labels of the legend, vary its position or suppress it completely.

To add a short text message to the chart, select Chart /Annotation: the resulting box allows you to type in the message and locate it at a set point defined by position on the vertical and horizontal axes.

To alter the layout or change the scales of the chart axes select Chart /Options and further dialogue boxes appropriate to the type of chart you are editing allow you specify how you want the chart to be constructed. The options offered depend on the type of chart you are editing, but this menu gives great flexibility in chart design.

To have a normal curve added to a histogram or add a regression line to a scatterplot, use the Charts /Options menu.

You can swap axes, so that histograms, for example, are oriented horizontally rather than vertically, by selecting Series/ Displayed or Attributes /Swap Axes, or by clicking on the icon in the icon bar which portrays a movement of the axes.

To alter the patterns used to fill areas of the chart, and similar features of the chart, select Attributes.

To alter the text fonts and sizes, select Attributes /Text.

To suppress the display of some of the variables you have previously selected for inclusion in the chart, select Series /Displayed.

To alter the sequence in which variables are grouped in a clustered barchart or a stacked chart, select Series /Displayed and alter the order in which variables are listed in the Display text box of the Displayed data dialogue box. (Click on the variable name, then click on the control box in the top left of the title bar. This opens a list containing the options to move the selected item up or down in the list.)

You can replace the current chart with another of a different type, using the same data, by selecting Gallery.

Line graphs, area charts, pie charts can be requested at the first stage of creating a chart. But more complex charts such as mixed bars and lines, exploded pie charts, dropped line charts are available once you have created a chart, put into a !Chart window, and selected Gallery from the menu bar. Experimenting with the possibilities is perhaps the best way to learn how to control these displays. As usual, the system provides appropriate dialogue boxes at every point.

32.12 Templates

A chart template allows you to save the style of a chart so that it can be applied to other charts, so you do not have to go through the process of designing a chart every time. Essentially, when you save a chart, the features of that chart can be applied when you create a new chart or can be applied to a chart already in the chart window.

Using a template when creating a chart

When you access the Define chart dialogue box, it contains an area titled Template, with the option Use chart specifications from:. If you select this and then click on the File button in the template area, a list of chart files, with the filename extension .CHT is shown. Select the one you want from the list so its name appears in the Chart Template File text box and click on OK. The chart you are creating will be assigned the attributes of the chart you are using as a template.

Assigning a template to an existing chart

If you have a chart in a chart window, and want to apply a template to it, select File from the menu and then Apply Chart Template... This has an option for Apply title and footnote text. If this is active, the titles and footnotes of the template will be added to the chart to which the template is being applied, over-riding any previous titles or footnotes.

32.13 Dealing with missing data when creating charts

When you are charting data that has some data missing, SPSS will omit any case that has data missing on the variables being plotted unless you specify that it should include them. This cannot be altered when you are plotting data for individual cases, nor if you are plotting a histogram. But for other charts, you do have a choice. To over-ride the default setting, you must select the Options button from the chart definition box. Exclude cases listwise means, although the name is rather confusing, that any row of data which has a missing data point for any of the variables selected for plotting will be omitted from the graph. This is the default condition. The alternative is Exclude cases variable by variable, which means that when a particular variable is plotted, any case with missing data is omitted, but the case is included when you analyse another variable if the case has a score on that variable.

For some charts, missing values are plotted as a separate category. For example, a barchart of the frequency of sex for the data from salesq has a bar for the case where the sex is unknown (sex had a value of 3 which was defined as a missing value). If any cases had the system-missing value, there would be a separate bar for them. You may wish to suppress the plotting of these missing value cases. To do so, select the Options button from the Define chart dialogue box and click on the button entitled Display groups defined by missing values, so the cross in the box is removed. Missing value cases will not then be plotted.

32.14 Adding grid lines to charts

You can ask for horizontal or vertical grid lines to be added to charts by selecting from the menu Edit /Preferences /Graphics. The dialogue box which will appear has one section headed Grid lines, and you use the check boxes to request horizontal lines (Scale axis) and/or vertical lines (Category axis).

33

Obtaining neat printouts

33.1 Obtaining a clean .LIS file in SPSS/PC+

The results from an SPSS/PC+ analysis are put into the .LIS file, and during a single SPSS/PC+ session, the .LIS file is built up with the results of later runs being added to it. If you wish to use the .LIS file for presenting the results of your analysis, you will need a 'clean' version of the file, containing just the results you want. There are various ways of obtaining a clean .LIS file.

One way is to get the command file perfect, so that it runs without error, enter the name of a new output .LIS file, run the command file. The .LIS file will contain only the clean output. A further method of obtaining a clean .LIS file is to edit it within SPSS/PC+, as described in section 15.5. Yet another way of obtaining a clean and tidy printout of the results of your analysis is to use the REPORT procedure.

33.2 Using REPORT in SPSS/PC+

To find REPORT *in the menu system, select* analyze data, *go right, select* reports and tables, *and go right again.*

Fig 33.1 shows the result of a REPORT command and the command lines that were used. REPORT creates tables from the data, and there is a wide variety of formatting commands. It is worth noting that REPORT can be criticised for being too flexible: there are so many variations one can use in laying out the table that even the menu help window suggests you may find it easier to type in the commands rather than using the menu! Also, tables can be obtained from other procedures such as CROSSTABS, and the resulting .LIS file edited to achieve a tidy tabular presentation without using REPORT at all.

Since REPORT has such a range of options, only the basic aspects of the command will be described. Once you have tried it out, you can explore further possibilities using the menus and/or the SPSS/PC+ manual.

The REPORT command reads the cases from the data file in sequential order. So it is usually necessary to re-order the data in the active file to put it in the order required to create the table. For example, to have a table showing all the males and then all the females, it is necessary to sort the file so that all the same-sex cases are together. This is done by:

```
SORT sex.
```

Further details on the SORT procedure are given in section 27.5.

```
Customers and sales per salesperson
```

		customers	
SEX	ID	visited	SALES
male	2	46	4984.42
	3	48	10432.82
	4	83	8235.21
	8	28	3819.00
	9	41	5723.52
	10	76	7937.45
	12	30	2005.30
	13	68	8914.50
	17	38	3449.35
	21	39	4004.80
Sum			59506.37
Mean	10	50	5950.64
female	1	43	3450.60
	6	72	6497.05
	7	42	3835.26
	11	39	4582.44
	14	33	3124.20
	15	36	4222.45
	16	79	8881.28
	18	48	7882.60
	19	58	8779.00
	20	60	5822.68
	22	40	5886.40
Sum			62963.96
Mean	14	50	5724.00
.	5	71	6441.38
Sum			6441.38
Mean	5	71	6441.38

```
GET /FILE 'a:ex1.sys'.
SET /LISTING 'a:ex17.lis'.
SET /LENGTH 70.
SORT sex.
REPORT /FORMAT AUTOMATIC LIST LENGTH (5,65) /VARIABLES id cust sales
/TITLE LEFT 'Customers and sales per salesperson' /BREAK sex /SUMMARY SUM
(sales) /SUMMARY MEAN.
```

Fig 33.1 An example of output from REPORT and the commands used to create it.

Once the data has been sorted, the REPORT command can be invoked. It produces tables in which the variables are set in columns, as shown in Fig 33.1. The table can list the variable values for individual cases from the data file, or it can list particular subgroupings of cases. The table can contain summary statistics such as the mean or sum for subgroups of cases. An example should help to make this clear.

In exdat there are data on males and females, and we want to obtain a table listing the sales data for each sex separately, with the means for the two sexes shown.

To obtain a list of the data file's cases, the report line must include a LIST subcommand:

```
REPORT /FORMAT AUTOMATIC LIST
```

The FORMAT AUTOMATIC entry means that the system uses a set of default formatting instructions. (These can be altered if one uses FORMAT MANUAL which invokes a different set of defaults.)

A REPORT command has to indicate which variable or variables are to be shown. To tabulate the id, customers visited and sales for each sex, the line would include:

```
REPORT /FORMAT AUTOMATIC LIST /VARIABLES id cust sales
```

(The order in which the variables are named determines the sequence of columns in the output table.)

When using Report, you usually want the table to subdivide the cases into groups (eg into males and females). To specify the variable which is to be used to create the subgroups, use /BREAK followed by the variable name. So to create subgroups based on sex:

```
REPORT /FORMAT AUTOMATIC LIST /VARIABLES id cust sales /BREAK sex
```

Various summary statistics can be requested including mean, variance, sd, sum, min, max, mode, median, but each must be preceded with the /SUMMARY subcommand. To obtain the totals and means for each of the subgroups, the complete line becomes:

```
REPORT /FORMAT AUTOMATIC LIST /VARIABLES id cust sales /BREAK sex
/SUMMARY SUM /SUMMARY MEAN.
```

To have summary statistics for some of the named variables only, use a line like this:

```
REPORT /FORMAT AUTOMATIC LIST /VARIABLES id cust sales /BREAK sex
/SUMMARY SUM (sales) /SUMMARY MEAN.
```

By default the table will have a title which is the same as the title of the pages in the .LIS file. To give the table its own title use:

```
/TITLE 'Title of table'
```

The positioning of the title can be centred on the page (the default) or left/right aligned:

```
/TITLE LEFT 'Table 1'
```

will produce a left-aligned title.

An example that includes all these options is:

```
REPORT /FORMAT AUTOMATIC LIST /VARIABLES id cust sales /TITLE LEFT
'Customers and sales per salesperson' /BREAK sex /SUMMARY SUM (sales)
/SUMMARY MEAN.
```

33.3 Setting REPORT table length for the printer

REPORT will automatically assume that a table can only be as long as the 25 lines used for screen displays. This is inappropriate for printed output, when you want to use the full depth of the paper. You can set the length of the printed table so that it is appropriate for the paper size on your printer, but must first alter the system page length, which is 25 lines unless altered by using a SET command such as:

```
SET /LENGTH 70.
```

The number tells the program how many lines there on a page, and 70 is appropriate for A4 paper.

Having set the system page length, you can then incorporate in the REPORT command a subcommand which tells the procedure where to start printing on a page and how long the page is:

```
/FORMAT AUTOMATIC LIST LENGTH (5,65)
```

The 5 tells REPORT to start printing on the fifth line of the page; the 65 tells it to print down to line 65 on a page. You should, of course, use the numbers you want in this subcommand. An example of the procedure for obtaining tables from REPORT that fit an A4 sheet is:

```
SET /LENGTH 70.
REPORT /FORMAT AUTOMATIC LIST LENGTH (5,65) /VARIABLES id cust sales
/TITLE LEFT 'Customers and sales per salesperson' /BREAK sex /SUMMARY SUM
(sales) /SUMMARY MEAN.
```

The output is shown in Figure 33.1.

As can be seen, the output does give neat tables. You may have noticed that Fig 33.1 gives the mean of the id values, a nonsensical figure. This could have been avoided by using /SUMMARY MEAN (cust sales) instead of merely /SUMMARY MEAN. You will also see that Figure 33.1 has one case shown by a full-stop in the left-hand column. This is the respondent whose sex is unknown and who therefore cannot be categorized as male or female.

33.4 Sending the output of REPORT to a separate file in SPSS/PC+

When using REPORT, the OUTFILE subcommand can be used to send the tables to a separate file so that they can be printed later. For example, the following sends the results of the REPORT command to a file called rep.lis on the floppy disc (drive a):

```
REPORT /FORMAT AUTOMATIC LIST /VARIABLES sales /OUTFILE 'a:rep.lis'
/TITLE 'Table 1' /BREAK sex /SUMMARY SUM.
```

The /OUTFILE subcommand must follow FORMAT but precede /BREAK.

From DOS, the tables can then be printed using the usual:

```
print a:rep.lis ⏎
```

or

```
type a:rep.lis >prn ⏎
```

33.5 Obtaining a clean .LST file in SPSS for Windows

If you wish to use the .lst file for presenting the results of your analysis, you will need a 'clean' version of the file, containing just the results you want. There are various ways of obtaining a clean .LST file. One way is to get the syntax file perfect, so that it runs without error, enter a new name for the output .lst file and run the syntax file. Only the clean output will then feature in the output file. A further method is to edit it the .lst file, either within SPSS as described in section 19.5 or by importing it into a word processor.

Yet another way of obtaining a clean and tidy printout of the results of your analysis is to use the REPORT procedure.

33.6 Using Report in SPSS for Windows

Version 4 of SPSS/PC included a Report facility of such complexity that few will have bothered to use it, as similar results could be obtained by importing the output file into a word processor and editing and formatting it there. In SPSS for Windows, an attempt has been made to provide a front-end which makes it feasible to consider using Report to provide presentation tables of the data and of the results of the analyses.

A data file includes the data organised into cases, and in many situations the case corresponds to a person. When dealing with the results of a survey, where one has obtained responses from a number of different types of respondent, one may well want to produce tables showing the responses of each subgroup of respondents (males and females, different age groups, different socio-economic groups etc) on some or all of the variables that were measured. Using Report, one can obtain tables that show the data from each subgroup of respondents, and/or the summary statistics of each subgroup (such as the mean or median response), with the table organised so that the various subgroups are divided from each other. The statistics for the whole set of data, referred to as grand totals, can also be shown.

The Report facility is obtained from the Statistics /Summarize /Report Summaries in Rows... menu in the SPSS window, which opens the Report dialogue box.

You specify which variables are to be shown in the tables by selecting variables from the list in the left hand box and inserting them into the Data Columns box by clicking on the left-pointing arrow in the usual way.

Report is usually used to get the data broken down into subgroups, and you specify the variables to be used to create the subgroups by entering the variables into the Break Columns box: select the appropriate variable(s) from the left-hand list of variables, and enter them into the Break Columns box by clicking on the arrow to the left of the Break Columns box. Suppose we wanted the data for males and females in salesq to be tabulated separately, then sex would be a Break Column variable. One can select ascending or descending order of levels of each Break Column variable by making the appropriate selection in the Sort Sequence box. Remember the data will be sorted according to the values of the variables in the data file. In salesq, 1 represents male and 2 represents female, so an ascending order will put the 1s (males) before the 2s (females). To have those with a sex score of 2 put first, one would select the Descending sort sequence.

If you wish to have statistics of the subgroups you have specified (e.g. for males and females in salesq), select the variable in the Break Columns list of variables, and then select Summary from the Break Columns area (not from the Report area). Another box is presented (Report: Summary Lines for division), and you can indicate which statistics you want, including sum, mean, number of cases, standard deviation and others. The Percentage above, Percentage below and Percentage inside options allow you to ask for the percentage of cases above, below or between specified values that you type into the boxes to the right of these entries. When you have made your selection, click on Continue.

To set the line spacing between break categories, between break headings and summary statistics, or to set it so that each break category is on a separate page, select a variable in the Break Columns list of variables and then select Options in the Break columns box (not in the Report section of the box).

When Report is used to produce a table in which the data is broken down by subgroups, there are headings for each subgrouping, referred to as break column headings. These can be modified if one selects Format from the Break columns box (not in the Report section of the box).

To specify the headings of the data columns, the alignment of the column headings, the width of the columns, whether the table shows the numbers or the value labels, select a variable in the Data Columns list of variables in the Report: Summaries in Rows dialogue box. (You created this list by selecting variables from the variable list and inserting them into Data Columns). Click on Format... in the Data Columns area of the Report dialogue box. This reveals a dialogue box in which you can type in a heading for the column. If you leave it blank, the variable label is used, and is wrapped to fit the column width. You can type in a fresh heading, but must use Ctrl+Enter at the end of each line if you want it to occupy more than one line. The column heading can be right-aligned, centered or left-aligned by selecting appropriately from the Column heading justification drop-down list. (Click on the down-pointing arrow to reveal the list.)

The column width can be set by typing a number into the Column width box. If you leave this blank, a default value will be used, and this varies according to whether or not you have specified a column heading and to the data that the column will contain. If you do not specify a column heading, the variable name is used as the heading, and the width of the column will be set to length of the longest word in the variable label. If you do specify a column heading, the column width is set to the length of the longest line in the heading. If the data is to be displayed as value labels (ie words, not the coded numbers), then the column width is set to the length of the longest value label.

The program will try to make allowances if you specify a column width which is too short for the data you want shown; for example, numbers will be converted to scientific notation or be replaced by asterisks if you specify a width less than 6 characters and the figures are too long for that. If you find these happening, you will need to increase the column width.

The Columns Content area allows you to say whether you want the table to show numbers or value labels.

The position of the data within the column is selected from the area headed Value position within column. By default, numbers are right aligned and letters [names] are left aligned with the column edge. One can specify how many character positions to offset the data from the edge of the columns or select the Centred within column option.

You may wish to obtain statistics on the whole set of data in addition to the various subgroups. These are requested by using the buttons in the Report area of the Report: Summaries in Rows dialogue box. To obtain statistics on the whole set of data, select the Summary button.

The margins of the table generated by Report and the number of lines per page can be specified by selecting the Layout button from the Report area of the Report: Summaries in Rows dialogue box. This box also allows you align the table within the margins you have set. NOTE that if you specify a width that is insufficient for the report table, it will not be generated.

33.7 Page headers and footers in Report for SPSS for Windows

To specify the titles you want printed on each page of the Report, or the message you want printed at the foot of each page, select the Titles... button from the Report area of the Report: Summaries in Rows dialogue box to reveal the Report: Titles dialogue box. You can type in page titles for the left, centre or right of the page. If you want a title to occupy more than one line, type in the text you want for Left, Center or Right position, and then click on Next in the upper right of the Report: Titles dialogue box.

To have the date or the page number as a title or footer, click on Date or Time in the Special variables box in the lower left of the Report: Titles dialogue box. Decide where you want the date or time to appear: left, center or right, and at the top (title) or foot of the page, and click on the right-pointing arrow adjacent to the appropriate text box heading.

You can have variable names included in titles and footers. Select the variable name from the list in the Report: Titles dialogue box, and click on the right-pointing arrow next to Left, Center or Right for the page title or page footer. The variable name will be inserted in the appropriate text box.

To specify the number of lines between headers and the Report table and between the bottom of the Report table and any page footer, select the Layout button from the Report area of the Report: Summaries in Rows dialogue box.

The titles and footers are left-aligned, right-aligned or centred according to the report width or – if you have specified them in the Report layout box – the report margins. They may not align with the table, because the table is narrower than the margins you have set, but you can shift the position of the titles and footers by changing the margins.

33.8 Page numbering in Report for SPSS for Windows

The pages of output from Report are numbered, and will start at 1 unless you alter this. To do so, select Options from the Report area of the Report: Summaries in Rows dialogue box. The dialogue box revealed includes a Number pages from option, and you can type in the value you require.

33.9 Missing data in Report for SPSS for Windows

When dealing with a set of data, there are likely to be instances where some cases are incomplete: respondents have not provided data on one of the variables which you are tabulating with Report. By default, such cases are deleted from the report. To alter this, so that missing cases are included in the tabled Report, select Options from the Report area of the Report: Summaries in Rows dialogue box, and cancel Exclude cases with missing values listwise. If you indicate that you want cases where the data is missing to be included, they will be shown as a full-stop, but you can specify a different character using the Missing values appear as option.

33.10 Saving the Report commands in SPSS for Windows

When you have made the (numerous) selections for Report, you can paste them into a syntax window, and then save that file so you get a copy of the commands which produced the layout that your various choices produced. The syntax file can be edited to allow further options to be invoked: these are described in the Syntax reference Guide to SPSS for Windows.

Merging data files in SPSS

You may find that you have two sets of data, in separate files, that you want to merge to form one file. There are two situations where this is likely to happen. First, you have collected data from a sample of respondents, and later obtain data from some more respondents which you want to add to your first set. The obvious way of doing this is to retrieve the original data file and simply add the new cases on the end, but this is not always feasible. (Perhaps you have the data from 1000 children in Mexico, and a colleague has data from 1000 children in Poland. Both of you have written a file containing the data you have collected, neither of you wants to type in another 1000 cases!) You can merge the two data files in SPSS/PC+ using the Join Add command, which is explained below (section 34.2). In SPSS for Windows you use Add Cases (section 34.5).

The second situation where you want to merge data is when you have data from a set of respondents, and then obtain another series of responses from the same respondents. For example, imagine we surveyed 500 adults on their alcohol drinking behaviour six months ago and yesterday. We want to add the data we collected yesterday to the file of their responses of six months ago, so we can look at changes in drinking behaviour over the six month period. We are not adding new cases to our data file, only adding new data to existing cases. We could go back and add the new data to our data file, but it may be that we have the two data sets in separate files and want to merge them. For this type of situation, in SPSS/PC+ you need the Join Match procedure (section 34.3, 34.4) and in SPSS for Windows you use Add Variables (section 34.6, 34.7).

34.1 Adding cases in SPSS/PC+: JOIN ADD

To find JOIN ADD *in the menu system, select* modify data or files, *go right, select* manipulate files *and go right again.*

The vital point to note at the outset is that the JOIN procedures can only be used with .SYS files, not ordinary data files. If you have not yet done so, make sure you understand the notion of .SYS files and how to create them (chapter 16).

The simplest method of explaining how to join data files is to give examples for you to work through. Suppose we have data from 3 additional respondents to add to our exdat file. This extra data is shown in Fig 34.1. These numbers are rather simple, but this example demonstrates how JOIN ADD works; the techniques apply just as easily to larger data sets.

```
23 1 1 1 3 2 3 055 03800.50 010691
24 2 2 2 4 2 4 060 04780.60 030690
25 2 1 2 3 2 5 078 06782.00 040690
```

Fig 34.1 Additional data from three respondents to be added to the data file

Write a new data file containing the lines shown in Fig 34.1, and save it as dat2 on the floppy disk. To merge this data with the data in exdat, the first task is to create .SYS files of each data set. You have already (chapter 16) created a .SYS file (ex1.sys) for exdat. To create a .SYS file of dat2, use this command file:

```
DATA LIST FILE 'a:dat2' /id 1-2 sex 4 employer 6 area 8 att1 10 att2 12
att3 14 cust 16-18 sales 20-27 (2) dstd 29-30 dstm 31-32 dsty 33-34.
SAVE /OUTFILE 'a:dat2.SYS'.
```

Write this command file, save it as dat2com, and run it. It creates a second .SYS file, dat2.sys, which contains the data from the dat2 file.

Now write another command file which merges the two .SYS files together and saves the merged file as ex2.sys. This file can be saved as jacom, and needs to contain these lines:

```
JOIN ADD /FILE 'a:ex1.sys' /FILE 'a:dat2.sys'.
SAVE /OUTFILE 'a:ex2.sys'.
```

This adds the contents of the dat2.sys file to the end of the ex1.sys file so that ex2.sys now contains both sets of data. To check that the merge has been successful, write and run another command file, mergcom, which will LIST the cases starting at number 20:

```
GET /FILE 'a:ex2.sys'.
SET /LISTING 'a:merg.lis'.
LIST /CASES FROM 20.
```

If all has gone well, the listing, stored in merg.lis, will be as shown in Fig 34.2.

ID	SEX	EMPLOYER	AREA	ATT1	ATT2	ATT3	CUST	SALES	DSTD	DSTM	DSTY
20	2	2	2	1	3	4	60	5822.68	31	5	91
21	1	2	2	3	4	3	39	5004.80	3	6	91
22	2	1	1	2	3	3	40	8886.40	5	6	90
23	1	1	1	3	2	3	55	3800.50	1	6	91
24	2	2	2	4	2	4	60	4780.60	3	6	90
25	2	1	2	3	2	5	78	6782.00	4	6	90

```
Number of cases read =    25    Number of cases listed =    6
```

Fig 34.2 The LIST of cases from 20 onward in ex2.sys, obtained by running mergcom.

As Fig 34.2 shows, the file ex2.sys has the additional 3 cases from dat2. The data in the joined file is in the order that comes from simply adding one file on to the end of the other. To obtain a different order, perhaps putting all the males (sex=1) together, use the SORT command (chapter 27). The cases can be stored in their sorted order by saving another .SYS file after the SORT command.

It is possible to join files and drop (delete) some of the variables from one of the files. This is unlikely to be needed by a beginner, and so the procedures will not be described here. They are, of course, described in the SPSS/PC+ Manual.

When joining files, the two data files have to be identical in the way the data is laid out. (The names of the variables id, sex, area etc need not be the same in the two files being joined, but if they differ the names used in the second file listed in the JOIN command will be the ones used in the joined file.)

34.2 Adding cases in SPSS/PC+ using 'Insert file'

The SPSS/PC+ manual asserts that you must use .SYS files when joining files. But if you press F3 you will find that the minimenu contains the entry Insert file. The section of the Manual describing what this does is hard to find, but it does say that this command is for inserting the contents of a DOS file into the current file (i.e. the one in the scratchpad).

It is possible to use this facility for merging data files. If you have two sets of data stored on the floppy disk as normal (i.e. not .SYS) files, and are editing one of these data files, then the other can be inserted into it by pressing F3, selecting the Insert file option and typing in the name of the file to be inserted. If the combined file is saved, it will be found to have both sets of data. This is somewhat easier than the JOIN ADD procedure described in 34.1. The absence of any comment on it in the official manual may imply that there are some limitations to its use, and that it is safer to rely on JOIN ADD.

34.3 Adding scores to existing cases in SPSS/PC+: JOIN MATCH

To find JOIN MATCH *in the menu system, select* modify data or files, *go right, select* manipulate files *and go right again.*

Imagine we have additional data for the respondents recorded in exdat: perhaps we now have their date of birth as a six-digit number like this: 050870 representing 5th August, 1970. This date could be assigned to three variables: dobd (day), dobm (month) and doby (year).

This additional data is stored in a data file (addat). An example of the data for the first two respondents is:

```
01 120870
02 221070
```

To add the data to that in the exdat file, you must use the JOIN MATCH command. As with JOIN ADD, you must use .SYS files, so it is necessary to create .SYS files for each of the data sets. The system file for exdat (ex1.sys) already exists on the floppy disk. To obtain a .SYS file for the data file of additional data, you would run a command file like this:

```
DATA LIST FILE 'a:addat' FIXED/ id 1-2 dobd 4-5 dobm 6-7 doby 8-9.
SAVE /OUTFILE 'a:add.SYS'.
```

This creates add.sys, the .SYS file version of the additional file of data. The two sets of data can be merged by writing and running another file containing these commands:

```
JOIN MATCH /FILE 'a:ex1.sys' /FILE 'a:add.sys'.
SAVE /OUTFILE 'a:full.sys'.
```

This creates a merged file formed by adding add.sys to ex1.sys, and saves the merged data as full.sys.

To determine whether the joining of the two files has been successful you would need a command file like this:

```
GET /FILE 'a:full.sys'.
SET /LISTING 'a:full.lis'.
LIST.
```

34.4 JOIN MATCH in SPSS/PC+ with incomplete data

The example of JOIN MATCH described in the previous section is simple, because every respondent in exdat and therefore in ex1.sys also appeared in addat and therefore in add.sys. Real data is often not so neat! What happens if you only have the second set of data on some of the respondents?

Suppose we have another set of additional data, which is the marital status of some of our respondents. The variable is named as marst, and 1 means unmarried, 2 is married. The data is shown in Fig 34.3, where the first two digits are the respondents' id. Write this data file and save it on your floppy disk as setxdat.

```
06 1
03 2
05 2
18 1
11 2
```

Fig 34.3 Additional data on the respondents to be added to the data file

Setxdat has scores on marst for 5 respondents. (Note that in setxdat the respondents are not in the same order as in the original data file; this is so you see how to cope with this situation.)

When one merges the data from the two files, it is obviously essential that the data from setxdat is added to the appropriate person in exdat. There must be some way of identifying which lines from exdat match which lines from setxdat, and in this example id lets us do that because id is included in both the data files.

The first step is to create .SYS files for each of the data files. We have ex1.sys, the .SYS file of exdat. To create a .SYS file for the setxdat file, write and run this command file (setcom):

```
DATA LIST FILE 'a:setxdat' FIXED/ id 1-2 marst 4.
SAVE /OUTFILE 'a:setx.sys'.
```

We now have on the floppy ex1.sys, the .SYS file of exdat, and setx.sys which is the .SYS file of setxdat. To merge the data, it is essential to make sure the data for respondent 05 from setx.sys is added to the data for that same subject from ex.sys, and similarly for the other respondents. We need therefore to match the data from the two files by id, and the first thing is to sort the cases into ascending order of id. For ex1.sys this is already done; the data starts with respondent 01 and goes up to respondent 22 in ascending order. But for setx.sys, the data is not in the correct order. So the next task is to put it in ascending order by writing and running this command file (sosetcom):

```
GET /FILE 'a:setx.sys'.
SORT id.
SAVE /OUTFILE 'a:setx.asf'.
```

This creates another .SYS file (setx.asf) of the data in setxdat with the cases in ascending order of id.

The two sets of data can now be joined, and the result listed, by writing and running this command file (jm2com):

```
JOIN MATCH /FILE 'a:ex1.sys' /FILE 'a:setx.asf' /BY id.
SAVE /OUTFILE 'a:mat.sys'.
```

The first line tells SPSS/PC+ which two files to merge (note that for setx it is setx.asf, the file which has the data sorted into an ascending sequence based on id). It also, with BY id, tells SPSS/PC+ to merge data according to id so that the data for respondent 05 in ex1.sys is matched to that from subject 05 in setx.asf.

The second line saves a new .SYS file (mat.sys) that contains the merged data.

To confirm that the new data has been added to the correct lines of the original data, you can LIST mat.lis. The output from the command LIST id sex marst. is shown in Fig 34.4, and demonstrates that the new data has been paired with the correct respondent.

```
ID SEX  MARST

 1   2       .
 2   1       .
 3   1       2
 4   1       .
 5   3       2
 6   2       1
 7   2       .
 8   1       .
 9   1       .
10   1       .
11   2       2
12   1       .
13   1       .
14   2       .
15   2       .
16   2       .
17   1       .
18   2       1
19   2       .
20   2       .
21   1       .
22   2       .


Number of cases read =   22    Number of cases listed =   22
```

Fig 34.4 The output of the command LIST id sex marst. applied to mat.sys.

34.5 Adding cases in SPSS for Windows

Suppose we have a file which contains data on additional respondents to be added to salesq and this additional data, shown in Fig 34.1, has been saved in a file called extra.sav, with the same names for the variables as were used in salesq.

To add these cases to salesq, retrieve salesq so it is in an active Data Editor window. From the menus, select Data /Merge Files /Add Cases, which opens a dialogue box entitled Add Cases Read File. Specify the file to be read (extra.sav in this example) in the Name text box, and click on the Define button.

This reveals another dialogue box (Add Cases from), and variables in the two data files which match are listed in the text box headed Variables in New Working Data File. So if both data files have a variable called sex, this will be listed in this box. The dialogue box also has a list of variables in a text box headed Unpaired Variables. Those variables followed by a * are present in the current, open data file and those variables followed by a + are present in the external file (extra.sav in this example). These are variables which do not have the same name in the two files. You can make a pair of them, so a variable called sex in the current file can be matched with a variable called gender in the external file, by clicking on these two names and then on the Pair button. (If the two variable names are not adjacent, hold down Ctrl while you click on the names.) If necessary, variables in the Unpaired Variable list can be renamed by selecting them and clicking on the Rename button.

If you want the merged file to include a variable that only exists in one of the files being merged, select its name and click on the right arrow button to add it to the list of Variables in New Working Data File.

When the definition is complete, click on OK. A file called Newdata will appear in the Data Editor.

34.6 Adding scores to existing cases in SPSS for Windows: Add Variables

This procedure merges two data files that contain different data on the same respondents. Imagine we have additional data for the respondents recorded in salesq: perhaps we now have their date of birth as a six-digit number like this: 050870, representing 5th August, 1970. This data has been assigned to three variables: dobd (day), dobm (month) and doby (year), and is stored in a data file (addat.sav). An example of the data for the first two respondents is:

```
01  120870
02  221070
```

We want to add this additional data on each respondent to the salesq file. First, the data in both files must have been sorted into the same order on the key variable which will be used to ensure the data is assigned to the correct case: this is one reason for having identification numbers (id) in data files such as salesq. Having sorted both salesq and addat.sav by id, ensure one of the files is in the active Data Editor. (Assume for this explanation that salesq is the active file). From the menu select Data /Merge Files /Add variables, and enter the name of the other file (addat.sav in this example) in the Name text box. Then click on Define.

Any variables which appear in either of the data files are shown in the New Working Data File list of the Add Variables from dialogue box. Those variables followed by a * are present in the current, open data file and those variables followed by a + are present in the external file (addat.sav in this example). Any variables which appear in both of the data files are shown in the Excluded Variables list, since one does not want them to appear twice in the merged file.

If the second file (addat.sav) has data on every case in the current file (salesq), you can click on OK, and the two sets of data will be merged and seen in the Data Editor window.

If the external file (addat.sav) does not have data for every one of the cases in the current file (salesq), see the next section.

34.7 Add Variables in SPSS for Windows with incomplete data

Suppose we have another set of additional data, which is the marital status of some of our respondents. The variable is named as marst, and 1 means unmarried, 2 is married. The data is shown in Fig 34.3, the first two digits being the respondent's id (identification number). This data has been saved in a data file called marry.sav.

Marry.sav has scores on marst for 5 respondents. (Note that in marry.sav the respondents are not in the same order as in the original data file; this is so you see how to cope with this situation.)

When one merges the data from the two files, it is obviously essential that the data from marry.sav is added to the appropriate person in salesq. There must be some way of identifying which lines from salesq match which lines from marry.sav, and in this example the variable id, preferred to as a key variable, lets us do that because id is included in both the data files.

The first step is to check that in both files the same name is used for the key variable. Then ensure that both data files have the cases sorted on the key variable (id, in this example); if necessary, retrieve each file, sort the data and then save the file.

Once the files have been sorted on the key variable, the procedure for matching salesq and marry.sav is similar to that for adding cases described in 34.6. The major difference is that when faced with the Add Cases From dialogue box you must click on the key variable name (id in our example) in the Excluded variables list, click the box entitled Match cases on key variables in sorted files and then enter the key variable into the Key Variable text box by clicking on the right arrow button. (The key variable must have the same name in both files, but you can if necessary use the Rename facility to bring this situation about by clicking on the Rename button in the Add Variables From dialogue box.)

Then click on OK: the files will be merged and the new merged set of data will appear in the Data Editor window where you can inspect it to ensure the data has been matched correctly.

Transferring files between SPSS and other programs

35.1 SPSS/PC+: Transferring the output file to a word processor

The .LIS files created by SPSS/PC+ can readily be imported into a word processing package. With Microsoft Word, for example, you simply use the normal Transfer Load procedure and, when asked which file to load, types in the name of the .LIS file, such as `ex1.lis`. The .LIS file is formatted with an 80-column line, so many of the lines wrap over, but it is quite straightforward to delete lines and to shorten lines by deleting characters so that the .LIS file takes on a neat appearance. When first loaded, the .LIS file has bold character formatting which can be turned off using the normal commands of the word processor. Once the editing has been done, the file can be saved in the normal way as a document file.

35.2 SPSS/PC+: Inputting data from other packages

With so many packages in use, it is impossible to give precise instructions here, but it is possible to import files from some other computer packages into SPSS/PC+, using the `Translate From` command. The Manual describes how to do this for 1 ·-3, Symphony and dBase files. Other packages may contain their own instructions on how their files can be imported. For example, EPIINFO is a package used for keeping medical records, and contains a procedure for converting files into a form that allows them to be imported into SPSS/PC+.

35.3 SPSS/PC+: Importing a command file

You can write the data and command files on a word processor, and then load them into SPSS/PC+ to run them and carry out the data analysis. When using a word processor, each line of data or commands must be ended with a carriage-return, and the file must be saved as an ASCII (non-document) file. To load the file into SPSS/PC+, use the normal F3 `Edit different file` procedure, and type in the name of the file when invited to do so.

35.4 SPSS for Windows: Transferring data and output (text) files to/from a word processor

The SPSS text output files can be loaded directly into word processing packages and edited from there.

Data can be prepared outside SPSS for Windows, in a word processor for example, and then saved in ASCII format. It can be imported into SPSS for Windows by selecting File /Read ASCII Data, specifying the file and clicking on the Define button. Here you have to specify the name of the variable and, if the data for each case extends over more than one line, you must indicate which line of the case has the variable you are defining by entering the line number in the box marked Record. You must also indicate the columns in the ASCII file which the variable occupies. (In salesq for example, id is in columns 1-2, sex in column 4 and so on.) The type of data must be specified in Data Type. (For the beginner, the default Numeric as is will be appropriate but other types are available in the drop-down list). Then click on the Add button, and the information you have provided will appear in the Defined variables list.

When you have entered the specifications for all the variables, click on OK. The file will be read and the data appear in the Data Editor window: before you do anything else, check that the data is as you expected!

If data is prepared in a word processor with values separated by tabs and the file saved in ASCII format, the data files can be imported into SPSS for Windows by selecting Tab-delimited in the dialogue box which is revealed when you select from the menus File /Open /Data.

One can write the syntax file on a word processor, and then load it into SPSS. When using a word processor, each line of data or commands must be ended with a carriage-return, and the file must be saved as an ASCII (non-document) file.

35.5 SPSS for Windows: Transferring data files to/from other packages

Data files can be saved in a number of formats so they can be read by other packages such a Excel, Lotus, dBase. The options are offered when you select File /Save As for a data file. Similarly, data files from these other packages can be read into SPSS for Windows.

SPSS/PC+ data files in the .SYS format can be loaded into SPSS for Windows directly without any conversion being required.

35.6 SPSS for Windows: Transferring chart files

A chart can be copied into other Windows applications, such as Word for Windows 2, by copying it to the windows clipboard using Edit /Copy Chart, opening a Word document and selecting Edit /Paste. Select in the dialogue box Picture and click on Paste. An alternative method is to have the chart open in SPSS for Windows, press the Print Screen key on the keyboard, open the Word for Windows document and then use Edit /Paste. The chart will be pasted into the document and can be altered using Microsoft Draw.

More technical details on exchanging information between SPSS for Windows and other Window applications are contained in the User's Guide.

When things go wrong

36.1 Faced with the unexpected in SPSS/PC+

SPSS/PC+ is a complex package, somewhat obscure for the beginner. It is easy to find yourself not where you expected, and with no obvious way of retrieving the situation. Some of the commoner errors, and how to correct them, are listed below.

Pressing ↵ when the cursor is on the last line of a file does not move it down to an empty line, and it stays on the last line of the file which scrolls up the screen.
You may inadvertently have come out of Insert mode by pressing the Ins key. Press the Ins key and see whether this corrects the problem. If you are still stuck, create a new empty line below the last line of the file by pressing F4 and select 'Insert after' ↵

Decimals in the data are not read
Ensure the DATA LIST line specifies the number of decimals in the scores on the particular variable e.g. `sales 20-27 (2)` is used to indicate that the data on sales is in columns 20-27 and has two decimal places such as: 11111.11

End of the line is reached when typing into a typing window
Press ↵ to paste the contents of the typing window into the scratchpad, and use Alt +T to get another typing window. Type in the rest of the material you want inserted into the file. See chapter 9.3.

'ERROR 34, Text: xxxx.
This command is not permitted until a file is defined via DATA LIST, IMPORT, GET, JOIN or TRANSLATE.
'This command not executed.' is shown when you try to run the command file.
You have tried to run a procedure command other than the DATA FILE LIST before the active file has been created. The screen shows MORE in the top right, so press keys until you are returned to the usual SPSS/PC+ screen. Retrieve the command file, move the cursor to the first line of the file (Ctrl+Home in edit mode), and try F10 again.

F9 will not operate
If you have chosen 'zoom' so that the whole screen is filled with the .LIS file, you must unzoom with Esc before the file can be saved.

'File not found' is shown when you try to load a file from DOS
See section 3.7

Menus disappear
Restore the menus with Alt+M

'Not found' is shown when you try to type in from the keyboard
Switch to edit mode with Alt+E and try again.

'Not available in menu mode' is shown when you press a Function key
Switch to edit mode with Alt+E and try again

Output shows more lines of data than you have cases
The data file contains empty line(s). Edit the data file to remove them. See section 12.4

Pressing the wrong Function key
Press Esc

SPSS/PC: is the only thing shown on the screen
You have exited to system prompt. Type

```
review.
```

and press F10 and ↵ to return to Review.

'Unsaved changes ok to exit? n' is shown when you try to invoke SPSS/PC+ (with F10) or when you try to retrieve a different file
You have made some changes to the file in the scratchpad and have not saved the altered version. If you need to save the contents of the scratchpad, press ↵ and then save the file before pressing F10 or F3 again. If you do not want to save the scratchpad, type y ↵.

You set an analysis running but want to stop it.
When the program is carrying out an analysis, it can be stopped by pressing Ctrl+Break.

You want the output to run on, not stopping and showing MORE
To turn off the routine that pauses the screen display of the output, insert the following command into the command file:

```
SET /MORE OFF.
```

This can be typed in, or can be created from the menus by selecting sessions control & info, then selecting operations.

36.2 When things go wrong in SPSS for Windows

SPSS for Windows is far easier to use, and if you do find it not operating as you expect, there is the extensive Help facility and the Cancel button which will take you back to the position you were in previously. Hence it does not seem necessary to provide here hints on how to retrieve errors for SPSS for Windows users.

It is wise to make a habit of pasting commands into a syntax file, at least while you are still learning the package, so that you can study which commands produced which output (or failed to produce the output!). Similarly, I recommend that you do not invoke the facility that suppresses a record of the commands in the output file until you feel thoroughly comfortable with using SPSS for Windows.

The main problem you may have is to launch the package on some lengthy analysis and suddenly realise it is the wrong one or there is some error and you want to stop the run. To do this, select from the menu File /Stop SPSS Processor.

37

Conclusion

You have now reached the end of this introduction to SPSS. The book set out with the aim of teaching you how to use the package, and to demonstrate most of the facilities available in the Base module. Some of the procedures have not been covered; for example, WEIGHT adjusts the weighting of cases for an analysis (the default is 1.00). (All the procedures and commands are, of course, described very fully in the manuals.) In addition, there has been no attempt to explain all the menu and submenu entries: there are literally hundreds, many of which are likely to be used very rarely.

In this book, one short set of data has been used to demonstrate how to achieve the statistical analyses available in SPSS. The principles apply to any set of data, so you should have little difficult in generalizing your skill to fresh sets of figures.

With the experience you now have of the way the package is driven, you should be able to investigate the additional facilities not covered in this book comparatively easily. Furthermore, you should now be able to approach the SPSS Manuals with more understanding than before. The manuals are not very helpful for the complete beginner, but now that you know how commands operate, the file structure used by the package, and how to inspect the output, you should be able to make sense of (most of) them, assuming you understand the statistical procedures a particular command invokes.

Although SPSS can be daunting when you first come across it, and SPSS/PC+ especially so, it does provide an enormously powerful tool. You may find that the Base module does not contain the procedures needed for your specific data analysis problem, but once you have mastered the Base module, you can face the Optional modules, such as Advanced Statistics with understanding of the principles upon which SPSS works.

Appendix A: Answers to SPSS/PC+ exercises

Exercise 14.1

```
TITLE 'Alcohol intake study'.
DATA LIST FILE 'a:alcdat' FIXED /id 1-4 age 6-7 sex 9 alcint 11.
VARIABLE LABELS alcint 'Alcohol intake per week'.
VALUE LABELS sex 1 'male' 2 'female'/alcint 1 'none' 2 'low' 3 'medium' 4
'high'.
MISSING VALUE age(-1) sex(-1) alcint(-1).
SET /LISTING 'a:alc.lis'.
FREQUENCIES /VARIABLES alcint.
```

One can have different names for the variables. Providing the variable names are used consistently throughout the file, and the file contains the lines shown, it would be successful.

Exercise 21.1

```
GET /FILE 'a:ex1.sys'.
SET /LISTING 'a:ex3.lis'.
EXAMINE /VARIABLES cust.
EXAMINE /VARIABLES cust BY area /FREQUENCIES FROM (20) BY (10).
EXAMINE /VARIABLES area /PLOT HISTOGRAM.
```

The first procedure, EXAMINE /VARIABLES cust., produces the output shown in Fig 38.1. The second EXAMINE procedure gives summary statistics and a stem-leaf plot for the whole set of data (thus repeating the output of the first EXAMINE command) and then the scores on cust for each area separately, as shown in Fig 38.1. The subcommand /FREQUENCIES..., following the BY area instruction, yields tables such as shown in Fig 21.3 for each area. (These are not shown in Fig 38.1.) Observe in Fig 38.1 that this EXAMINE command gives separate box-plots, on one graph, for each area. (The meaning of box-plots is described in section 31.4.)

The final EXAMINE command produces summary statistics and a simple histogram of the frequency of scores which can be seen at the end of Fig 38.1. The histogram gives the frequency, the number of cases in each score interval, and plots the appropriate number of asterisks. But the central value of each interval, referred to in the printout as 'bin center', which should be 1 and 2 since these are the two values of the variable area, are printed as 2 and 3.

Another aspect of Fig 38.1 deserves mention. The final command line produces summary statistics on area, which is a nominal variable: the two areas of the country are coded as 1 or 2, but the magnitude of the numbers is meaningless, they are simply used as labels. The printout shows the mean of the area variable to be 1.5909: this is nonsensical, and the investigator needs to examine the printout carefully to ensure there is no misinterpretation of the numbers.

```
EXAMINE /VARIABLES cust BY area /FREQUENCIES FROM (20) BY (10).

       CUST
By   AREA      1            north

Valid cases:    9.0   Missing cases:    .0    Percent missing:   .0

Mean   51.2222  Std Err  6.1639  Min   30.0000  Skewness 1.0009
Median 43.0000  Varian 341.9444  Max   83.0000  S E Skew   .7171
5% Trim50.6358  Std Dev 18.4917  Range 53.0000  Kurtosis -.2788
                                 IQR   29.0000  S E Kurt 1.3997

-------------------------------------------------------------------


       CUST
By   AREA      1            north

  Frequency    Stem &  Leaf
     2.00       3  .  09
     4.00       4  .  0138
     1.00       5  .  8
      .00       6  .
     1.00       7  .  9
     1.00       8  .  3

Stem width:   10
Each leaf:        1 case(s)

-------------------------------------------------------------------


       CUST
By   AREA      2            south

Valid cases:   13.0   Missing cases:    .0    Percent missing:   .0

Mean   50.5385  Std Err  4.6266  Min   28.0000  Skewness   .3601
Median 46.0000  Varian 278.2692  Max   76.0000  S E Skew   .6163
5% Trim50.3761  Std Dev 16.6814  Range 48.0000  Kurtosis-1.5159
                                 IQR   32.5000  S E Kurt 1.1909

-------------------------------------------------------------------


       CUST
By   AREA      2            south

  Frequency    Stem &  Leaf
     1.00       2  .  8
     4.00       3  .  3689
     3.00       4  .  268
      .00       5  .
     2.00       6  .  08
     3.00       7  .  126

Stem width:   10
Each leaf:        1 case(s)
-------------------------------------------------------------------
```

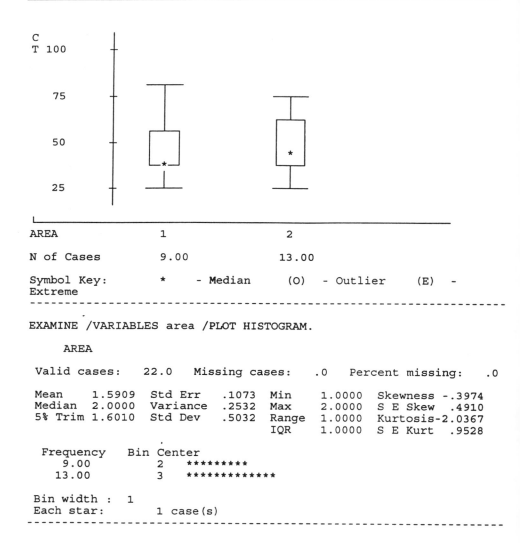

```
AREA                  1                   2

N of Cases          9.00               13.00

Symbol Key:       *   - Median     (O)  - Outlier    (E)  -
Extreme
```

```
EXAMINE /VARIABLES area /PLOT HISTOGRAM.

        AREA

Valid cases:    22.0  Missing cases:    .0   Percent missing:   .0

Mean      1.5909   Std Err     .1073  Min    1.0000  Skewness  -.3974
Median    2.0000   Variance    .2532  Max    2.0000  S E Skew   .4910
5% Trim   1.6010   Std Dev     .5032  Range  1.0000  Kurtosis-2.0367
                                      IQR    1.0000  S E Kurt   .9528

  Frequency    Bin Center
    9.00          2    *********
   13.00          3    *************

Bin width :   1
Each star:       1 case(s)
```

Fig 38.1 Extract of the output from the Exercise 21.1 command file.

Exercise 22.1

```
GET /FILE 'a:ex1.sys'.
SET /LISTING 'a:ex4.lis'.
FREQUENCIES /VARIABLES sex employer.
FREQUENCIES /VARIABLES employer /FORMAT DVALUE.
FREQUENCIES /VARIABLES cust /FORMAT NOTABLE /STATISTICS ALL.
```

The first FREQUENCIES command produces a simple table showing the number of cases with each score on the variable named, as shown in Fig 14.3. The second FREQUENCIES line illustrates the /FORMAT DVALUE subcommand. As Fig 38.2

shows, the effect is to have the values of the variable (employer in this example) given in descending order. The last FREQUENCIES command does not provide a table of frequencies, because the /FORMAT NOTABLE subcommand suppresses it. The /STATISTICS ALL subcommand gives the summary statistics shown in Fig 38.2.

```
FREQUENCIES /VARIABLES employer /FORMAT DVALUE.

EMPLOYER
                                                Valid     Cum
      Value Label            Value  Frequency  Percent  Percent Percent

                               3         6       27.3     27.3     27.3
                               2         8       36.4     36.4     63.6
                               1         8       36.4     36.4    100.0
                                      -------  -------  -------
                            TOTAL       22      100.0    100.0

Valid Cases      22     Missing Cases      0
-----------------------------------------------------------------------


FREQUENCIES /VARIABLES cust /FORMAT NOTABLE /STATISTICS ALL.

CUST        customers visited

Mean          50.818    Std Err       3.627    Median      44.500
Mode          39.000    Std Dev      17.012    Variance
<$ob>289.394
Kurtosis      -1.000    S E Kurt       .953    Skewness      .605
S E Skew        .491    Range        55.000    Minimum     28.000
Maximum       83.000    Sum        1118.000


Valid Cases      22     Missing Cases      0
-----------------------------------------------------------------------
```

Fig 38.2 Extract of the output from the Exercise 22.1 command file

Exercise 22.2

```
GET /FILE 'a:exl.sys'.
SET /LISTING 'a:ex5.lis'.
CROSSTABS /TABLES= area BY employer /OPTIONS 5.
CROSSTABS /TABLES= sex BY employer /STATISTICS= CHISQ .
CROSSTABS /TABLES= sex BY employer BY area.
```

The output is shown in Fig 38.3. The first CROSSTABS line gives a table showing the number of cases from each area/employer, and the /OPTIONS 5 subcommand gives each frequency is expressed as a percentage of the total number of cases.

The second CROSSTABS produces a table similar to Fig 22.2, but employer forms the columns and sex forms the rows; this shows how easy it is to have the table rotated simply be choosing the appropriate order of naming the variables in the /TABLES=... section of the command line. The /STATISTICS= CHISQ subcommand gives a chi-square test, although it is not valid as the printout shows that 6 of 6 cells in the table have an Expected frequency (E.F.) of less than 5.

The last CROSSTABS demonstrates the use of a control variable: separate sex by employer tables are given for each value of area.

```
CROSSTABS /TABLES AREA BY EMPLOYER /OPTIONS 5.

Crosstabulation:      AREA
                   By EMPLOYER

EMPLOYER->  Count                                      Row
            Tot Pct        1  |     2  |     3  |    Total
AREA        ---------------------------------------
               1          5   |    1   |    3   |      9
     north            22.7    |  4.5   | 13.6   |   40.9
            ---------------------------------------
               2          3   |    7   |    3   |     13
     south            13.6    | 31.8   | 13.6   |   59.1
            ---------------------------------------
            Column        8        8        6        22
            Total      36.4     36.4     27.3     100.0

Number of Missing Observations =         0
```

```
CROSSTABS /TABLES SEX BY EMPLOYER /STATISTICS= CHISQ.

Crosstabulation:      SEX
                   By EMPLOYER

EMPLOYER->  Count                                      Row
                           1  |     2  |     3  |    Total
SEX         ---------------------------------------
               1          4   |    3   |    3   |     10
     male                                           47.6
            ---------------------------------------
               2          4   |    4   |    3   |     11
     female                                         52.4
            ---------------------------------------
            Column        8        7        6        21
            Total      38.1     33.3     28.6     100.0


Chi-Square   D.F.   Significance    Min E.F.    Cells with E.F.< 5
---------    ----   ------------    --------    ---------------
 .09545       2        .9534         2.857       6 OF 6 (100.0%)

Number of Missing Observations =             1
```

Fig38.3 Output from the Exercise 22.2 command file (Part 1)

```
CROSSTABS /TABLES SEX BY EMPLOYER BY AREA.
```

Crosstabulation: SEX
             By EMPLOYER
     Controlling for AREA
                                              = 1   north

EMPLOYER->	Count	1	2	3	Row Total
SEX					
male	1	2		1	3 33.3
female	2	3	1	2	6 66.7
Column Total		5 55.6	1 11.1	3 33.3	9 100.0

Crosstabulation: SEX
             By EMPLOYER
     Controlling for AREA
                                              = 2   south

EMPLOYER->	Count	1	2	3	Row Total
SEX					
male	1	2	3	2	7 58.3
female	2	1	3	1	5 41.7
Column Total		3 25.0	6 50.0	3 25.0	12 100.0

```
Number of Missing Observations =       1
```

Fig 38.3 Output from the Exercise 22.2 command file (Part 2)

Exercise 23.1

```
GET /FILE 'a:ex1.sys'.
SET /LISTING 'a:ex6.lis'.
MEANS /TABLES sales BY sex area.
MEANS /TABLES sales BY sex /OPTIONS 6 8 12.
```

The first MEANS command produces tables showing the mean scores on sales for each level of sex (the same table as Fig 23.1) and then a similar table for each level of area. The second MEANS command demonstrates the use of the /OPTIONS subcommand: the output is shown in Fig 38.4. With options 6 and 12, the table includes the sum and variance for each group. Option 8 is included to suppress the printing of value labels; without it, the command will fail. The 'missing case' mentioned in the printout is the respondent whose sex was recorded in the original data file as 3, indicating that their sex was not known.

```
MEANS /TABLES sales BY sex /OPTIONS 6 8 12.

Summaries of    SALES
By levels of    SEX

Variable        Value      Sum        Mean       Std Dev    Variance     Cases

Population:            122470.330  5831.9205  2377.9699  5654740.79       21

SEX                 1  59506.3700  5950.6370  2772.4555  7686509.34       10
SEX                 2  62963.9600  5723.9964  2089.1906  4364717.18       11

   Total Cases =       22
Missing Cases =        1 OR    4.5 PCT.
-------------------------------------------------------------------------
```

Fig 38.4 Extract of output from the Exercise 23.1 command file

Exercise 27.1

```
GET /FILE 'a:ex1.sys'.
SET /LISTING 'a:ex9.lis'.
RANK cust sales.
CORRELATIONS /VARIABLES rcust rsales.
RANK cust BY employer /RANK INTO rnkbyem.
SORT employer.
LIST id employer rnkbyem.
```

The output from these commands is given in Fig 38.5. The RANK command produces two new variables, rcust and rsales, which are the ranked values of cust and sales as the printout indicates. The CORRELATIONS yields the rank correlation between cust and sales as it calculates the correlation between rcust and rsales. In this instance the correlation is .8153, and the two asterisks indicate this is significant at the .001 level.

The second RANK command illustrates the use of the /RANK INTO subcommand. The scores on the variable cust are ranked for each employer separately, as a result of the RANK cust BY employer instruction, and the name of the new variable created by this ranking procedure is defined as rnkbyem (standing for 'rank-by-employer').

In order to obtain a clearer printout of these rnkbyem values, the SORT command is used to have the data sorted according to employer, and the data is then printed out using the LIST command. As can be seen in Fig 38.5, the data for respondents from employer 1 are all listed, then the data for respondents from employer 2 and finally the data for respondents from employer 3.

The column of rnkbyem values in Fig 38.5 shows how the RANK cust BY employer instruction operated: the 8 respondents from employer 1 were ranked from 1 to 8, the 8 respondents from employer 2 were ranked from 1 to 8, and the 6 respondents from employer 3 were ranked from 1 to 6. Some of the rnkbyem values are not whole numbers (e.g. in the employer 1 set, two scores are 7.5000); this is because when two respondents had the same score on cust, they were given the mean value of the ranks appropriate to their scores. For example, the two largest scores on cust for respondents from employer 1 were both 48, corresponding to rank values of 7 and 8; so both these scores are assigned a rank of 7.5.

```
RANK cust sales.

From      New
variable  variable  Label
--------  --------  -----
CUST      RCUST     RANK of CUST
SALES     RSALES    RANK of SALES
----------------------------------------------------------------------

CORRELATIONS /VARIABLES rcust rsales.

Correlations:  RCUST      RSALES
  RCUST        1.0000     .8153**
  RSALES        .8153**   1.0000

N of cases:    22         1-tailed Signif:  * - .01  ** - .001

" . " is printed if a coefficient cannot be computed
----------------------------------------------------------------------

RANK cust BY employer /RANK INTO rnkbyem.

From      New
variable  variable  Label
--------  --------  -----
CUST      RNKBYEM   RANK of CUST by EMPLOYER
----------------------------------------------------------------------

SORT employer.
LIST id employer rnkbyem.

ID EMPLOYER   RNKBYEM
 1        1    6.000
 3        1    7.500
 7        1    5.000
 9        1    4.000
12        1    1.000
17        1    2.000
18        1    7.500
22        1    3.000
 2        2    6.000
 5        2    8.000
 8        2    1.000
11        2    4.500
14        2    2.000
15        2    3.000
20        2    7.000
21        2    4.500
 4        3    6.000
 6        3    3.000
10        3    4.000
13        3    2.000
16        3    5.000
19        3    1.000

Number of cases read =    22   Number of cases listed =    22
```

Fig 38.5 Extract of the output from the Exercise 27.1 command file.

Exercise 28.1

```
GET /FILE 'a:ex1.sys'.
SET /LISTING 'a:ex11.lis'.
RECODE sales (7000 THRU HI = 2) (LO THRU 7000 = 1).
LIST id sales.
```

The output from this command file is shown in Fig 38.6.

```
RECODE sales (7000 THRU HI = 2) (LO THRU 7000 = 1).
LIST id sales.
```

ID	SALES
1	1.00
2	1.00
3	2.00
4	2.00
5	1.00
6	1.00
7	1.00
8	1.00
9	1.00
10	2.00
11	1.00
12	1.00
13	2.00
14	1.00
15	1.00
16	2.00
17	1.00
18	2.00
19	2.00
20	1.00
21	1.00
22	1.00

```
Number of cases read =      22     Number of cases listed =      22
-----------------------------------------------------------------
```

Fig 38.6 Output from the Exercise 28.1 command file

One may wish to confirm that the RECODE has operated as one expected, and list both the original scores and the recoded ones. Once the scores have been recoded, the original scores are lost from the Active File, and so cannot be listed. The way round this is to COMPUTE a new variable, which is simply a copy of the original scores, before the RECODE is carried out. The recoding will not, of course, affect the new variable, and so one retains in the Active File both the original scores and the recoded ones. The command file shown in Fig 38.7 shows how this is achieved. A new variable, osales, is computed by the COMPUTE line. The sales data is then RECODEd, and both osales and the recoded sales are LISTed. The listing (Fig 38.7) shows that the original sales figures from 7000 upward have been recoded as 2, lower values being recoded as 1.

```
COMPUTE osales = sales.
RECODE sales (7000 thru hi = 2)(lo thru 7000 = 1).
LIST id osales sales.
```

```
ID    OSALES      SALES
 1   3450.60       1.00
 2   4984.42       1.00
 3  10432.82       2.00
 4   8235.21       2.00
 5   6441.38       1.00
 6   6497.05       1.00
 7   3835.26       1.00
 8   3819.00       1.00
 9   5723.52       1.00
10   7937.45       2.00
11   4582.44       1.00
12   2005.30       1.00
13   8914.50       2.00
14   3124.20       1.00
15   4222.45       1.00
16   8881.28       2.00
17   3449.35       1.00
18   7882.60       2.00
19   8779.00       2.00
20   5822.68       1.00
21   4004.80       1.00
22   5886.40       1.00

Number of cases read =     22    Number of cases listed =     22
```

Fig 38.7 A command file and output that RECODEs and retains original scores.

Exercise 28.1

```
GET /FILE 'a:ex1.sys'.
SET /LISTING 'a:ex12.lis'.
COMPUTE newv1 = (att1 + att2).
LIST id att1 att2 newv1.
```

In this command file the LIST instruction asks for a listing of the respondents' id and the original att1 and att2 scores as well as newv1, the sum of att1 and att2. The output, shown in Fig 38.8, allows one to check that the program has calculated newv1 in the way one intended.

```
ID ATT1 ATT2   NEWV1
 1    4    5    9.00
 2    4    4    8.00
 3    2    3    5.00
 4    2    3    5.00
 5    2    2    4.00
 6    3    3    6.00
 7    3    2    5.00
 8    4    5    9.00
 9    2    3    5.00
10    1    2    3.00
11    2    3    5.00
```

```
12      2    3      5.00
13      2    2      4.00
14      1    2      3.00
15      5    4      9.00
16      2    2      4.00
17      3    4      7.00
18      2    3      5.00
19      4    3      7.00
20      1    3      4.00
21      3    4      7.00
22      2    3      5.00
```

Number of cases read =   22   Number of cases listed =   22

Fig 38.8 Output from the command file for Exercise 28.1.

Exercise 30.1

```
GET /FILE 'a:ex1.sys'.
SET /LISTING 'a:ex13.lis'.
PROCESS IF (att1 = 1).
DESCRIPTIVES /VARIABLES att3.
PROCESS IF (area = 2).
FREQUENCIES /VARIABLES att2.
```

The output is shown in Fig 38.9. The first table shows the mean, standard deviation, minimum and maximum of scores on att3 for those respondents who scored 1 on att1 (selected by the first PROCESS IF command).

The second table shows the scores on att2 for those respondents who had a score of 2 on the variable area. Note the use of PROCESS IF, not SELECT IF, to achieve this outcome.

```
PROCESS IF (att1=1).
DESCRIPTIVES /VARIABLES att3.
```

Number of Valid Observations (Listwise) =   3.00

Variable	Mean	Std Dev	Minimum	Maximum	N	Label
ATT3	4.33	.58	4	5	3	

```
PROCESS IF (area=2).
FREQUENCIES /VARIABLES att2.
```

ATT2

Value Label	Value	Frequency	Percent	Valid Percent	Cum Percent
	2	5	38.5	38.5	38.5
	3	3	23.1	23.1	61.5
	4	4	30.8	30.8	92.3
	5	1	7.7	7.7	100.0
	TOTAL	13	100.0	100.0	

Valid Cases   13   Missing Cases   0

Fig 38.9 Output from the Exercise 30.1 command file

Appendix B: The basics of statistical analysis

B1 Fundamental definitions
B1.1 Population and sample
B1.2 Descriptive and inferential statistics
B1.3 Scales of measurement
    B1.3.1 Nominal scales
    B1.3.2 Ordinal scales
    B1.3.3 Interval scales
    B1.3.4 Ratio scales
B1.4 Parametric and non-parametric data and tests
B1.5 Dependent and independent variables
B1.6 Within-subjects and between-subjects variables

B2 Measures of central tendency: Mode, Median, Mean

B3 Measures of Variability
B3.1 The concept of variability
B3.2 Range; Interquartile range
B3.3 Variance and standard deviation

B4 Standard error and confidence limits

B5 Frequency distributions
B5.1 Histograms and barcharts
B5.2 The normal distribution curve
B5.3 z scores

B6 Statistical significance and testing hypotheses
B6.1 The concept of statistical significance
B6.2 Significance level
B6.3 Type I and type II errors
B6.4 One and two-tailed hypotheses

B7 Parametric and non-parametric tests

B8 Analyzing nominal data: Chi-square
B8.1 The two-way chi-square
B8.2 The one-sample chi-square
B8.3 Essential requirements for the chi-square test

B9 Parametric tests
B9.1 The t-test
    B9.1.1 The independent t-test
    B9.1.2 The related, paired or within-subjects t-test
B9.2 Analysis of Variance
    B9.2.1 Basic concepts
    B9.2.2 Two-way anovar
    B9.2.3 Range tests

B10 Correlation
B10.1 The concept of correlation
B10.2 Parametric correlation: Pearson product moment correlation
B10.3 Non-parametric correlation: Spearman Rank (rho)
B10.4 Regression
B10.5 Multiple regression

B11 Nonparametric tests
B11.1 Deciding which test to use
B11.2 Wilcoxon test
B11.3 Friedman test
B11.4 Mann-Whitney test
B11.5 Kruskal-Wallis test

B12 Interpreting the outcome of a significance test

The main body of this book assumes that the user knows the statistical analyses that are needed, and describes the procedures for getting SPSS to provide particular statistics and apply specific statistical tests. The aim of this appendix is to remind readers of the principles of statistical analysis, so that they can decide which statistics they need for their particular sets of data. It is not intended as a substitute for a text on statistics, but should be seen rather as an aide-memoire for those who have temporarily forgotten what the various statistical procedures are used for.

B1 Fundamental definitions

B1.1 Population and sample

A population is an entire set of objects or people, such as the residents of France or Australian nine-year olds. A sample is a subset of a population, and in the majority of research analysis one works with a sample of a population. Usually one hopes to generalize from the sample to the population, as in opinion polls where perhaps 1,000 people are asked for their opinion, the results obtained from this sample are generalized to the whole voting population of the country, and statements are made about the popularity of political parties in the country as a whole.

Whether it is valid to generalize from the sample to the population depends upon the size of the sample and whether it is representative of the population: does it have the same characteristics as the population of which it is a subset?

B1.2 Descriptive and inferential statistics

Descriptive statistics are used to describe and summarize sets of data. They answer questions such as "What was the average age of the patients who were admitted to the local hospital with a heart attack in the last six months?"

Inferential statistics are used in generalizing from a sample to a wider population, and in testing hypotheses, deciding whether the data is consistent with the research prediction.

B1.3 Scales of measurement

B1.3.1 Nominal scales

Nominal scales are where the numbers are used merely as a label. For example, we may code sex of respondent as 1 or 2, with 1 meaning male and 2 meaning female. The size of the numbers is meaningless, and 2 is not bigger or better than 1 (we could just as easily used 1 to indicate female and 2 to indicate male).

B1.3.2 Ordinal scales

In ordinal or rank scales there is some correspondence between the size of the numbers and the magnitude of the quality represented by the numbers. A common ordinal scale is position in a race. One knows that the person who came first (position 1) was faster than the person who came second (position 2), who was in turn faster than the person who came third (position 3). But the numbers 1, 2 and 3 do not tell you anything about the size of the differences between the three people. The winner, number 1, may have been well ahead of numbers 2 and 3, or number 1 may have just beaten number 2 with number three trailing far behind.

B1.3.3 Interval scales

With interval scales, the numbers do represent the magnitude of the differences. A frequently-cited example is the Celsius temperature scale, where the difference between 20 and 30 degrees is the same as the difference between 30 and 40 degrees. But note that the Celsius scale is not a ratio scale: something with a temperature of 40 degrees is not twice as hot as something with a temperature of 20 degrees.

B1.3.4 Ratio scales

In ratio scales, there is a true zero point and the ratio of the numbers reflects the ratios of the attribute measured. For example, an object 30 cm long is twice the length of an object 15 cm long.

B1.4 Parametric and non-parametric data and tests

The distinction between types of scale is important as the type of scale determines which type of statistical analysis is appropriate. In order to use the parametric statistical tests, one should have used an interval or ratio scale of measurement. If the data is measured on an ordinal scale, one should use non-parametric tests. For nominal scales, some of the non-parametric tests, such as chi-square, are appropriate.

B1.5 Dependent and independent variables

In experiments, the experimenter manipulates the independent variable, and measures any consequential alterations in the dependent variable. If the experiment has been designed and carried out properly, it is assumed that the changes in the dependent variable are the results of the changes in the independent variable.

The distinction between dependent and independent variables is not restricted to research using the experimental method. When correlational studies are performed, one also has a dependent variable and independent variables. For example, there has been a considerable amount of research into the factors associated with students' success and failure at their courses. This research has correlated students' study habits and personality to their course grades; the grades form the dependent variable and the study habits and personality are independent variables.

B1.6 Within-subjects and between-subjects variables

If the same respondents are used in two or more conditions of an experiment, one has a within-subjects, or repeated-measures, design. When different respondents feature in the different conditions, one has a between-subjects, or independent groups, design. It is, of course, possible to combine the two into a mixed design. For example, one might have data on men and women's ability to drive when they have had no alcohol and when they have had a certain amount of alcohol. If one used the same subjects in the no-alcohol and the with-alcohol conditions, sex would be a between-subjects variable and alcohol would be a within-subjects variable.

Different statistical tests are appropriate for within-subjects and between-subjects variables, and it is important to ensure one is using the proper test for the data being analysed.

B2 Measures of central tendency: mode, median, mean

Given a set of scores or readings, one usually requires a single figure which indicates the 'typical' value of the set. There are three alternative figures one can use: mode, median and mean. Table B1 shows the scores of 22 respondents on an attitude-scale question, where the possible responses were coded as 1, 2, 3, 4 or 5 (it is taken from the file of data used in the main text of this book).

Table B1. Scores on an attitude scale question

Respondent	Response
01	1
15	1
19	1
02	3
06	3
08	3
11	3
17	3
21	3
22	3
04	4
05	4
09	4
12	4
13	4
14	4
16	4
18	4
20	4
03	5
07	5
10	5

The MODE is the most frequently occurring value, in this instance 4.

The MEDIAN is the value that divides the distribution of scores in half: 50% of the scores fall below the median and 50% fall above it. When the scores are in ascending order, if there are an odd number of scores, the median is the middle score. If there are an even number of scores, average the two middle scores. In Table B1, there are 22 scores, so the median is obtained by taking the average of the 11th and 12th scores; in Table B1 these are both 4, so the median is 4.

The arithmetic MEAN is obtained by totalling the scores and dividing the sum by the number of scores. In Table B1, the total of the scores is 75, and the mean is therefore 75/22 = 3.41.

B3 Measures of Variability

B3.1 The concept of variability

An important feature of a set of data is the spread or variation of the scores in the set. We need to be able to express the variation within a set of scores as well as the central value (mode, median or mean) of the set. Table B2 shows the number of customers visited by male and female sales personnel (the figures are again taken from the file used in the main text of this book).

Table B2. Customers visited by male and female personnel

Males subject	n visits	Females subject	n visits
2:	46	1:	43
3:	48	6:	72
4:	83	7:	42
8:	28	11:	39
9:	41	14:	33
10:	76	15:	36
12:	30	16:	79
13:	68	18:	48
17:	38	19:	58
21:	39	20:	60
		22:	40

B3.2 Range; Interquartile range

The RANGE of a set of scores is simply the difference between the highest and lowest scores. So for the males in Table B2, the range is 83 –28 = 55 and for females the range is 79 − 33 = 46. Range gives an indication of the spread of the scores, but of course it depends completely on just two figures from the whole set, the highest and the lowest. One very low or very high score will produce a large increase in the range, and this might be quite misleading.

One alternative measure is the Interquartile Range. As mentioned earlier, the MEDIAN is that score which divides the set into two halves, with half the scores falling below the median and half the scores falling above it. The median is the 50th percentile, which means 50% of the scores fall below it. We can also have a 25th percentile, which is the score below which 25% of the scores fall, a 75th percentile, a 90th percentile etc. The interquartile range is the difference between the 25th and 75th percentiles. The Interquartile Range for the two sets of data shown in Table B2 are 34 for males and 21 for females. The semi-interquartile range is the interquartile range divided by 2.

Unlike the range, the interquartile range is not affected by a single score which is much greater or much less than the others. But it does use only two figures from the set to express the variability in the set, and so ignores most of the numbers.

B3.3 Variance and standard deviation

A better measure of variation would be one that used all the numbers in the set, not just two of them. This problem is tackled by looking at the mean of the set of scores, and taking the difference between each score and the mean. If one adds these deviations from the mean, the total is zero: so this figure is not going to be very helpful as an indication of the variation in the set of scores! The way round this is to square each of the deviations, which gets rid of all the negative numbers, and then add them up to obtain a sum of squared deviations. In order to get an idea of the variation in the set, it is sensible to take the average of the squared deviations. The sum of the squared deviations divided by n is known as the VARIANCE of the set of scores.

(Note: If you are using data from a sample as an estimate of a wider population, then divide by n-1 to obtain a better estimate of the population variance.)

The square root of the variance is the STANDARD DEVIATION, and is the number used to express the variation in the set of scores.

B4 Standard error and confidence limits

Inferential statistics involve estimating the characteristics of a population from the data obtained from a sample of that population. For example, one uses the mean of the sample to estimate the population mean. If one took a large set of samples from the population, the means of the samples would form a normal distribution. The standard deviation of that distribution is given by taking the standard deviation of the sample and dividing it by the square root of n, the number in the sample. This is the

Standard Error, and it allows one to state the probability that the true mean of the population is within specified limits. From the properties of the normal distribution, it can be deduced that there is a 95% probability that the true mean of the population is within plus or minus approximately 2 standard errors of the sample mean. Suppose you have taken a sample of 100 subjects from a population and found that the mean of the sample is 50, and the standard deviation is 10. The standard error is 1.0 (10/square root of 100). One can conclude that the true mean of the population has a 95% probability of being within the limits 50 +or- (1 multiplied by 2) = 50 +or- 2 i.e between 48 and 52. So the 95% confidence interval means that there is a 95% probability that the true mean is between the limits specified.

B5 Frequency distributions

B5.1 Histograms and barcharts

A frequency distribution shows the number of times each score occurs in the set of scores under examination. Histograms and barcharts are graphical displays of the frequency distribution of the scores. In SPSS, a histogram shows values of the variable where there are no instances of that value being obtained, but these zero-frequency values are not shown in a barchart.

A frequency distribution can be symmetrical or skewed. If it is roughly symmetrical, the mean can be used as the measure of central tendency but if it is skewed the median should be used rather than the mean. A normal distribution, which is symmetrical, has a skewness statistic of zero. Kurtosis measures the extent to which observations are clustered in the tails; for a normal distribution, the kurtosis statistic is zero.

B5.2 The normal distribution curve

The normal distribution curve is fundamental to statistical analysis. It is a frequency distribution: if we take large sets of data for biological functions such as body height, the resulting frequency distribution is a normal curve.

The normal distribution curve is symmetrical, with the 'middle' being equal to the mean. One can measure off the horizontal axis in standard deviations from the mean. Very nearly all the distribution lies between −3sd and +3sd from the mean. Tables of the normal curve, found in most statistics texts, give the proportion of the curve falling above and below any position on the horizontal axis. From such tables, it is easy to find the proportion of the curve between any two points on the horizontal axis.

B5.3 z scores

When a series of parametric data is transformed so that it has a mean of zero and a standard deviation of 1.00, the scores are known as z-scores.

B6 Statistical significance and testing hypotheses

B6.1 Statistical significance

The data in Table B3, taken from the data file used in the main part of this book, shows the number of customers visited by the sales personnel of two employers (labelled 2 and 3).

Table B3 Customer visits by sales personnel from two employers

Employer 2 subject	n visits	Employer 3 subject	n visits
2:	46	4:	83
5:	71	6:	72
8:	28	10:	76
11:	39	13:	68
14:	33	16:	79
15:	36	19:	58
20:	60		
21:	39		
Mean:	44.00	Mean:	72.67

The question that the researcher asks is: "is there a statistically significant difference between the means of the scores of the two groups of sales personnel?"

In Table B3, group 2 has the smaller mean, and so you might wish to conclude that these people made fewer visits. But look at subject 5 in group 2 and subject 19 in group 3: the group 3 member has a smaller score than the group 2 member. So if you took just those two subjects, you could not say that group 2 had the lower score.

If there were no difference between the two groups, their mean scores would be the 'same'. This does not imply, of course, that they would be identical, because responses almost always show some variance (variability). This random, unexplained variation is due to chance. For example, the variation in the scores for group 2 in Table B3 is variation due to chance. The mean for subjects 2, 5, 8 and 11 in group 2 is 46 and the mean for subjects 14, 15, 20 and 21 from the same group is 42. The difference between these two means is simply due to chance, random variation. It arises even though both these subgroups come from one 'population' (the complete set of scores given by group 2 subjects).

Our question now is: is the difference between the means of group 2 and group 3 also simply due to chance?

If the difference between the means of group 2 and group 3 is due to chance, then groups 2 and 3 are samples from the same 'population', just as subjects 2-11 and 14-21 of group 2 are samples from one population.

To decide whether groups 2 and 3 are samples from one population or are 'really' different and come from different populations, one applies a test of statistical significance. The significance tests let you estimate how likely it is that the data from the separate groups of subjects come from one population. If it is unlikely that they came from the same population, you can conclude that they didn't, and that they came from separate populations.

In significance testing we look at the difference between the scores and compare it with the amount of variation in the scores which arises due to chance. If the chance variation is likely to have produced the difference between our groups, we say the difference is non-significant, which means the difference probably did arise from chance variation. We have to conclude there is no 'real' or statistically significant difference between the groups, and they are both from the same underlying population.

B6.2 Significance level

If the difference between two groups is likely to have arisen from chance variation in the scores, we conclude there is no real 'significant' difference between them. On the other hand, if the difference between the groups is unlikely to have been brought about by the chance variation in scores, we conclude there is a real, statistically significant difference between the groups.

But what do we mean by likely? It is conventional to use the 5% probability level (also referred to as alpha-level): what does this mean? If there is a 5% (also written as 0.05) or smaller probability that the difference between the groups arose from chance variation, we conclude it did not arise from chance and that there is a 'real' difference. If there is more than 5% (0.05) probability that the difference arose from chance, we conclude the difference is not a real one.

You may well ask why we use 5%; and the answer is that it is merely convention. We could use 10% (.10), 1% (.01), .5% (.005).

B6.3 Type I and type II errors

A significance test allows us to say how likely it is that the difference between the groups of subjects' scores was due to chance. If there is a 5% or smaller probability that the difference is due to chance variation, we conclude that it was not caused by chance. But we can never be sure: there is always a possibility that the difference we find was due to chance even when we conclude that it was not. Conversely, we may find a difference and conclude that it is not significant (that it was due to random or chance variability in the scores) when in fact it was a 'real' difference. So there are two types of error we may make. These are referred to as type I and type II errors.

A Type I error occurs when we reject a null hypothesis when it is true i.e we say there is a 'real' difference between the groups when in fact the difference is not 'real'. The probability that we shall make a type I error is given by the significance level we use. With an alpha or significance level of 5%, on 5% of occasions we are likely to make a type I error and say the groups differ when they do not.

We can reduce the probability of making a type I error by using a more stringent level of significance: 1%, say, rather than 5%. But as we reduce the chances of making a type I error, we increase the likelihood that we shall make a type II error, and say there is no difference between the groups when there is one.

B6.4 One and two-tailed hypotheses

Referring back to Table B3, the aim of the study was to test the hypothesis that there is a difference between the scores of the two groups of subjects. (The null hypothesis is that there is no difference between the scores of the two groups of subjects.)

Note that the hypothesis is that there is a difference. It does NOT say group 3 will score higher or lower than group 2, merely that group 3 and group 2 will differ. This is a two-tailed hypothesis: group 3 could score less than group 2 or group 3 could score more than group 2.

If we had stated the hypothesis that group 2 will score less than group 3 (i.e if we predict the direction of the difference between the groups), then we would have had a one-tail hypothesis. Similarly, if our hypothesis were that group 2 would score more than group 3, this would also be a one-tailed hypothesis since we would still be predicting the direction of the difference between the groups.

The distinction between one and two-tailed hypotheses is important when applying significance tests. Most SPSS printouts show the two-tailed probability of the calculated statistic. If you have stated a one-tailed hypothesis before examining the data, you can use the one-tailed probabilities, which are the two-tailed probabilities divided by 2.

B7 Parametric and non-parametric tests

Parametric significance tests rest upon assumptions that the data has certain characteristics. The assumptions for using parametric tests are:

1. Observations are drawn from a population with a normal distribution; (note that

the population is normally distributed, not necessarily the sample of scores taken from it)

2. The sets of data being compared have approximately equal variances (this is referred to as homogeneity of variance). If the groups are of equal size (n1 = n2), then this assumption is not so important as it is when the two groups have unequal n's. If the groups being compared have an n of 10, it is acceptable for the variance of one group to be up to three times as large as that of another. With larger groups, you can still use the parametric tests if one group has a variance double that of another.

3. The data is measured on an interval scale.

If the data does not meet these assumptions, you can convert the data into a non-parametric form and then apply one of the non-parametric tests. The commonest way of converting data into a form for non-parametric analysis is to rank it.

B8 Analysing nominal data: Chi-square

B8.1 The two-way chi-square

The chi-square test is used with nominal (frequency) data, where subjects are assigned to categories. For example, a recent survey asked adults whether they thought 'adult' films should be shown uncut on TV. Data was reported for different age groups and sexes. The results for men might have looked like this:

Table B4. Male respondents' views on showing uncut films on TV (hypothetical data).

Respondents' age	Number saying 'yes'	Number saying 'no'
under 60	75	35
over 60	50	30

The cell entries show the number of respondents of that age-group giving the response indicated at the top of the column.

The chi-square test is used for analyzing this type of frequency data, and is concerned with answering the question: Is there a relationship between the variable that distinguishes the rows (age, in the example above) and the variable that distinguishes the columns (response 'yes' or 'no' in the example)?

The test rests upon comparing the observed frequencies with the 'expected' frequencies which would be obtained if there were no relationship between the row variable and the column variable. (The expected frequencies are calculated for each cell in the table by multiplying the appropriate row and column totals and dividing by N.)

The SPSS output from a chi-square test states the probability of the value of chi-square having arisen by chance.

B8.2 The one-sample chi-square

The test can be used with just one sample of data. In chapter 26, the example of suicide rates for different months is used to explain the way one would employ the one-sample chi-square.

B8.3 Essential requirements for the chi-square test

The chi-square test is only valid if three conditions are met. First, the data must be independent: no subject can appear in more than one cell of the table. In Table B4, this condition is met since any person is either under or over 60 and any person responded yes or no.

Secondly, no more than 20% of the Expected Frequencies in the table can be less than 5. So if you have a 2 x 5 table which has 10 cells, the test will be invalid if 3 expected frequencies are below 5. If your data fails to meet this criterion, you have to collect more data or it may be possible to change the table; for example you could merge groups together. SPSS output from the two-way chi-square test indicates the number of cells with an expected frequency of less than 5, and shows the number of cells as a percentage, so you can readily see if the data meets this criterion or not.

Thirdly, no cell should have an expected frequency of less than 1. The output from SPSS tells you the minimum expected frequency so it is simple to check whether this condition has been met.

B9 Parametric tests

B9.1 The t-test

The t-test is a parametric test which is used to test whether the difference between the means of two sets of scores is statistically significant.

There is one important feature of the t-test. If you have more than two sets of data, it is not acceptable to do multiple t-tests. For example, assume we have measured the performance of three groups of subjects (groups A, B and C) on a test of memory. It is not valid to do one t-test to compare groups A and B, another to compare B and C and another to compare A and C. The reason is that multiple t-testing distorts the probability levels: when you believe you are using the 5% level, you are not. If you have data from three groups, you should use a test designed to cope with that situation. For parametric data, this is the analysis of variance. For non-parametric data you can use Friedman's test (repeated measures) or the Kruskal-Wallis test (independent groups).

You need to be sure about when it is appropriate to use the independent t-test and when to use the related test. (Essentially, if you use a related t-test when you should have used an independent one, you may conclude that the difference is significant when it is not- a type I error).

B9.1.1 The independent t-test

The independent t-test is used to compare the means of two groups of subjects i.e when different individuals were allocated to group 1 and group 2. It involves taking the difference between the means, and expressing that difference as a ratio of the variability of the scores in the two sets.

B9.1.2 The related, paired or within-subjects t-test

Use the related t-test when comparing the means of two sets of scores obtained with the same subjects in both conditions. This form of t-test involves calculating the difference between the two scores for each respondent, finding the mean of these differences and expressing it as a ratio of the variability of the difference scores.

B9.2 Analysis of Variance

B9.2.1 Basic concepts

When you have three or more sets of parametric data, you may want to test the hypothesis that the scores of the various groups differ. You cannot use the t-test, as that only compares two groups and it is not proper to carry out multiple t-tests on three sets of data. The parametric analysis of variance is the technique to employ; it makes the same assumptions as the t-test, so should only be used when those assumptions (see section B7 above) can be made.

As the name implies analysis of variance examines the variance within the whole sets of scores. Imagine we have sets of data from three separate groups of subjects, and want to know whether there is a difference between the three groups. If there were no difference between the groups (the null hypothesis is true) their data would all come from the same population, and the three sets of data would all have the same means and the same variances. The variance of each group would be an estimate of the population variance (variance due to random fluctuations between subjects, known as error variance because it arises due to chance alterations in our readings). Our best estimate of the population variance is given by calculating the mean of the variances of the three groups. So by looking at the average variance of the three groups, we can get an estimate of the error variance.

Again, if the null hypothesis is true, the means of the three groups will be the same, and the variance of the means (i.e how much the means differ from each other) will be very small. (We would expect it to be the same as the population variance.) The variance of the means of the three groups is known as the treatment variance. So if the null hypothesis were true, and the three groups did not differ from each other, the variance between the means (the treatment variance) would equal the error variance; if we divided the treatment variance by the error variance, the answer would be 1.00.

If the null hypothesis is not true, there is a difference between the three groups. The variance of the means will be larger than the error variance. If we divide the variance of the means (the treatment variance) by the error variance, we shall get a number bigger than 1.00.

In the analysis of variance, we compare the treatment variance with the error variance to test the hypothesis that there is a significant difference between the means.

The one-way anovar is obtained using either the MEANS or the ONEWAY procedures. The crucial statistic is the value of F, the ratio of the mean square due to treatments (between groups) and the mean square due to error (within groups). The output shows the value of F and the probability of it arising by chance; if this value is less than 0.05 one can conclude there is a significant difference between the groups.

B9.2.2 Two-way anovar

Analysis of variance can be extended to experiments in which there are two or more independent variables. Imagine we have measured the performance of young (under 30) and old (over 50) subjects at two different times of day (2 am and 2 pm), and used different subjects in each group so there were four separate groups altogether. We might be interested in knowing whether performance differed according to the subject's age, differed according to time of day, and whether there was an interaction between these variables. Interaction means that the effect of one variable was influenced by the other; for example, we might find that the difference between performance at 2 pm and 2 am was less for the younger subjects than for the older ones. If this were so, the analysis of variance would show a significant interaction term.

When both variables are between-subjects, as in the example just given, the ANOVA procedure is used.

The analysis of variance can be applied to within-subjects (repeated measures) studies, where the same subjects are used in different conditions. For example, we would have a repeated measures experiment if we had carried out our time-of-day / age of subjects experiment, and tested the same respondents at 2 am and 2 pm. To analyse this kind of experiment requires the MANOVA procedure not covered here as it is not part of the base module of SPSS/PC+ or SPSS for Windows.

B9.2.3 Range tests

If the analysis of variance indicates a significant F value, you can conclude there is a difference between the three or more groups that were compared. But the anovar does not indicate which groups differed from which: was group A different from both B and C, or were A and B very similar but both different from group C? To answer these questions, one needs to use multiple comparison procedures. A number of these are available, including the Tukey test, the Scheffe test, the Duncan test. The relative merits of these tests is too advanced to be considered here, but the Tukey HSD (Honestly Significant Differences) test is widely used.

B10 Correlation

B10.1 The concept of correlation

A correlation expresses the extent to which two variables vary together. A positive correlation means that as one variable increases so does the other. For example, there is a strong positive correlation between size of foot and height, and a weak positive correlation between how much one is paid and one's job satisfaction. A negative correlation is when one variable increases as the other decreases; for example, there is a negative correlation between job satisfaction and absenteeism: the more satisfied people are with their job, the lower the amount of absenteeism they show.

Correlations vary between –1.00 and +1.00; a correlation of 0.00 means there is no relationship between the two variables. For example, one would expect the correlation between size of foot and job satisfaction to be about 0.00 (although I have never seen any data on this relationship!).

There are two vital factors about correlations which one should bear in mind. The first is summarized in the aphorism "Correlation does not equal causation": if variables A and B are correlated, one cannot say that A causes B. It could be that B causes A, or they may both be related to some other factor that produces the variation in A and B. Some examples: absenteeism and job satisfaction are negatively correlated, but one cannot conclude that low job satisfaction causes absenteeism; it is possible that being absent a lot causes the feelings of low job satisfaction. The positive correlation between foot size and height does not mean that having a large foot makes you grow; foot size and overall height are both caused by a common genetic factor. However, correlations are used to predict one variable from another. Knowing someone's foot size, one can predict how tall they are better than one could if you did not know their foot size.

The second crucial point about simple correlations is that they indicate how far there is a linear relationship between the two variables. In a curvilinear relationship, low scores on x are associated with low scores on y, medium scores on x are associated with high scores on y and high scores on x are associated with low scores on y. This relationship would not appear in a correlation coefficient, which would have a low value (about 0). It is wise to plot the two variables in a scattergram, even if the correlation coefficient is low, in case the two variables are related in a non-linear fashion.

B10.2 Parametric correlation: Pearson product moment correlation

This is the parametric measure of correlation, and measures the relationship between two variables which have both been measured on an interval scale.

B10.3 Non-parametric correlation: Spearman Rank (rho)

This is a non-parametric correlation and can be used when data is ordinal rather than interval.

B10.4 Regression

When two variables are correlated, one can predict the level of an individual on variable x from their standing on variable y (or vice versa: one can predict height from foot size or one can predict foot size from height). When you have a scattergram it is possible to draw in the best-fitting straight line that represents the relationship between x and y. The best-fitting line is known as the regression line and it can be expressed as an equation of the form x = c + by, where c is the intercept and b the slope.

The correlation coefficient squared ($r2$) indicates how much of the variance in y is explained by x. So if x correlates with y 0.6, then .36 (36%) of the variance in y is explained by the variance in x.

B10.5 Multiple regression

This refers to using more than one variable to predict the dependent variable. Job satisfaction is correlated with pay and with level of occupation. So one can predict job satisfaction from pay and one can predict it from job satisfaction; but one may get a better prediction if one uses both pay and job level as predictors. So one would have an equation of the form:

job satisfaction = pay multiplied by a + level of job multiplied by b

This is an example of a multiple regression equation, where the dependent variable is related to a number of independent, or predictor, variables. Each predictor variable is multiplied by a weighting, reflecting its importance in determining the dependent, or predicted, variable. The weighting is known as the regression coefficient for that variable. In multiple regression analysis, one investigates which variables add to one's ability to predict the dependent variable, and the weighting they should have.

There are a number of alternative techniques that one can use in solving a multiple regression problem, using the /METHOD subcommand of the REGRESSION procedure. For example, one can force all the predictor variables to be included in the equation, or one can have the program calculate the predictive power of each one and only include those which add to the accuracy with which the dependent variable is predicted. The SPSS Manuals provides full details on the various methods.

B11 Nonparametric tests

B11.1 Deciding which test to use

When the assumptions underlying parametric tests are not met, non-parametric tests can be applied. The chi-square test (section 8 above) deals with nominal (frequency) data. The four non-parametric tests described in this section are used to analyze the subjects' dependent variable measures.

To decide which test to apply you can follow this decision tree:

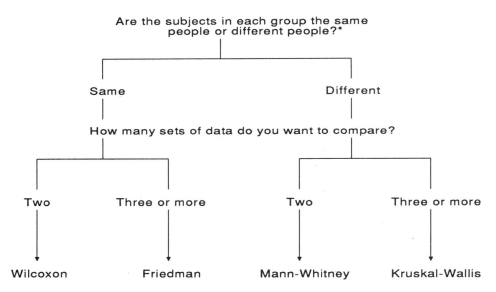

*If you have formed matched groups of subjects, you can assume you have the 'same' people in the groups i.e it is a within-Ss experiment.

B11.2 Wilcoxon test

If you have carried out a within-subjects experiment, and have two scores for each subject, the Wilcoxon test is used to see whether there is a significant difference between the subjects' scores under the two conditions.

It involves calculating the differences between the scores for each subject, and ranking the difference scores, giving rank 1 to the smallest difference etc, but ignoring the sign of the difference. Any subjects where the difference score is 0 are dropped from the analysis. The + or – signs of the difference scores are assigned to the rank values, and the sum of the rank-values obtained for the + and − signed ranks separately.

The Wilcoxon test rests on the argument that if there is no difference between the two sets of scores, there will be about the same number of small + differences as there are small − differences, and about the same number of large + differences as there are large − differences. So the sum of the ranks for + differences will be about the same as the sum of the ranks for the − differences. If the sums of + differences are very dissimilar to the sum of the − differences, then it is likely there is a reliable difference between the two sets of scores.

B11.3 Friedman test

This is used to compare three or more groups of matched subjects. A table is created where each row is the data for one subject, and the data within each row is ranked. The sum of ranks (T) for each column is calculated.

Friedman's test is concerned with establishing whether the rank totals of each column differ more than would be expected by chance; if there were no difference between the conditions, the rank totals would be more or less the same.

B11.4 Mann-Whitney

This is used to compare two sets of data obtained from independent groups. The whole collection of scores are ranked, the sum of the rank values of each subgroup is calculated, and a U statistic is then calculated. The value of U is transformed into a z-value in the SPSS output for this test.

B11.5 Kruskal-Wallis

This test is used with three or more independent groups (between subjects design). The method is reminiscent of the Mann-Whitney, in that it involves ranking all the scores and then calculating the sum of ranks for each group. The SPSS output gives a value of chi-square and its probability.

B12 Interpreting the outcome of a significance test

Understanding what a significance test tells you is the most important part of statistical analysis: doing all the proper tests and getting the correct answers is no good if you then misunderstand what the outcome means! Unfortunately, in the drive to do the computations, some investigators forget that the interpretation is the rationale for the whole procedure. So try to remember some basic principles:

1. If the test tells you the difference between groups is not significant, you must conclude there is no difference, even though the mean scores are not identical.

2. If the difference between groups is statistically significant, this does NOT necessarily mean that it is practically meaningful or significant in the everyday sense. For example, in a study of people's ability to remember car licence plates, one group's score remained the same on two test occasions so the increase was 0, whereas another group's score increased from 3.22 to 3.42, an increase of 0.20; the difference was statistically significant. But it is a subjective judgement, not a statistical one, as to whether the increase of 0.20 for the second group has any practical importance.

3. The assumption behind the experimental method is that one can conclude that significant changes in the dependent variable are caused by the changes in the independent variable. But the validity of this assumption depends on one having used a properly designed and controlled experiment: just because one has a significant difference between group A and group B doe NOT mean you can necessarily conclude the difference was due to the changes in the independent variable. If the experiment was confounded, and the different groups differed systematically on another variable in addition to the independent variable, no clear explanation of the differences in the dependent variable can be given. Imagine we compare two schemes for teaching reading: group A has one scheme and group B the other. We find that group B learn to read after a shorter period of instruction. Can we conclude that the scheme used by group B is 'better'? We now discover that all the children in group B are from a higher socio-economic group than the children in group A (i.e the experiment was confounded). This means that differences between the group's reading may have been due to home background, not the reading scheme they were given. So the statistical significance of the result does not by itself give us any grounds for concluding that the independent variable brought about the changes in the dependent variable.

4. Avoid the temptation to take the level of significance as an index of the magnitude of the experimental effect. By convention one usually uses the 5% significance level, but one can use a more stringent one, and find that a difference between groups is significant not only at 5% but also at 1% or 0.1%. Even eminent researchers have been known to argue that a difference significant at 1% is somehow more 'real' than one significant at 5%. This is NOT a valid interpretation. If the result of your analysis is significant at the level you are using (usually 5%), just accept that and do not give in to the temptation to conclude that a difference significant at 1% is 'better'!

Appendix C: The menu structures

One of the oddities about the SPSS manuals, even that for version 5, is that they do not include a simple diagram of the menu structure so that one can see where the various procedures are located. This omission is more annoying as related procedures are not always located in the same menu: for example, the one-way analysis of variance is, in version 5, in the Compare Means subsection of the Statistics menu, but the two-way analysis of variance is under a separate ANOVA Models submenu. Users tend, not unreasonably, to think of analysis of variance first, and then decide whether it is a one-way or two-way one they want. So it would be more helpful if both were in the same menu. But the user has to work within the system as provided, and so the listings below are intended to assist you find the procedures you need.

40.1 Summary of the menu structure in SPSS/PC+

This summary only shows a small section of the menu system of SPSS/PC+ which goes to at least six levels, and contains hundreds of entries, so that a complete map would be unwieldy. Once you are familiar with the system you can explore the various entries at the different levels.

In the menus, a word in CAPITALS is a command you can paste into the scratchpad by putting the cursor over it and pressing ⏎. If an entry is preceded by ~, it is a compulsory component of that command. When using ANOVA, for example, the command line must include /VARIABLES and the variables must be specified by name. A menu entry in lower case letters cannot be pasted into the scratchpad by pressing ⏎; they may lead to submenus. When items have to be typed in, a typing window may be presented automatically or you can obtain a typing-in window with Alt +T and then key in the details needed.

The main commands mentioned in the text are shown in the left-hand column, in alphabetical order. The second column shows the main menu entry and submenu entries to select to reach the submenu that contains the command shown in the left-hand column. The right hand column shows the more important entries in the submenu below the entry in the left-hand column. So, for example, to find the command COMPUTE from the main menu top level, select the 'modify data or files' entry; from the submenu then revealed, select the 'modify data values' entry. COMPUTE will be in the submenu then shown. If you move the menu cursor so it is over COMPUTE and press the right-arrow key, another submenu will be revealed, and it contains (among other items) '~target', '~=' and '~instructions'. The presence of useful items in the next sublevel down is shown by ----.

PROCEDURE COMMAND	ROUTE FROM TOP LEVEL OF MAIN MENU	SUBMENU'S MAIN CONTENTS
AGGREGATE	modify data or files manipulate files	~/OUTFILE --- ~/BREAK --- ~aggregate variables ---
ANOVA	analyze data comparing group means	~/VARIABLES --- /OPTIONS --- /STATISTICS ---
AUTORECODE	modify data or files	~/VARIABLES modify data values~/INTO
CHISQUARE (one-sample)	analyze data other NPAR TESTS	~variable list
COMPUTE	modify data or files modify data values	~target ~= ~instructions ---
CORRELATIONS	analyze data correlation & regression	~/VARIABLES --- /STATISTICS ---
COUNT	modify data or files modify data values	~target ~= ~variables ~() ---
CROSSTABS	analyze data descriptive statistics	~/TABLES --- /OPTIONS --- /STATISTICS ---
DATA LIST	read or write data	FILE* FIXED/ ---
DESCRIPTIVES	analyze data descriptive statistics	~/VARIABLES /OPTIONS --- /STATISTICS ---
DOS	run DOS or other pgms	
EXAMINE	analyze data descriptive statistics	~/VARIABLES --- /PLOT --- /STATISTICS ---
FINISH		
FLIP	modify data or files manipulate files	/VARIABLES

FREQUENCIES	analyze data descriptive statistics	~/VARIABLES /FORMAT — /BARCHART — /HISTOGRAM — /PERCENTILES /STATISTICS —
FRIEDMAN	analyze data other NPAR TESTS	~variable list
GET	read or write data	~/FILE* /DROP
IF	modify data or files modify data values	~condition — ~target ~= ~instructions —
JOIN ADD	modify data or files manipulate files	~/FILE —
JOIN MATCH	modify data or files manipulate files	~/FILE —
KRUSKAL-WALLIS	analyze data other NPAR TESTS	~variable list ~BY ~grouping variable
LIST	analyze data reports and tables	/VARIABLES /CASES —
MANN-WHITNEY	analyze data other NPAR TESTS	~test variable ~BY ~grouping variable
MEANS	analyze data descriptive statistics	~/TABLES — /OPTIONS — /STATISTICS —
MISSING VALUE	read or write data labels and formatting	~variables ()
MODIFY VARS	read or write data	/RENAME —
N	modify data or files select or weight data	~n of cases
ONEWAY	analyze data comparing group means	~/VARIABLES — /RANGES — /OPTIONS — /STATISTICS —
PLOT	graph data	/FORMAT — /TITLE* /VERTICAL — /HORIZONTAL — /VSIZE /HSIZE ~/PLOT —

PROCESS IF	modify data or files select or weight data	~() ---
RANK	modify data or files modify data values	~variables order --- BY ranking functions ---
RECODE	modify data or files modify data values	~variables () ---
REGRESSION	analyze data correlation & regression	~/VARIABLES --- /DESCRIPTIVES --- ~/DEPENDENT ~/METHOD --- residual analysis ---
REPORT	analyze data reports and tables	/FORMAT --- ~/VARIABLES --- /TITLE --- /BREAK --- /SUMMARY --- /OUTFILE"
SAMPLE	modify data or files select or weight data	sampling fraction FROM
SAVE	read or write data	/OUTFILE"
SELECT IF	modify data or files select or weight data	~() ---
SET	session control and info	output --- operations ---
SORT	modify data or files manipulate files	sort variable(s) (A) (D)
SPSS MANAGER	session control and info	STATUS
SUBTITLE"	session control and info titles and comments	
TITLE"	session control and info titles and comments	
T-TEST	analyze data comparing group means	/GROUPS --- /VARIABLES /PAIRS ---
VALUE LABELS	read or write data labels and formatting	~variables ~value "
VARIABLE LABELS	read or write data labels and formatting	~variables ~"

WILCOXON	analyze data other NPAR TESTS	~variable list
WRITE	read or write data	/VARIABLES /CASES
YRMODA	modify data or files modify data values IF ~instructions functions	

40.2 Summary of the menu structure in SPSS for Windows

The menu bar of the main SPSS window varies according to which type of window is active, but most of the time you will be using the normal setting. The main procedures and statistical tests are shown in alphabetical order in the left-hand column of the list below. The second column shows the menu entries you need to select in order to reach the procedure. For example, to find Frequencies, select Statistics /Summarize.

Add Cases	Data /Merge Files
Add Variables	Data /Merge Files
Aggregate	Data

Analysis of Variance
    Oneway
    Two-way
	
	Statistics /Compare Means /Oneway
	Statistics /ANOVA Models /Simple factorial

Binomial (test)	Statistics /Nonparametric Tests
Bivariate (correlation)	Statistics /Correlate
Chi-Square (one-sample)	Statistics /Nonparametric Tests
Chi-square (independent samples)	Statistics /Summarize /Frequencies
Cochrans's Q	Statistics /Nonparametric Tests /K Related Samples
Compute	Transform
Correlation	Statistics /Correlate /Bivariate
Count	Transform /Count Occurrences
Crosstabs	Statistics /Summarize
Descriptives	Statistics /Summarize
Explore	Statistics /Summarize
Frequencies	Statistics /Summarize

Friedman (test)	Statistics /Nonparametric Tests /K Related Samples
Kendall's W (test)	Statistics /Nonparametric Tests /K Related Samples
Kolmogorov-Smirnov (test for 1 sample)	Statistics /Nonparametric Tests/ 1-Sample K-S
Kolmogorov-Smirnov (test for 2 samples)	Statistics /Nonparametric Tests /2 Independent Samples
Kruskal-Wallis (test)	Statistics /Nonparametric Tests /K Independent Samples
Linear (Regression)	Statistics /Regression
List Cases	Statistics /Summarize
Mann-Whitney U test	Statistics /Nonparametric Tests /2 Independent Samples
McNemar (test)	Statistics /Nonparametric Tests /2 Related Samples
Median (test)	Statistics /Nonparametric Tests /K Independent Samples
Means	Statistics /Compare Means
Moses (test)	Statistics /Nonparametric Tests /2 Independent Samples
Multiple Response	Statistics
One-Way Anova	Statistics /Compare Means
Paired-Samples T-Test	Statistics /Compare Means
Partial (correlation)	Statistics /Correlate
Rank	Transform /Rank Cases
Rank correlation	Statistics /Correlate /Bivariate
Recode	Transform
Regression	Statistics
Reports Summaries in Rows	Statistics /Summarize
Runs (test)	Statistics /Nonparametric Tests
Select Cases	Data
Sign (test)	Statistics /Nonparametric Tests /2 Related Samples
Simple Factorial (ANOVA)	Statistics /ANOVA Models
Sort Cases	Data
Split File	Data
T-Test for Independent-Samples	Statistics /Compare Means
T-Test for Paired data	Statistics /Compare Means
Wilcoxon (test)	Statistics /Nonparametric Tests /2 Related Samples

INDEX

Words for the wise - from
Sigma Press

Sigma publish what is probably the widest range of computer books from any independent UK publisher. And that's not just for the PC, but for many other popular micros – Atari, Amiga and Archimedes – and for software packages that are widely-used in the UK and Europe, including Timeworks, Deskpress, Sage, Money Manager and many more. We also publish a whole range of professional-level books for topics as far apart as IBM mainframes, UNIX, computer translation, manufacturing technology and networking.

A complete catalogue is available, but here are some of the highlights:

Amstrad PCW
The Complete Guide to LocoScript and Amstrad PCW Computers – Hughes – £12.95
LocoScripting People – Clayton and Clayton – £12.95
The PCW LOGO Manual – Robert Grant – £12.95
Picture Processing on the Amstrad PCW – Gilmore – £12.95
See also Programming section for *Mini Office*

Archimedes
A Beginner's Guide to WIMP Programming – Fox – £12.95
See also: *Desktop Publishing on the Archimedes* and *Archimedes Game Maker's Manual*

Artificial Intelligence
Build Your Own Expert System – Naylor – £11.95
Computational Linguistics – McEnery – £14.95
Introducing Neural Networks – Carling – £14.95

Beginners' Guides
Computing Under Protest – Croucher – £12.95
Alone with a PC – Bradley – £12.95
The New User's Mac Book – Wilson – £12.95
PC Computing for Absolute Beginners – Edwards – £12.95

DTP and Graphics
Designworks Companion – Whale – £14.95
Timeworks Publisher Companion (3rd Edn.) – Morrissey – £12.95
Timeworks for Windows Companion – Sinclair – £14.95
PagePlus V2.0 Publisher Companion – Sinclair – £12.95
Express Publisher for Windows DTP Companion – Sinclair – £14.95
Amiga Real-Time 3D Graphics – Tyler – £14.95
Atari Real-Time 3D Graphics – Tyler – £12.95

European and US Software Packages
Mastering Money Manager PC – Sinclair – £12.95
Using Sage Sterling in Business – Woodford – £12.95
Mastering Masterfile PC – Sinclair – £12.95
All-in-One Business Computing (Amstrad PCW and Mini Office
Professional) – Hughes – £12.95

Game Making and Playing
PC Games Bible – Matthews and Rigby – £12.95
Archimedes Game Maker's Manual – Blunt – £14.95
Atari Game Maker's Manual – Hill – £14.95
Amiga Game Maker's Manual – Hill – £16.95
Adventure Gamer's Manual – Redrup – £12.95

General
Music and New Technology – Georghiades and Jacobs – £12.95
Getting the Best from your Amstrad Notepad – Wilson – £12.95
Computers and Chaos (Atari and Amiga editions) – Bessant – £12.95
Computers in Genealogy – Isaac – £12.95
Multimedia, CD-ROM and Compact Disc – Botto – £14.95
Advanced Manufacturing Technology – Zairi – £14.95

Networks
$25 Network User Guide – Sinclair – £11.95
Integrated Digital Networks – Lawton – £24.95
Novell Netware Companion – Croucher – £16.95

PC Operating Systems and Architecture

Working with Windows 3.1 – Sinclair – £16.95
Servicing and Supporting IBM PCs and Compatibles – Moss – £16.95
The DR DOS Book – Croucher – £16.95
MS-DOS Revealed – Last – £12.95
PC Architecture and Assembly Language (3rd Edn) – Kauler – £16.95
Programmer's Technical Reference – Williams – £19.95
MS-DOS File and Program Control – Sinclair – £12.95

Programming

C Applications Library – Pugh – £16.95
Starting MS-DOS Assembler – Sinclair – £12.95
Programming in ANSI Standard C – Horsington – £14.95
Microsoft Visual Basic: programmer's companion – Penfold – £16.95
For **LOGO**, *see Amstrad PCW*

UNIX and mainframes

UNIX – The Book – Banahan and Rutter – £11.95
UNIX – The Complete Guide – Manger – £19.95
RPG on the IBM AS/400 – Tomlinson – £24.95

HOW TO ORDER

Order these books from your usual bookshop, or direct from:

SIGMA PRESS,
1 SOUTH OAK LANE, WILMSLOW, CHESHIRE, SK9 6AR

PHONE: 0625 – 531035; FAX: 0625 – 536800

PLEASE ADD £1 TOWARDS POST AND PACKING FOR ONE BOOK.
POSTAGE IS FREE FOR TWO OR MORE BOOKS.

CHEQUES SHOULD BE MADE PAYABLE TO SIGMA PRESS.

ACCESS AND VISA WELCOME

24 HOUR ANSWERPHONE SERVICE.

Overseas customers: payment by credit card only;
airmail postage will be added at cost.